EASY•PIANO

THE BEST SONGS EVER

6TH EDITION

ISBN-13: 978-0-7935-7739-2
ISBN-10: 0-7935-7739-X

HAL•LEONARD®
CORPORATION
7777 W. BLUEMOUND RD. P.O. BOX 13819 MILWAUKEE, WI 53213

Visit Hal Leonard Online at
www.halleonard.com

EASY PIANO

THE BEST SONGS EVER

ALL I ASK OF YOU

from THE PHANTOM OF THE OPERA

Music by ANDREW LLOYD WEBBER
Lyrics by CHARLES HART
Additional Lyrics by RICHARD STILGOE

Slowly, in 2
RAOUL:

No more talk of dark - ness, for - get these wide - eyed

With pedal

fears; I'm here, noth - ing can harm you, my

words will warm and calm you. Let me be your free - dom, let

day - light dry your tears; I'm here, with you, be -

5

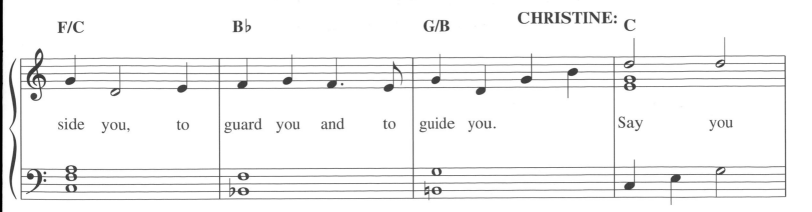

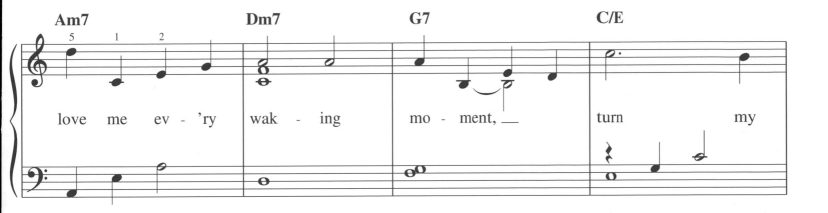

prom-ise me that all you say is true, that's all I ask of

rit.

RAOUL:

Let me be your shel - ter, let me be your light; you're
you.
a tempo

safe, no one will find you, your fears are far be -

CHRISTINE:

hind you. All I want is free - dom, a world with no more

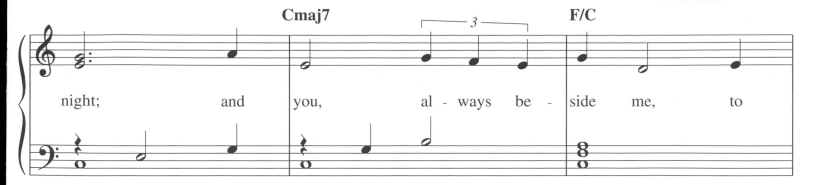

night; and you, al - ways be - side me, to

hold me and to hide me. Then say you'll share with me one

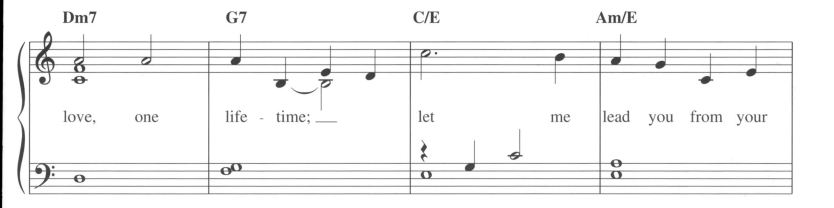

love, one life - time; ___ let me lead you from your

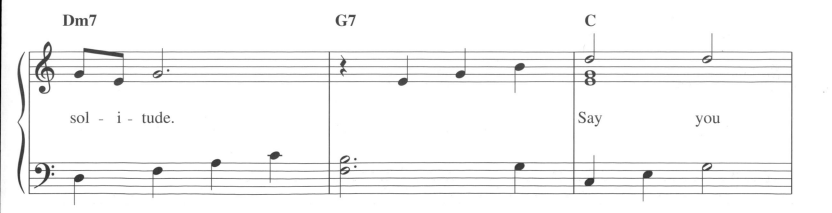

sol - i - tude. Say you

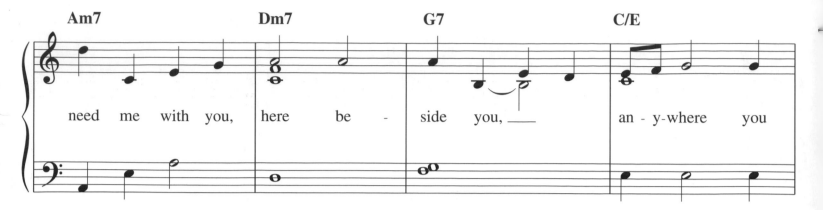

need me with you, here be - side you, ___ an - y-where you

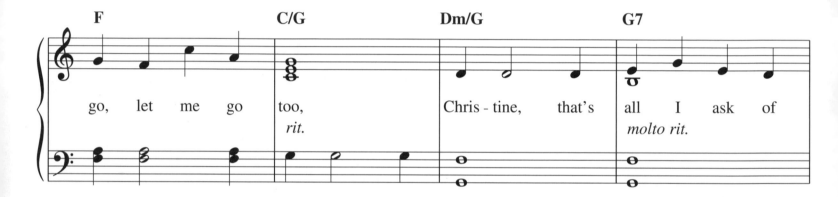

go, let me go too, Chris - tine, that's all I ask of
rit. *molto rit.*

CHRISTINE:

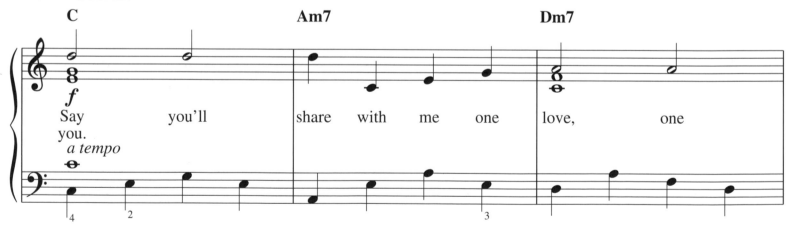

Say you'll share with me one love, one
you.
a tempo

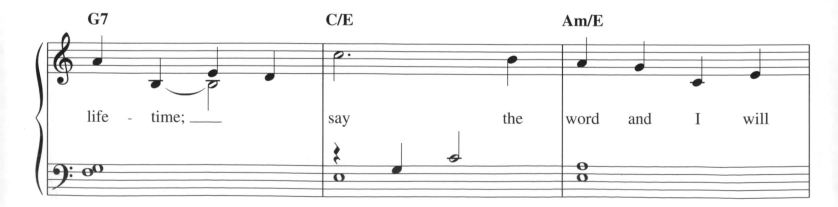

life - time; ___ say the word and I will

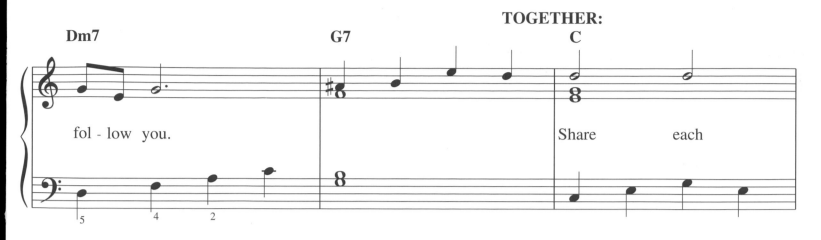

fol - low you.   Share   each

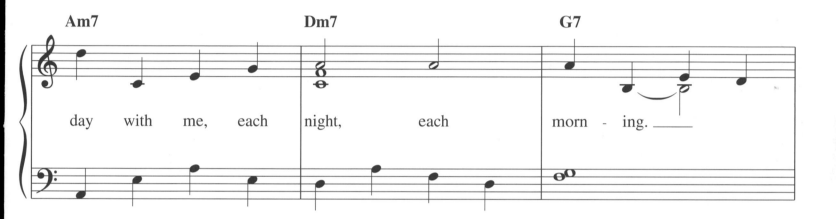

day   with   me,   each   night,   each   morn - ing. _____

Slower

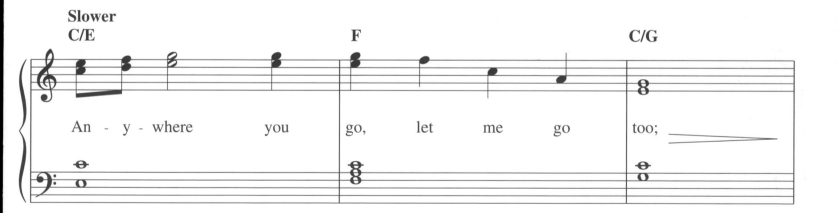

An - y - where   you   go,   let   me   go   too;

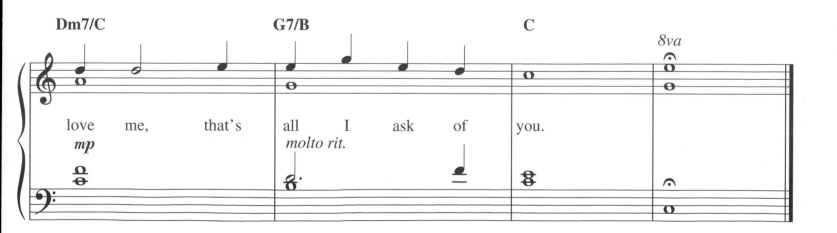

love   me,   that's   all   I   ask   of   you.

ALL THE THINGS YOU ARE
from VERY WARM FOR MAY

Lyrics by OSCAR HAMMERSTEIN II
Music by JEROME KERN

All that I want in all of this world is you.

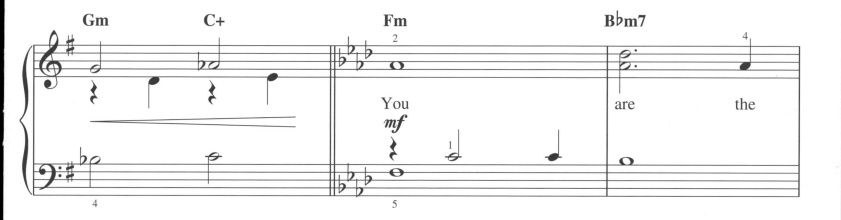

You are the

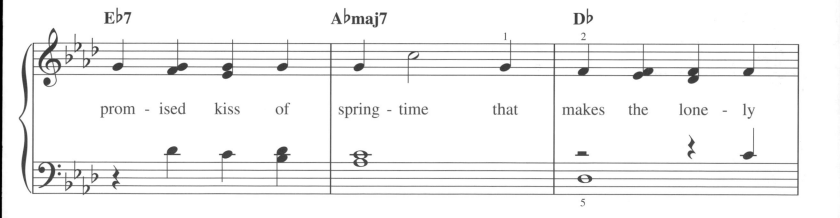

prom - ised kiss of spring - time that makes the lone - ly

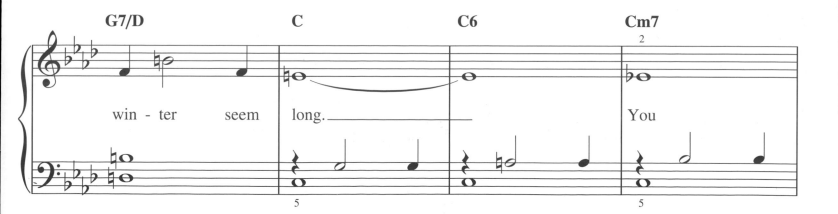

win - ter seem long. You

Fm7 Bb7 Ebmaj7

are the breath - less hush of eve - ning that

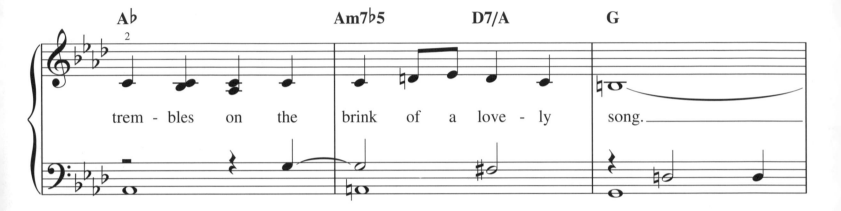

Ab Am7b5 D7/A G

trem - bles on the brink of a love - ly song.___

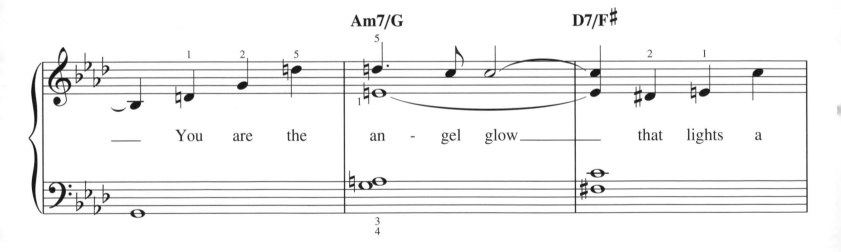

Am7/G D7/F#

___ You are the an - gel glow___ that lights a

G F#m7b5/E

star,___ the dear - est things I know___

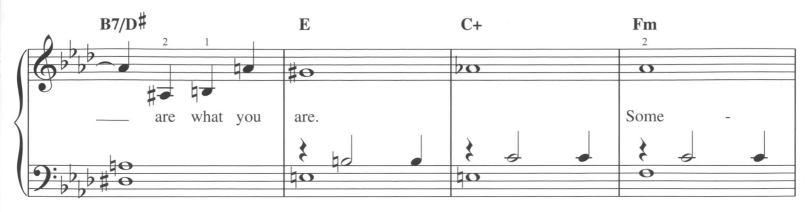

_____ are what you are.   Some -

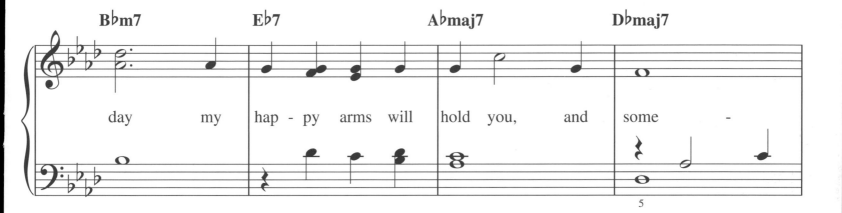

day   my   hap - py arms will   hold   you,   and   some -

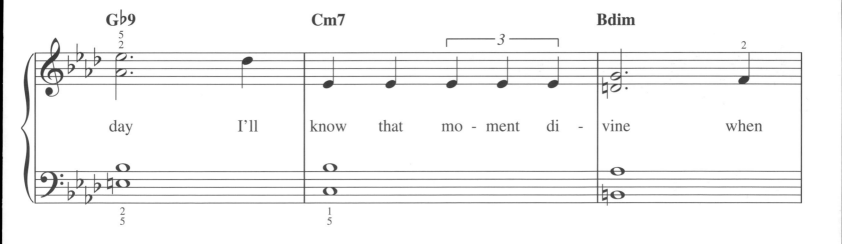

day   I'll   know   that   mo - ment di - vine   when

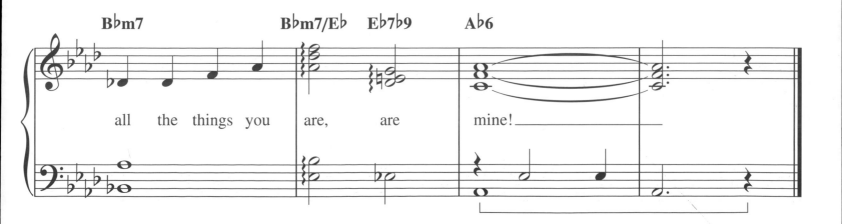

all   the things you   are,   are   mine! _____

ALWAYS

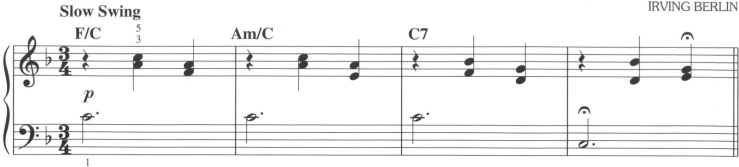

Words and Music by
IRVING BERLIN

Slow Swing

I'll   be lov - ing   you,   al - ways

with   a love that's   true,

al - ways.   When   the things you've

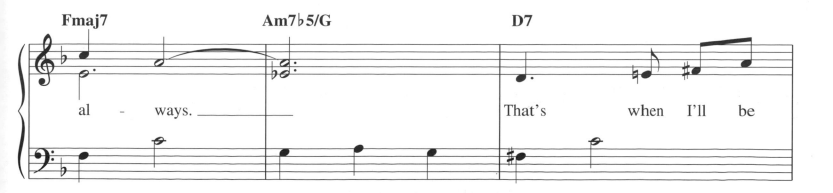

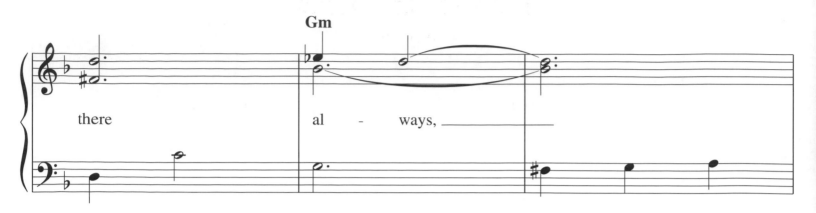

there   al - ways, _____

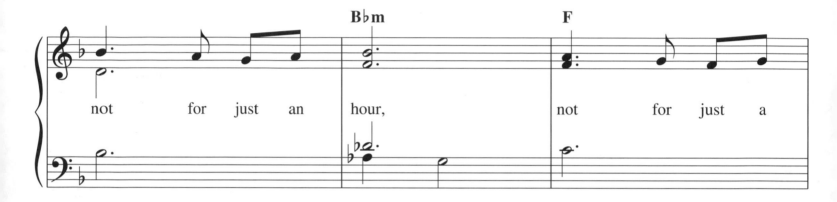

not   for just an   hour,   not   for just a

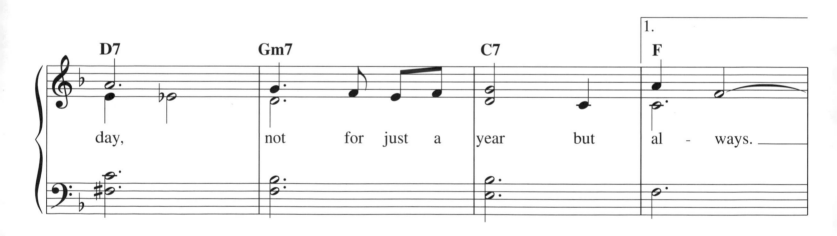

day,   not   for just a   year   but   al - ways. ___

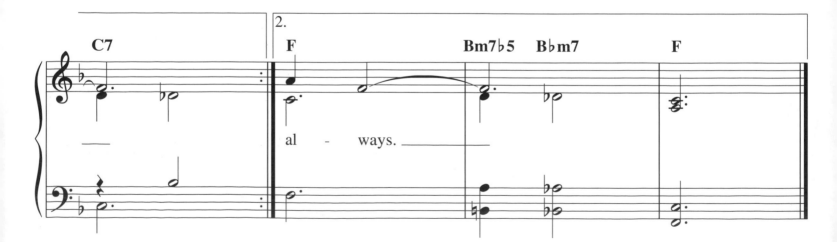

___   al - ways. ___

BLUE SKIES

from BETSY

Words and Music by
IRVING BERLIN

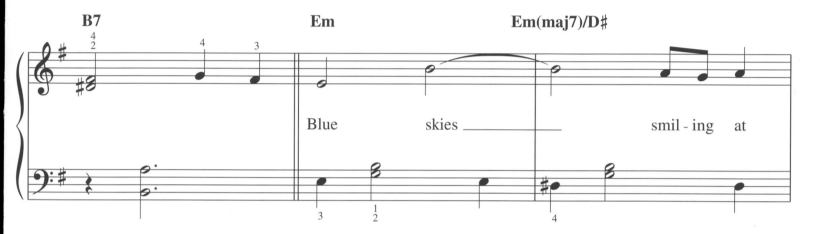

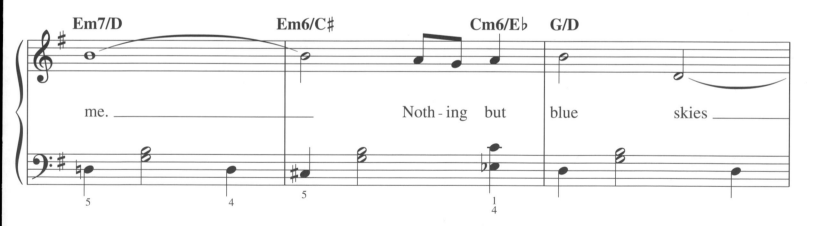

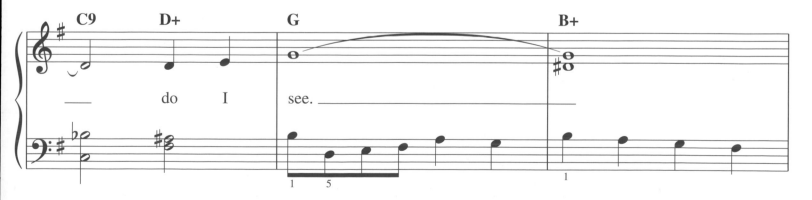

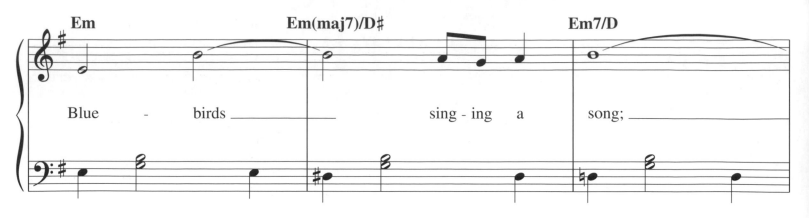

Blue - birds _____ sing - ing a song; _____

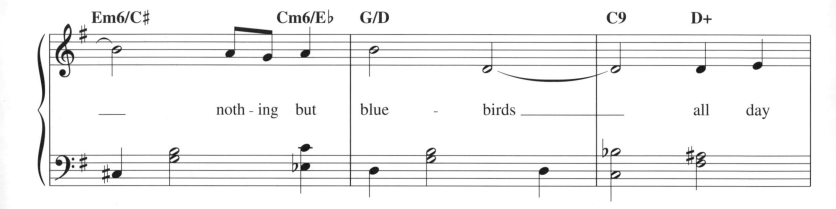

_____ noth - ing but blue - birds _____ all day

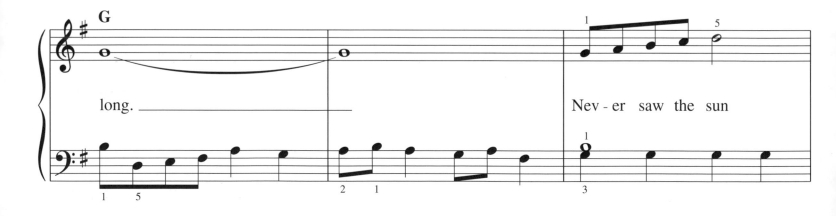

long. _____ Nev - er saw the sun

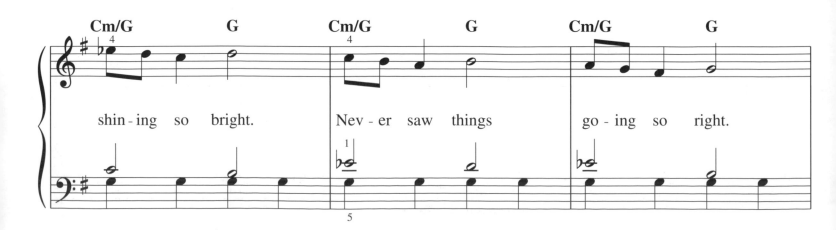

shin - ing so bright. Nev - er saw things go - ing so right.

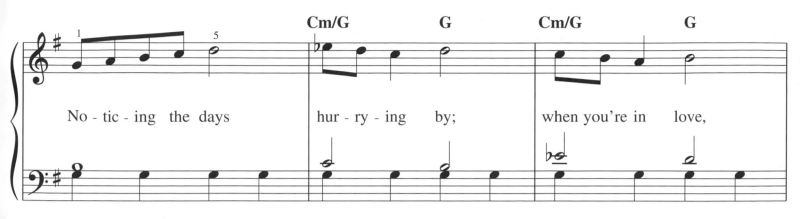

No - tic - ing the days hur - ry - ing by; when you're in love,

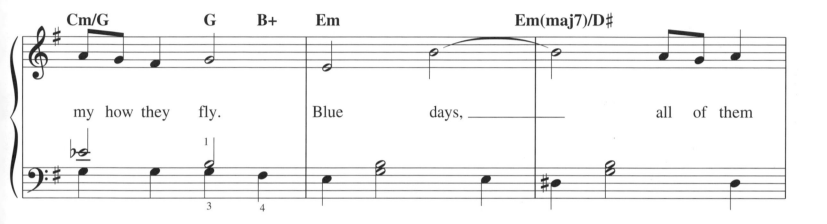

my how they fly. Blue days, _____ all of them

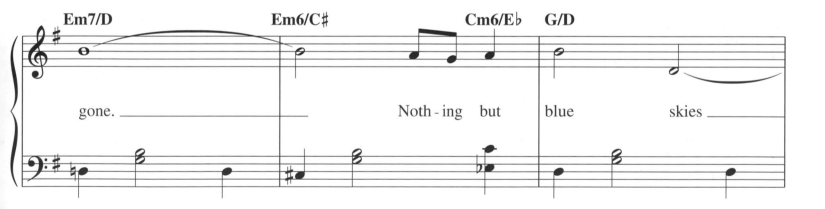

gone. _____ Noth - ing but blue skies _____

___ from now on.

BEWITCHED
from PAL JOEY

Words by LORENZ HART
Music by RICHARD RODGERS

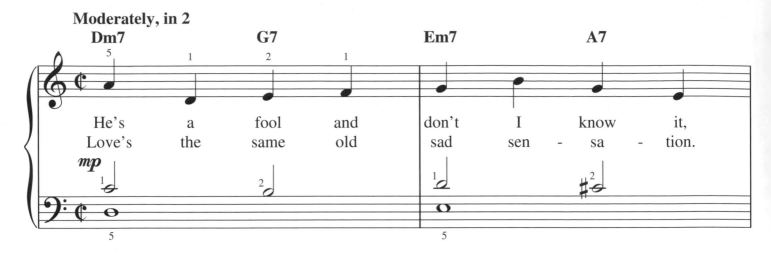

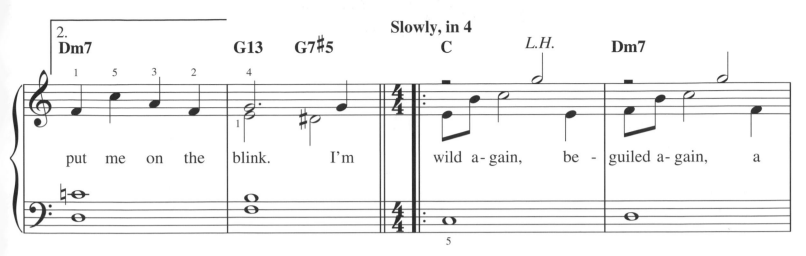

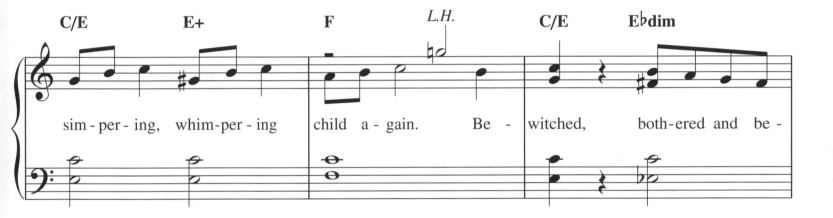

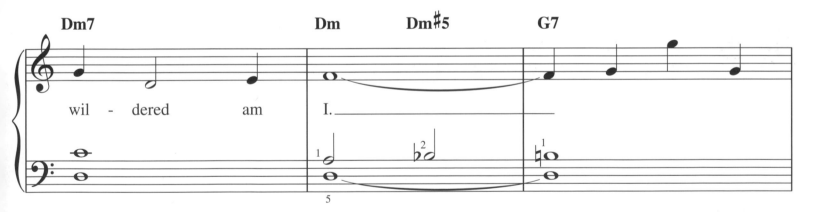

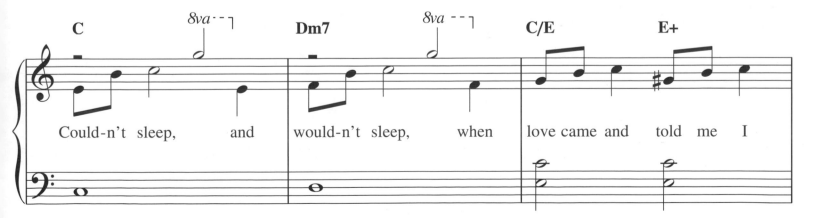

22

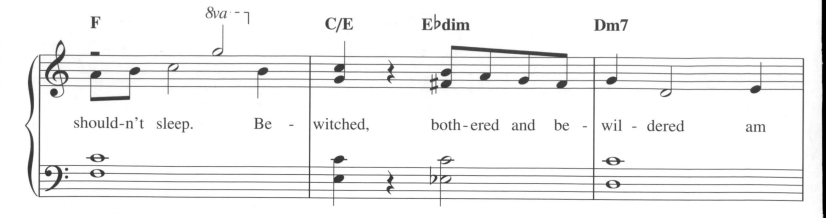

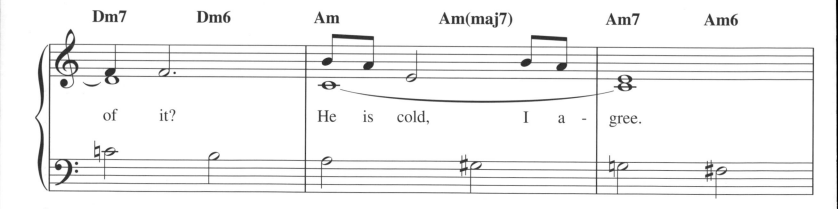

23

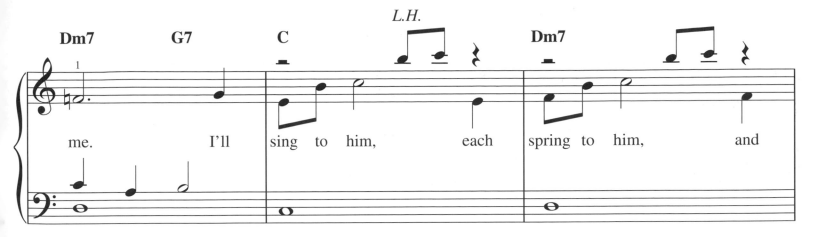

me. I'll sing to him, each spring to him, and

long for the day when I'll cling to him. Be - witched, both-ered and be -

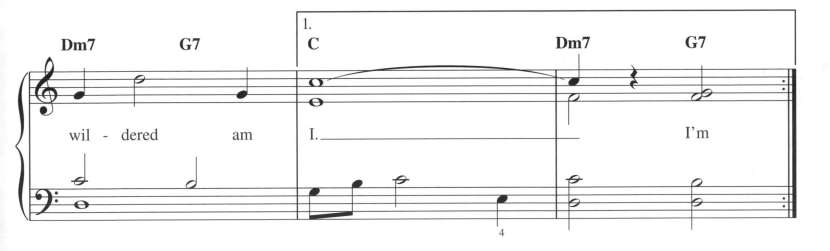

wil - dered am I. I'm

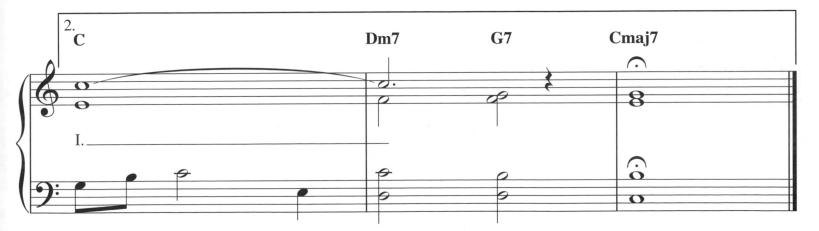

I. I'm

BODY AND SOUL

Words by EDWARD HEYMAN,
ROBERT SOUR and FRANK EYTON
Music by JOHN GREEN

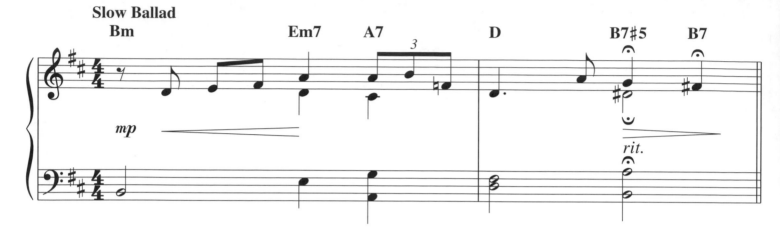

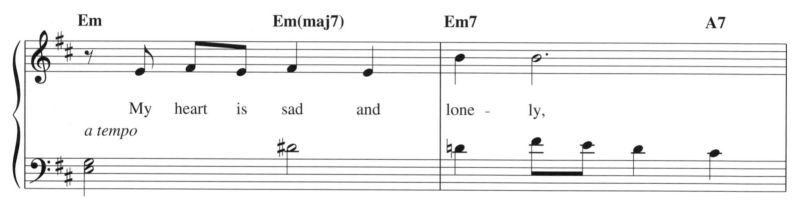

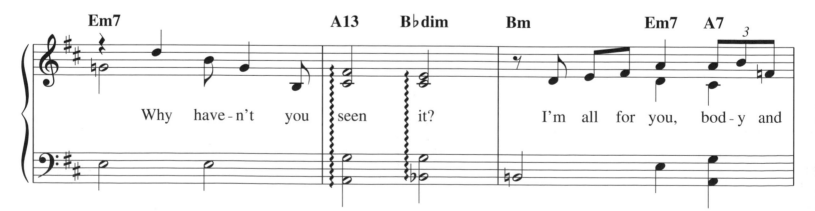

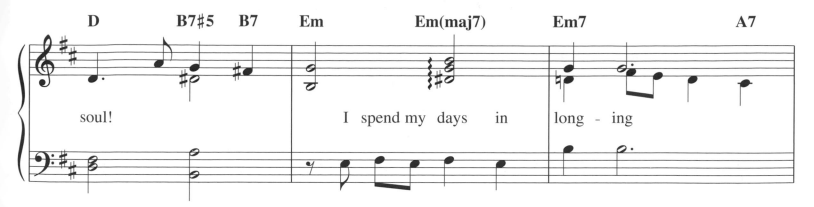

soul!   I spend my days in   long - ing

and won-d'ring why   it's   me   you're wrong - ing,   I   tell you   I

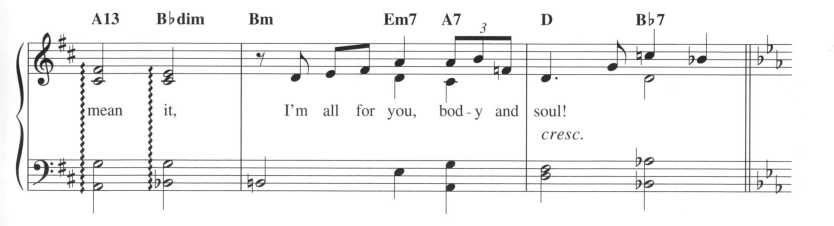

mean   it,   I'm all   for   you,   bod - y   and   soul!
cresc.

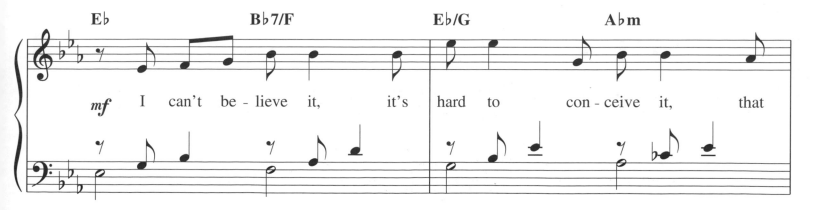

mf   I   can't   be - lieve   it,   it's   hard   to   con - ceive   it,   that

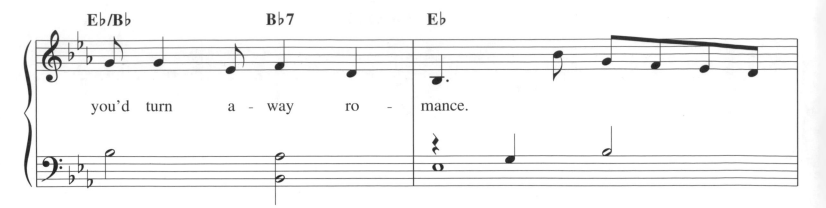

you'd turn a - way ro - mance.

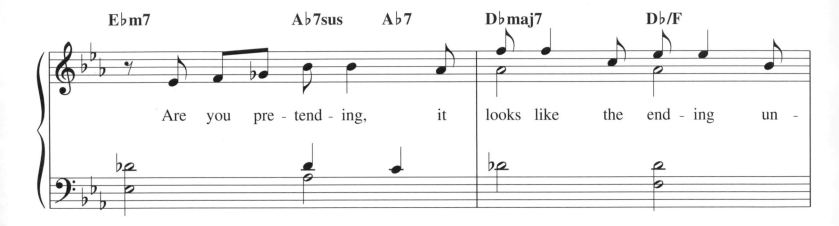

Are you pre - tend - ing, it looks like the end - ing un -

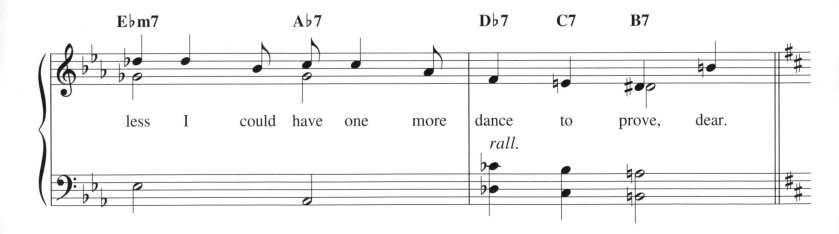

less I could have one more dance to prove, dear.

rall.

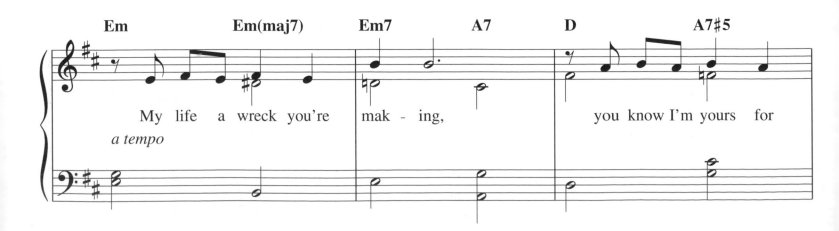

My life a wreck you're mak - ing, you know I'm yours for

a tempo

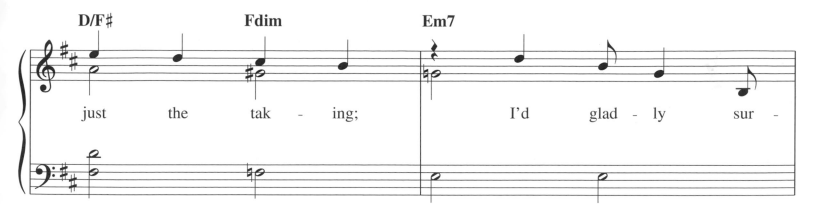

just the tak - ing; I'd glad - ly sur -

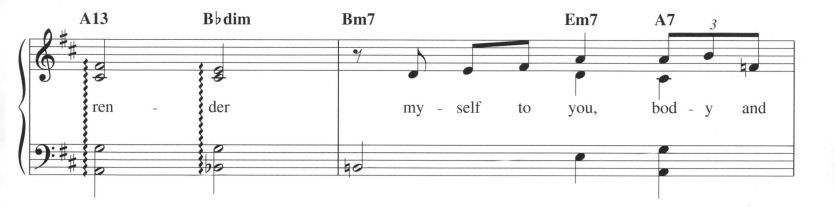

ren - der my - self to you, bod - y and

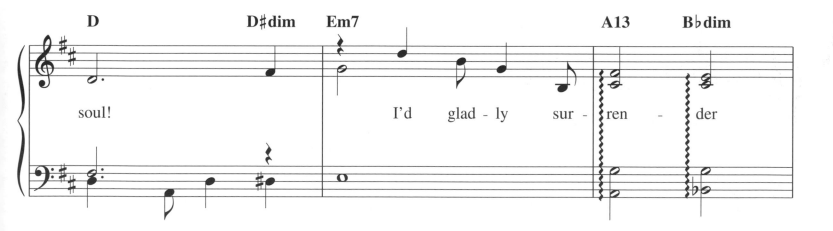

soul! I'd glad - ly sur - ren - der

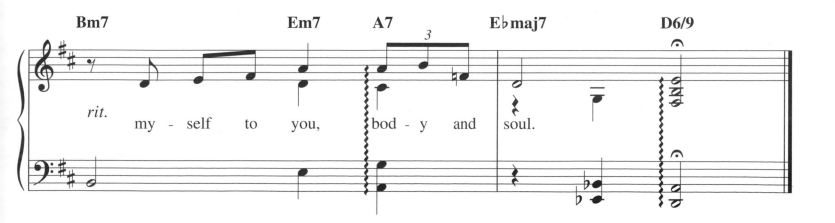

rit. my - self to you, bod - y and soul.

CALL ME IRRESPONSIBLE

from the Paramount Picture PAPA'S DELICATE CONDITION

Words by SAMMY CAHN
Music by JAMES VAN HEUSEN

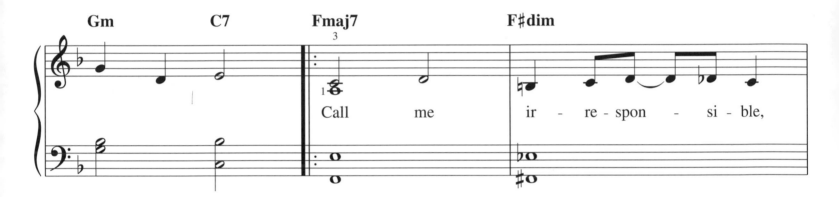

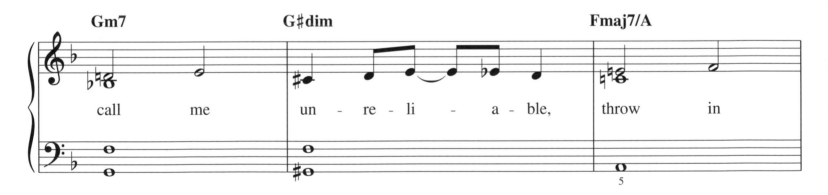

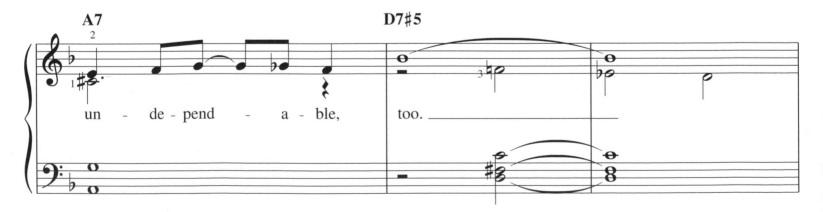

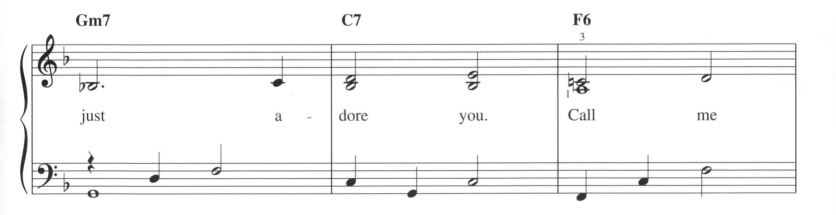

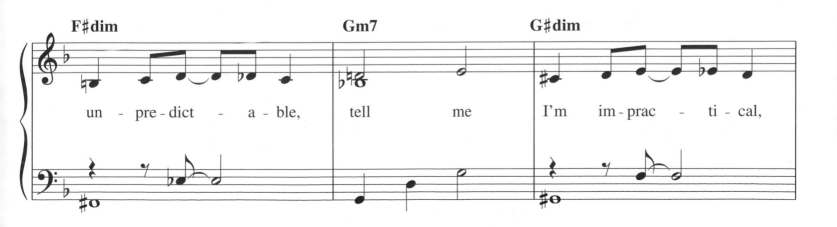

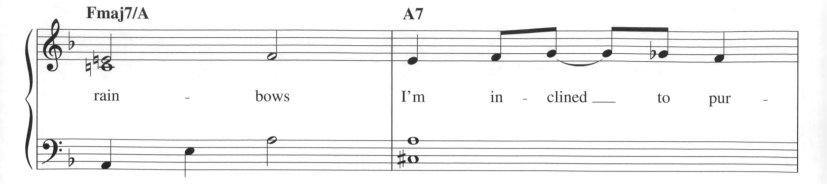

rain - bows   I'm in - clined ___ to pur -

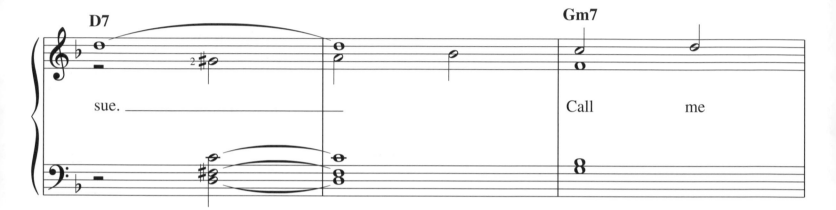

sue. ___   Call   me

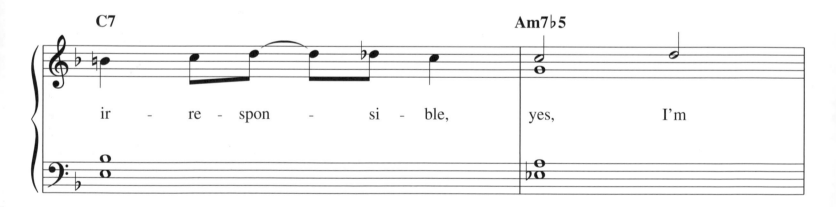

ir - re - spon - si - ble,   yes,   I'm

un - re - li - a - ble,   but   it's

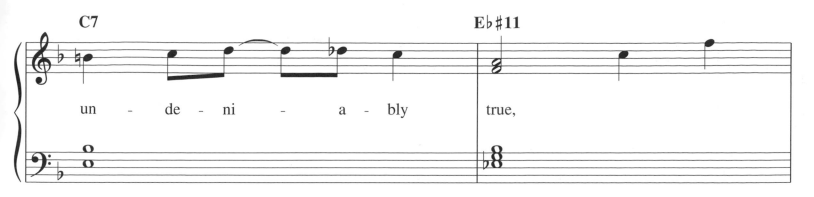

un - de - ni - a - bly   true,

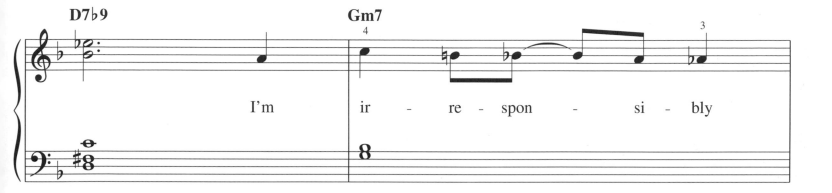

I'm   ir - re - spon - si - bly

mad   for   you!

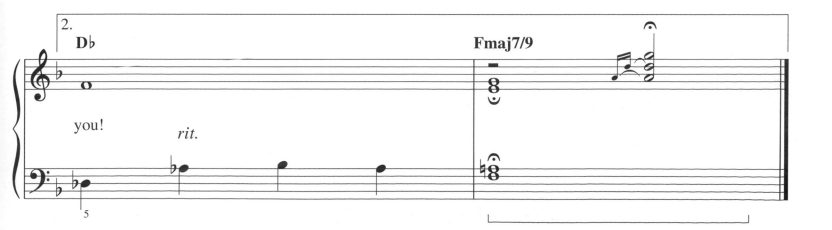

you!   *rit.*

CAN YOU FEEL THE LOVE TONIGHT

from Walt Disney Pictures' THE LION KING

Music by ELTON JOHN
Lyrics by TIM RICE

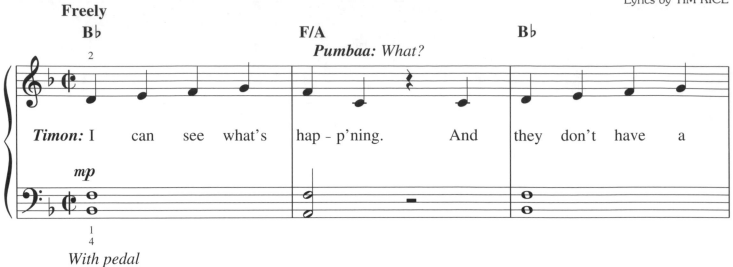

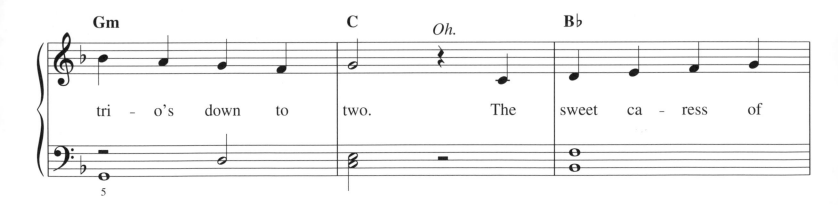

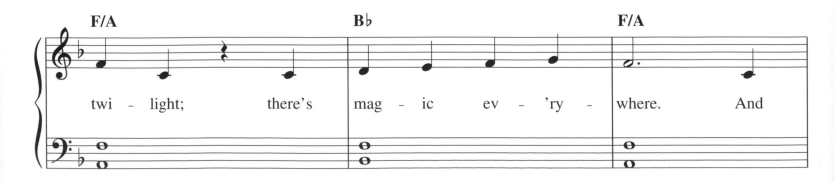

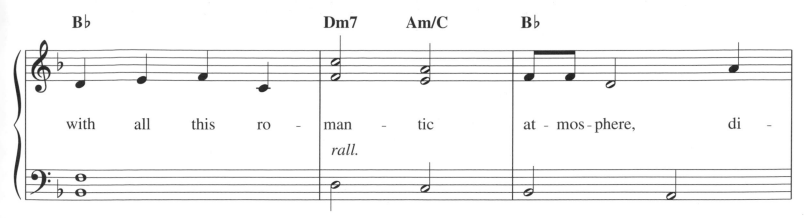

with all this ro - man - tic at - mos - phere, di -
rall.

Moderately (in two)

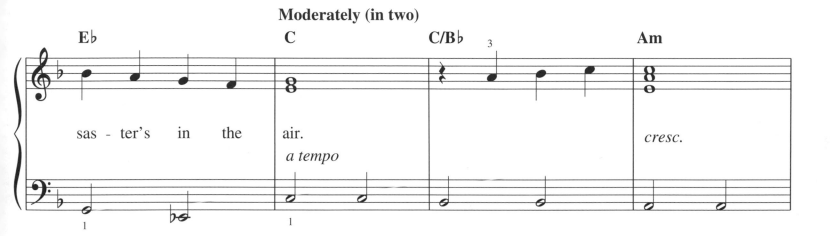

sas - ter's in the air. cresc.
a tempo

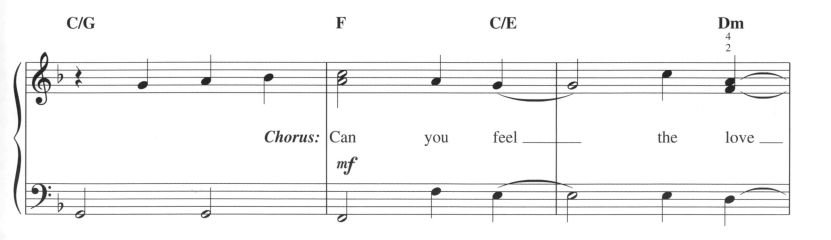

Chorus: Can you feel the love
mf

to - night, the peace the

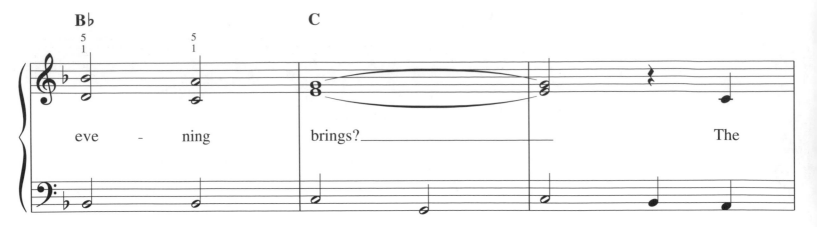

eve - ning brings?   The

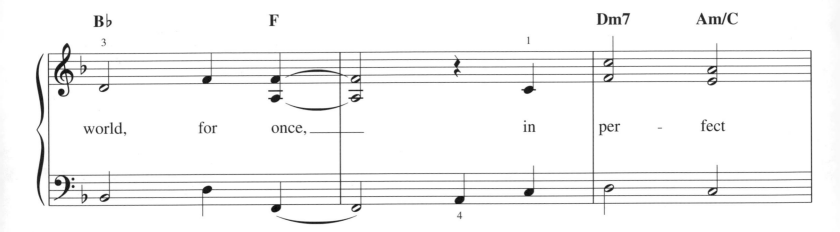

world, for once,   in per - fect

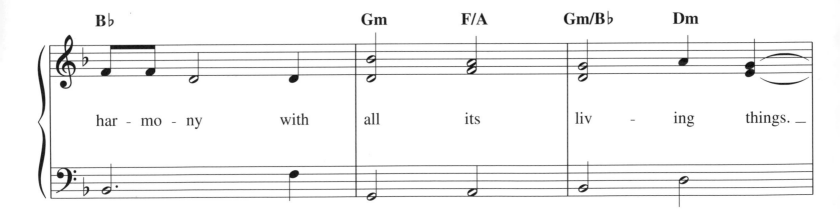

har - mo - ny with all its liv - ing things.

dim.

Simba: So man - y things to

mp

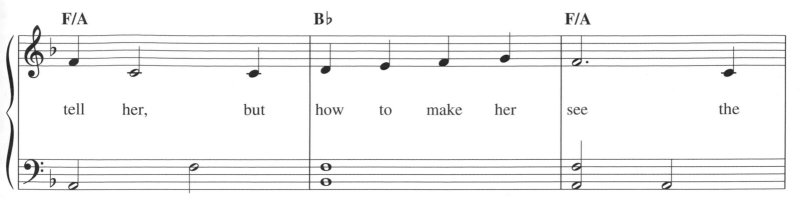

tell her, but how to make her see the

truth a - bout my past? Im - pos - si - ble. She'd turn a - way from

me. _____ *Nala:* He's hold - ing back, he's hid - ing. But

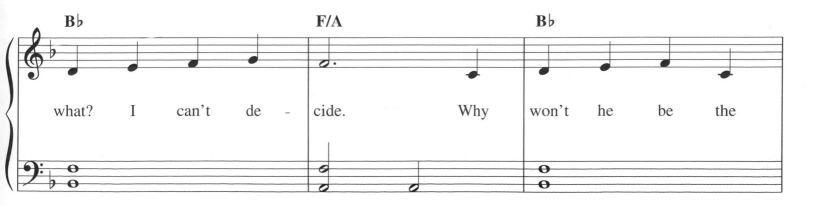

what? I can't de - cide. Why won't he be the

36

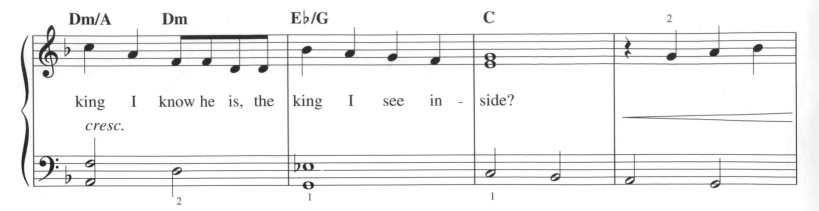

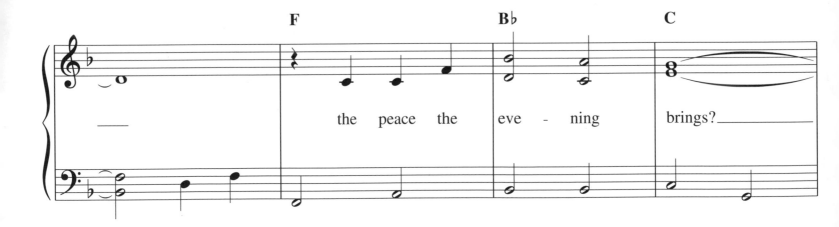

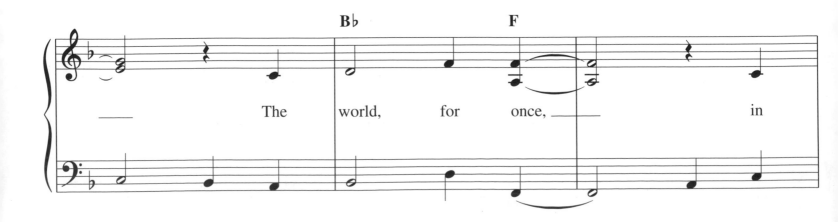

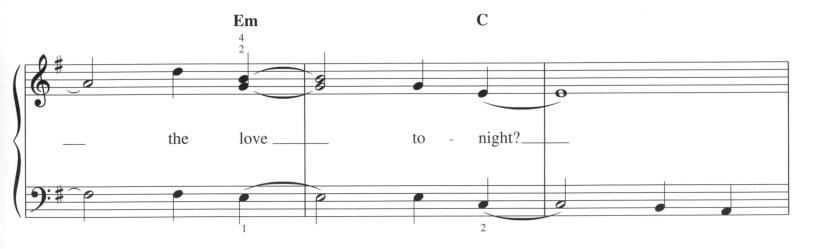

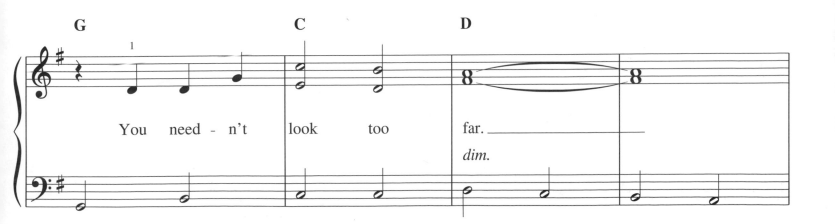

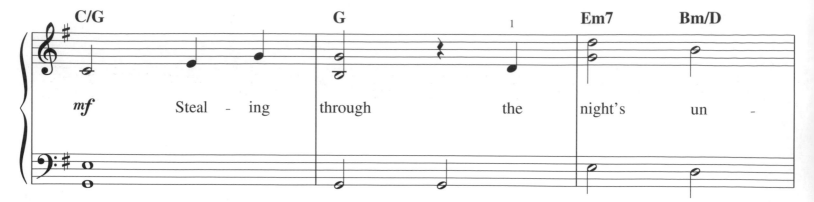

Steal - ing through the night's un -

cer - tain - ties, love is where they are. ___

___ Timon: And if he

mp

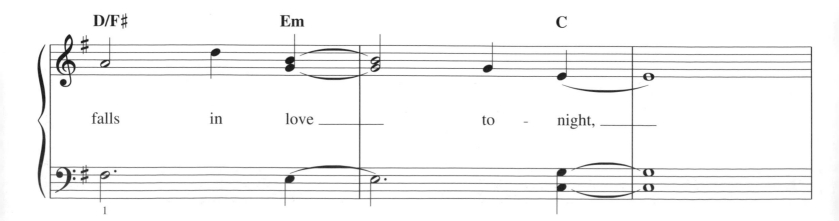

falls in love ___ to - night, ___

39

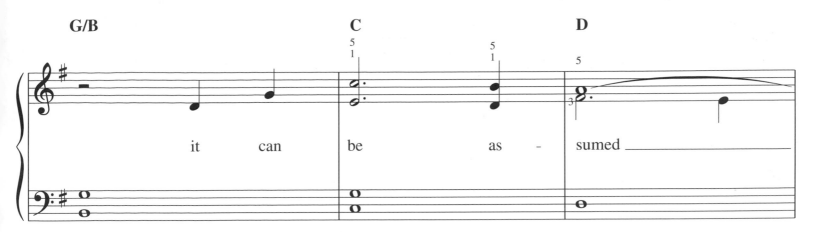

it can be as - sumed

_____ *Pumbaa:* his care - free days with

us are his - tory, *Timon & Pumbaa:* in short, our

rall.

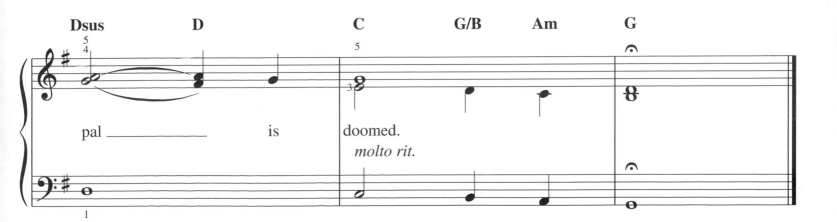

pal _____ is doomed.

molto rit.

CAN'T HELP FALLING IN LOVE

from the Paramount Picture BLUE HAWAII

Words and Music by GEORGE DAVID WEISS,
HUGO PERETTI and LUIGI CREATORE

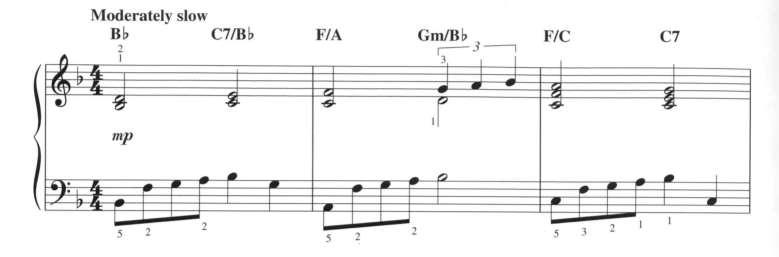

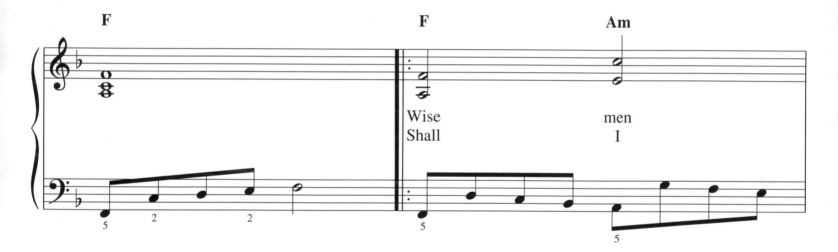

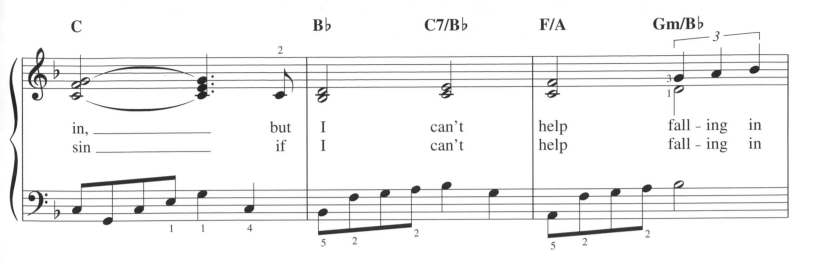

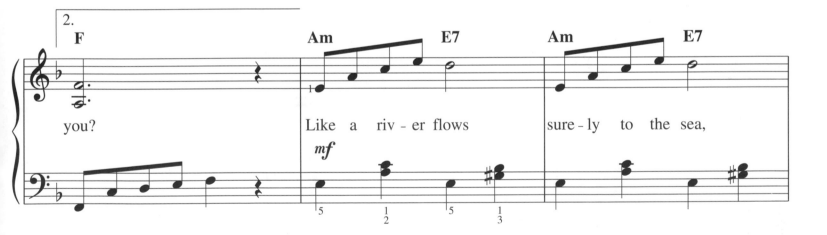

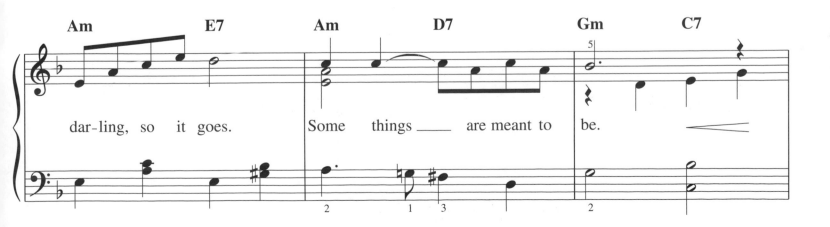

Take   my   hand,   take my whole   life,

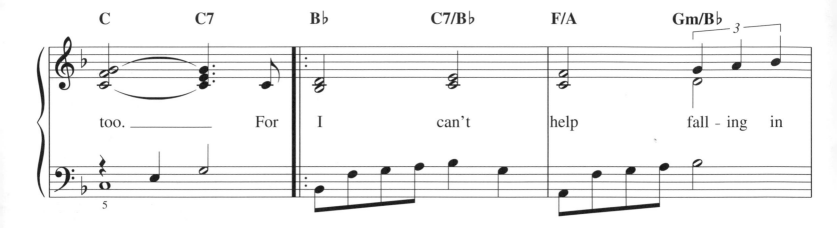

too. _____ For   I   can't   help   fall - ing   in

love   with   you. _____   For

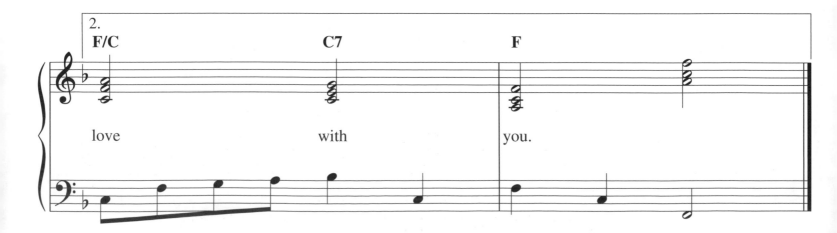

love   with   you.

CANDLE IN THE WIND

Music by ELTON JOHN
Words by BERNIE TAUPIN

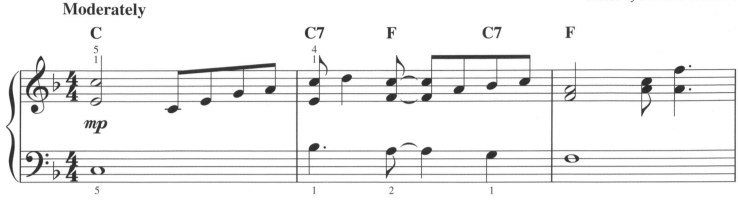

Good-bye, Nor - ma Jean,___ though I nev - er
Lone - li - ness___ was tough,___ the tough-est role you

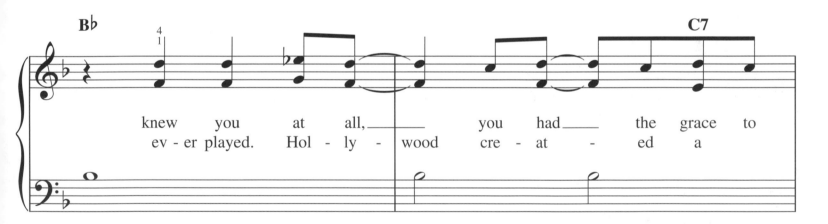

knew you at all,___ you had___ the grace to
ev - er played. Hol - ly - wood cre - at - ed a

hold your-self___ while those a-round___ you crawled.___
su - per-star___ and pain was the price you paid.___

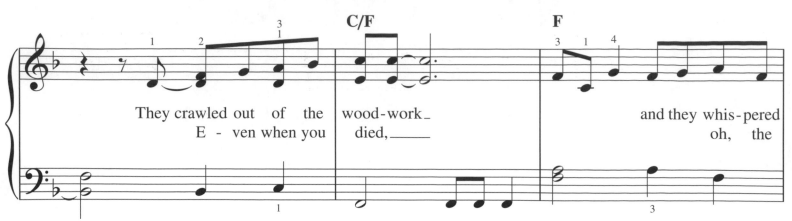

They crawled out of the wood-work and they whis-pered
E - ven when you died, oh, the

in - to your brain, they set you on a tread - mill and they
press still hound - ed you, all the pa - pers had to say was that

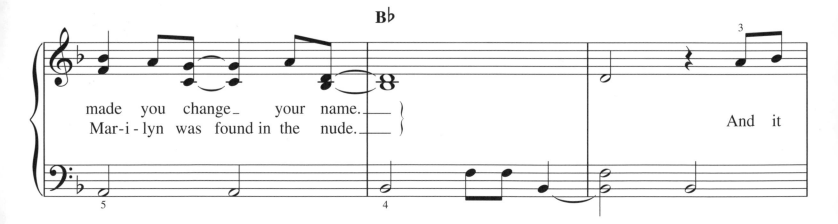

made you change your name.
Mar-i-lyn was found in the nude.

And it

seems to me you lived your life like a can - dle in the wind.

Nev-er know-ing___ who to cling___ to___ when the rain___

___ set in.___ And I would have liked___ to have known___

___ you, but___ I was just___ a kid.___ Your can-dle had burned___ out

To Coda ⊕

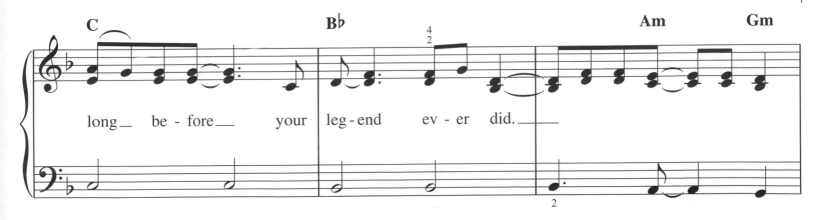

long___ be-fore___ your leg-end ev-er did.___

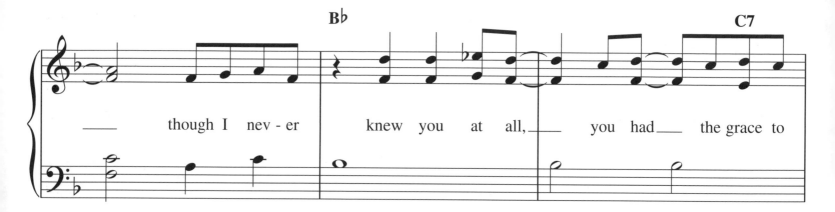

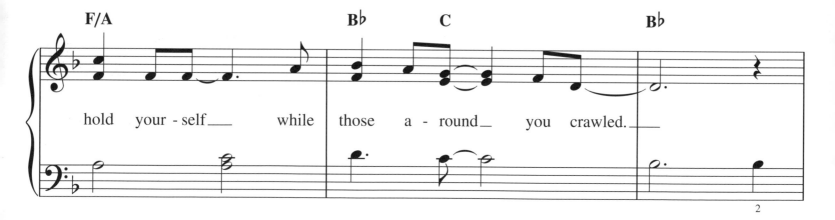

47

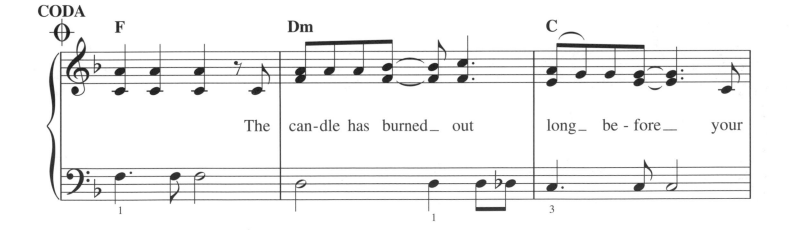

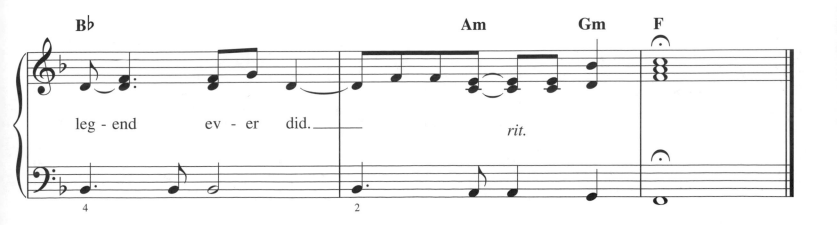

CLIMB EV'RY MOUNTAIN
from THE SOUND OF MUSIC

Lyrics by OSCAR HAMMERSTEIN II
Music by RICHARD RODGERS

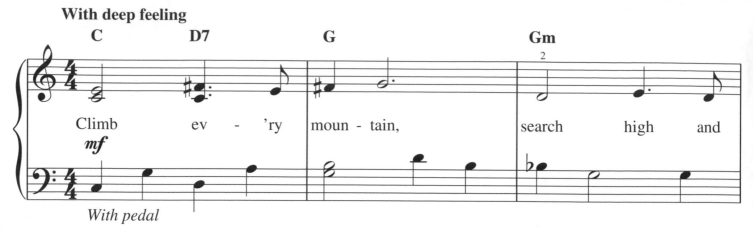

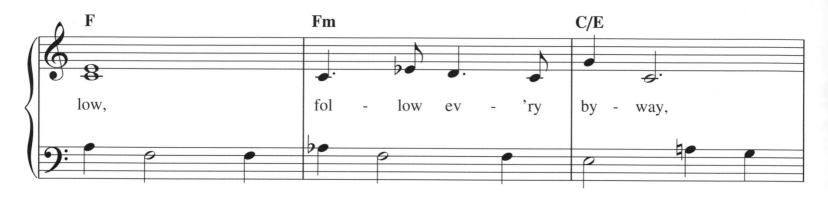

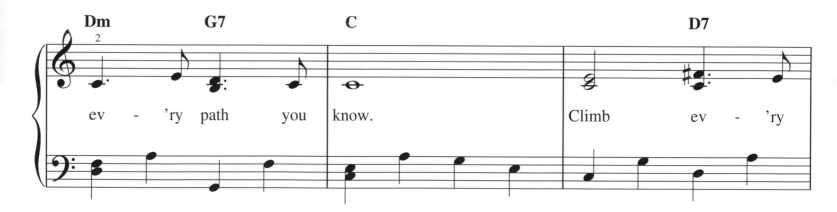

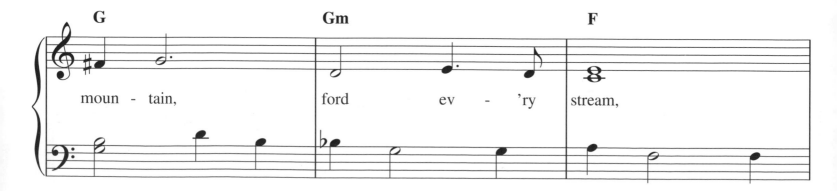

49

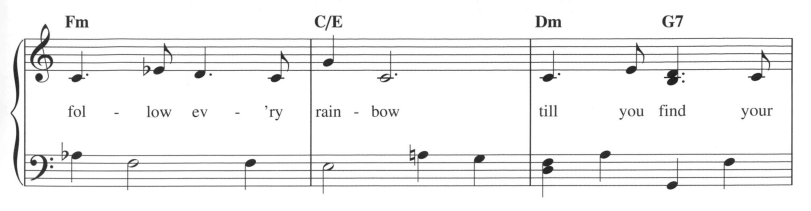

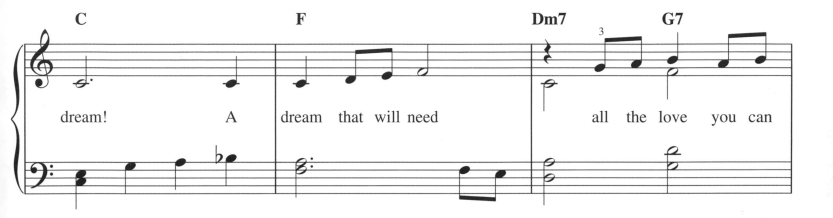

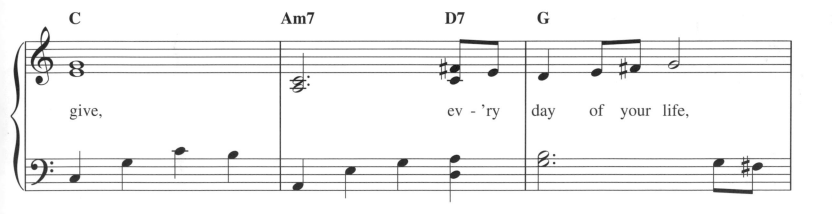

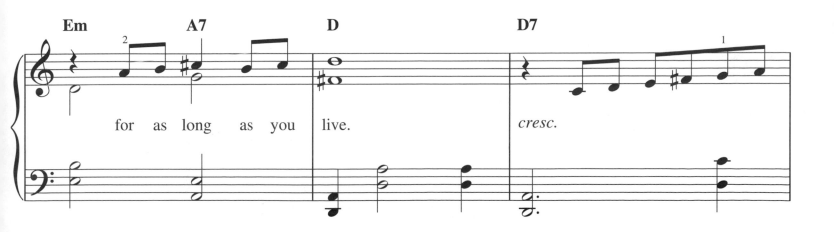

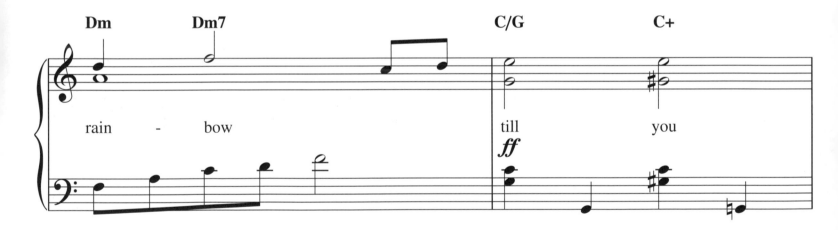

CRAZY

Words and Music by
WILLIE NELSON

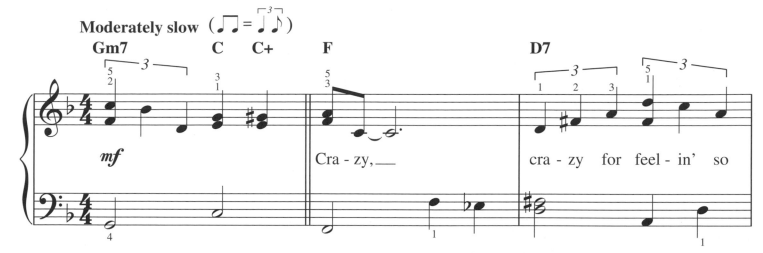

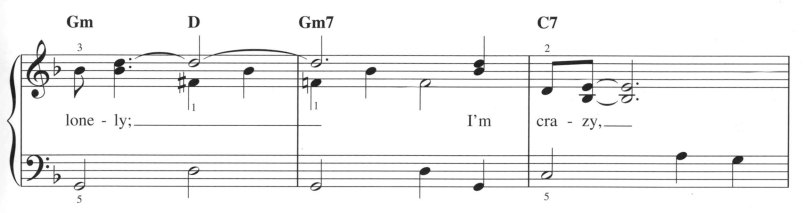

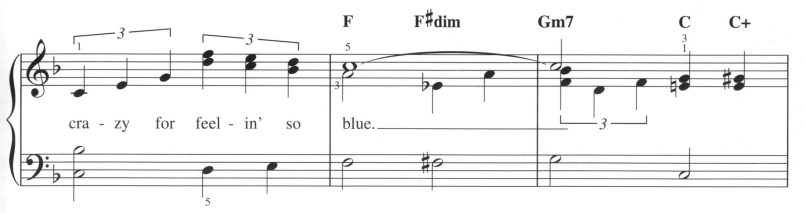

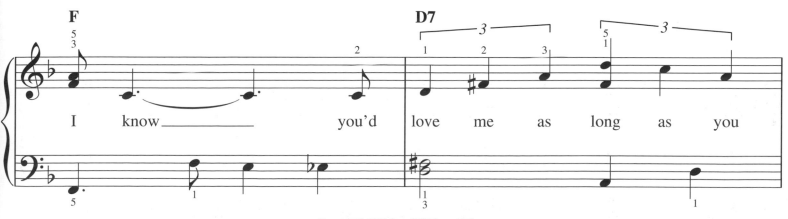

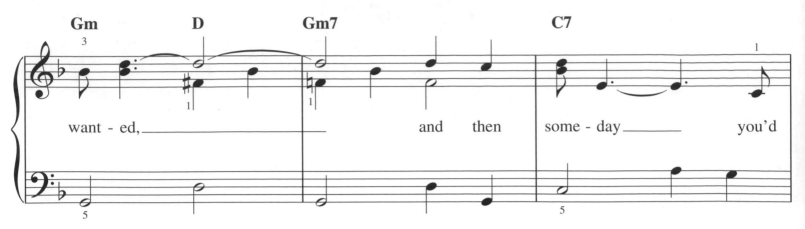

want - ed, _____ and then some - day _____ you'd

leave me for some - bod - y new. _____

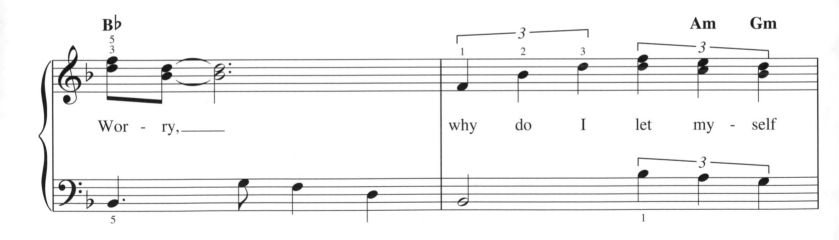

Wor - ry, _____ why do I let my - self

wor - ry, _____ won - d'rin' _

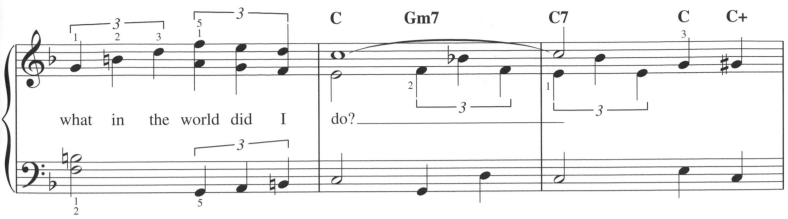

what in the world did I do?

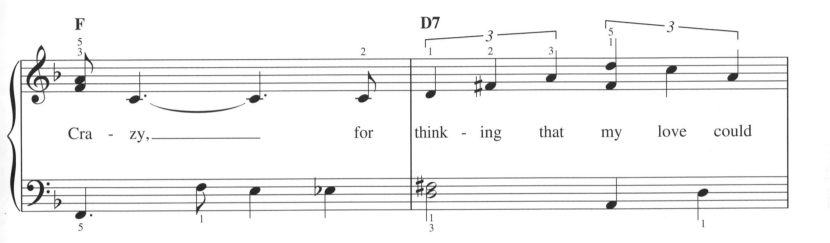

Cra - zy, _____ for think - ing that my love could

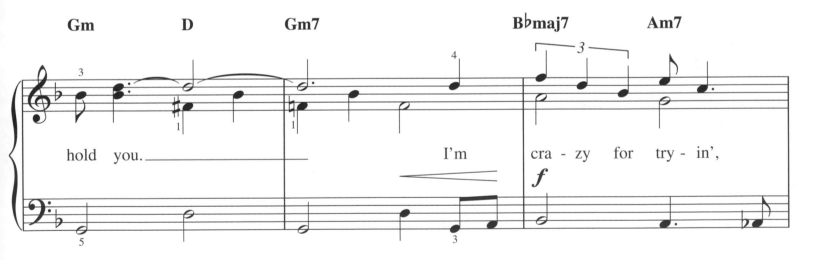

hold you. _____ I'm cra - zy for try - in',

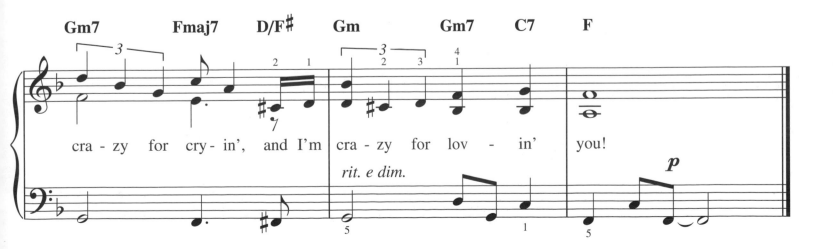

cra - zy for cry - in', and I'm cra - zy for lov - in' you!

rit. e dim.

EDELWEISS
from THE SOUND OF MUSIC

Lyrics by OSCAR HAMMERSTEIN II
Music by RICHARD RODGERS

Slowly, with expression

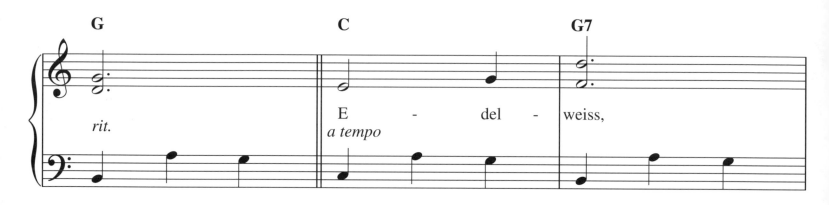

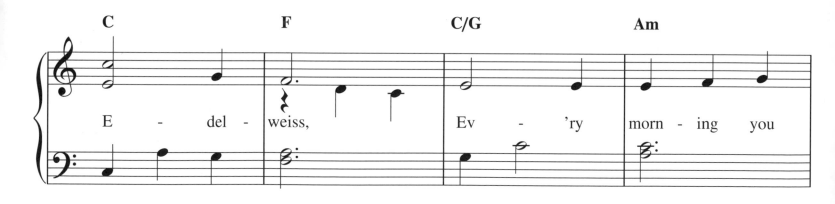

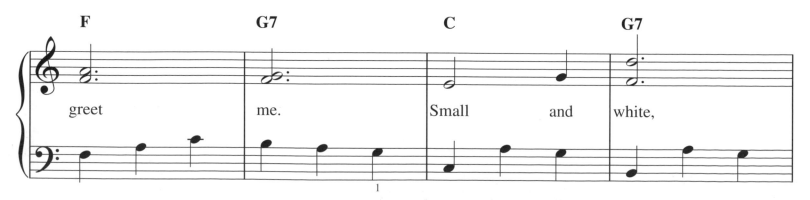

1

Clean and bright, You look

hap - py to meet me.

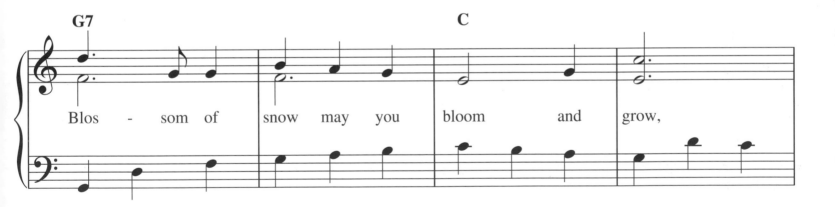

Blos - som of snow may you bloom and grow,

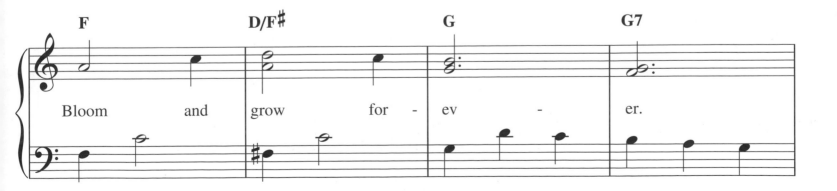

Bloom and grow for - ev - er.

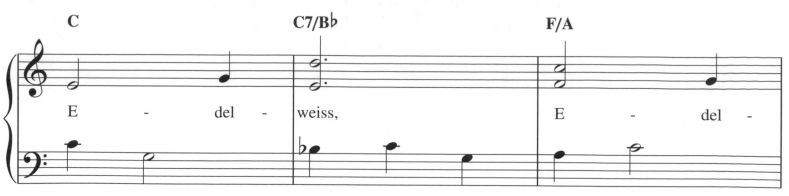

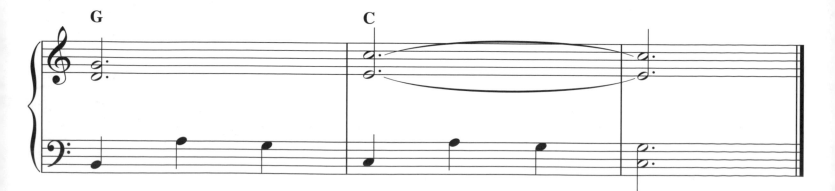

FLY ME TO THE MOON
(In Other Words)

Words and Music by
BART HOWARD

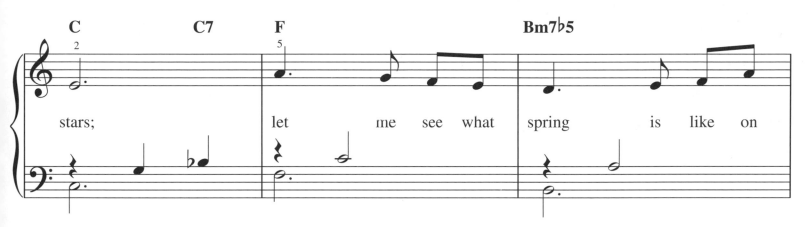

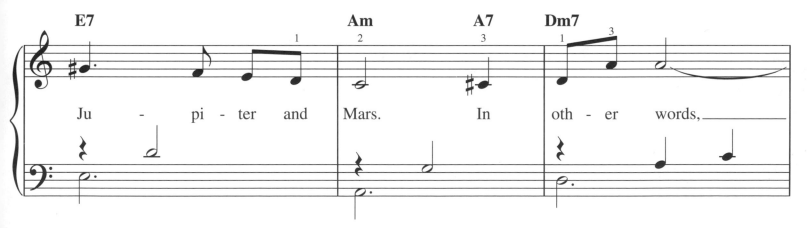

dar - ling, kiss me!

Fill my life with song and let me sing for - ev - er

more; you are all I long for, all I

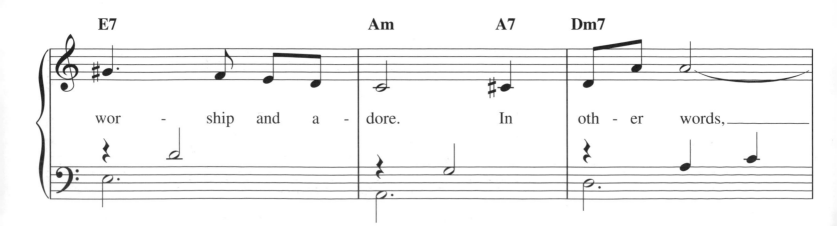

wor - ship and a - dore. In oth - er words,____

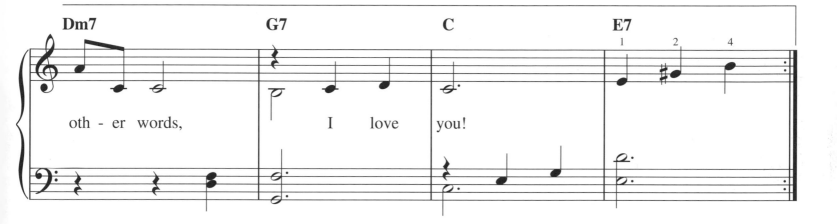

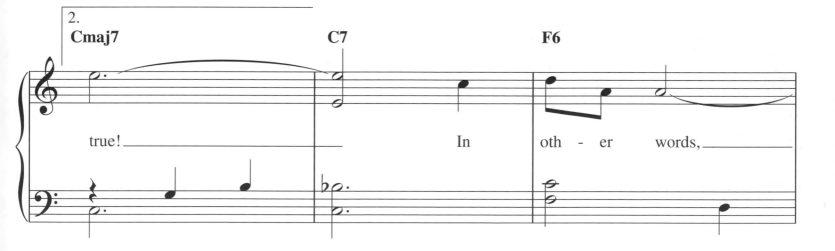

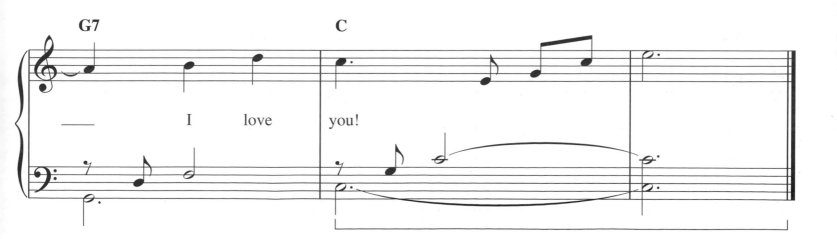

FROM A DISTANCE

Words and Music by
JULIE GOLD

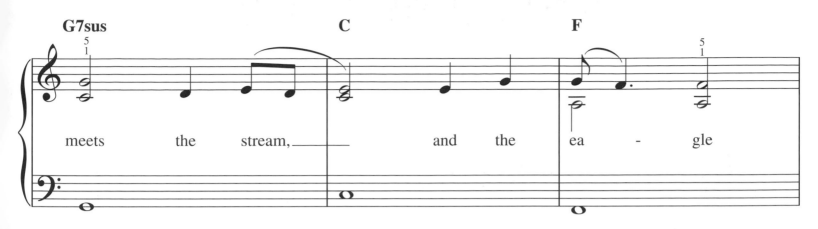

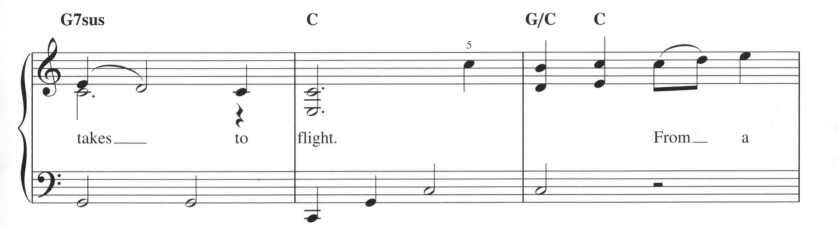

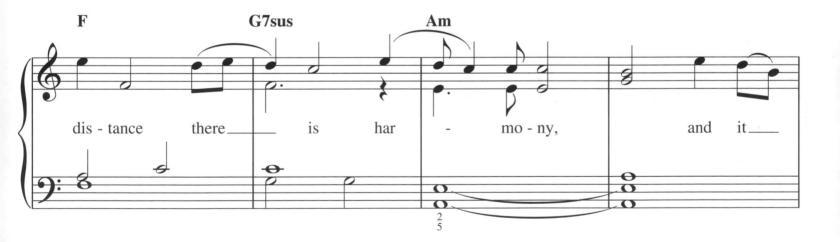

voice   of____   hope,_____ it's   the   voice   of____

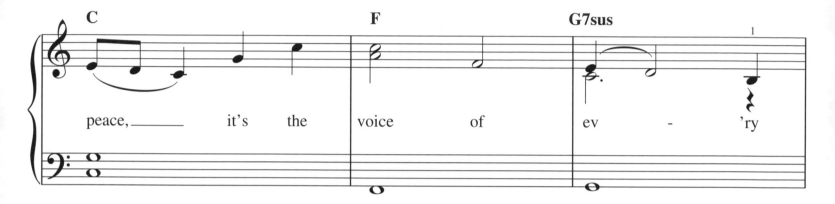

peace,_____   it's   the   voice   of   ev   -   'ry

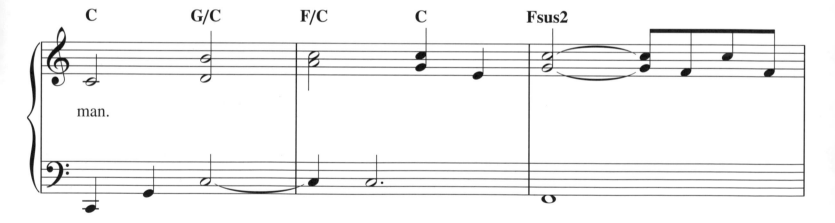

man.

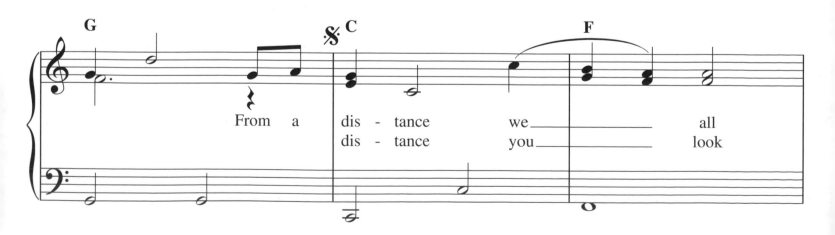

From   a   dis - tance   we_____   all
          dis - tance   you_____   look

63

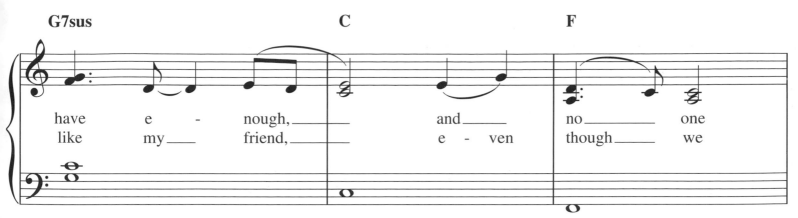

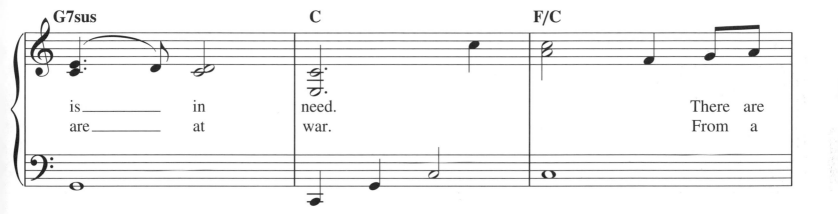

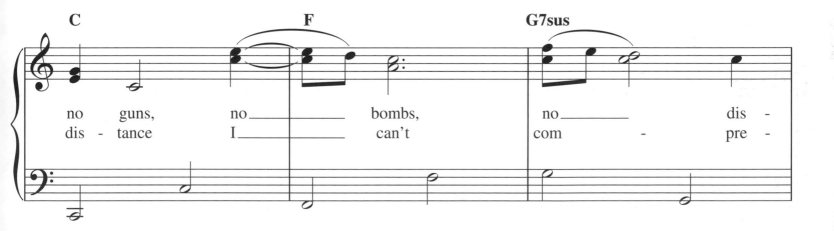

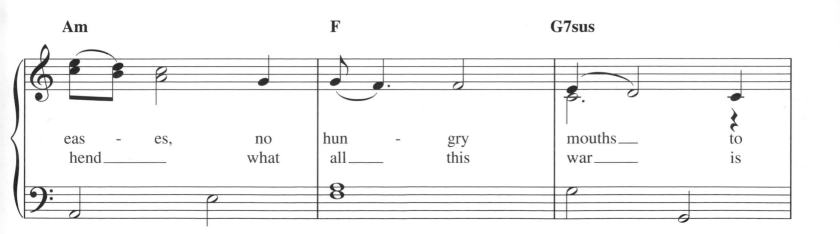

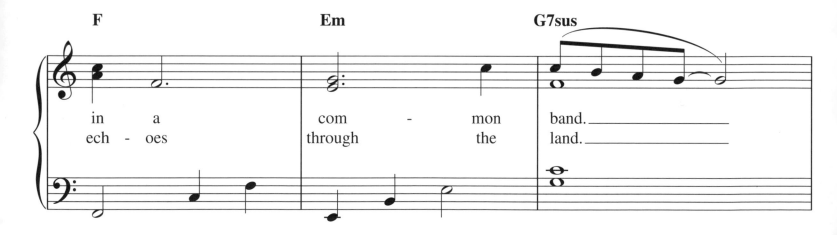

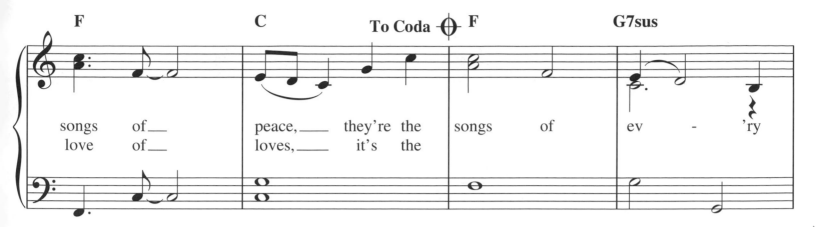

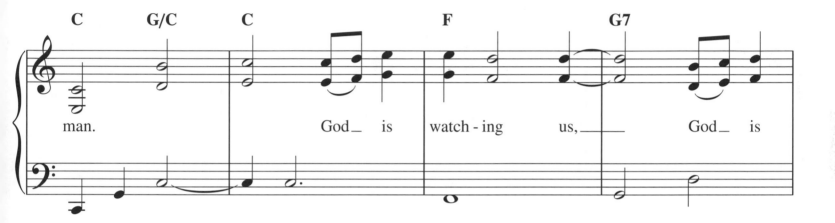

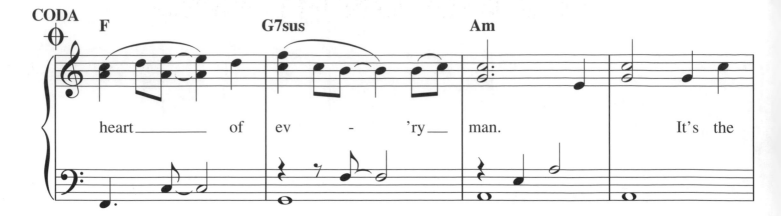

heart _____ of ev - 'ry ___ man. It's the

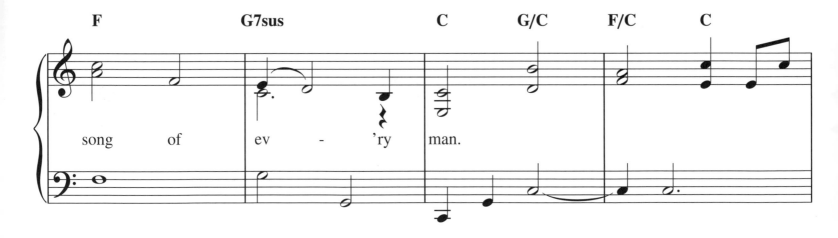

hope of ___ hopes, ___ it's the love of ___ loves, ___ it's the

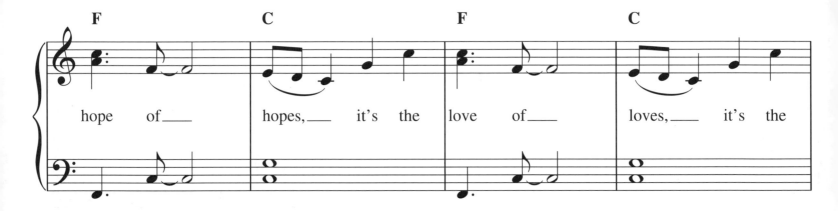

song of ev - 'ry man.

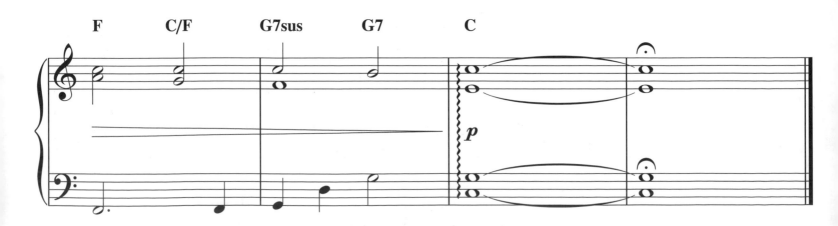

GEORGIA ON MY MIND

Words by STUART GORRELL
Music by HOAGY CARMICHAEL

Moderately slow

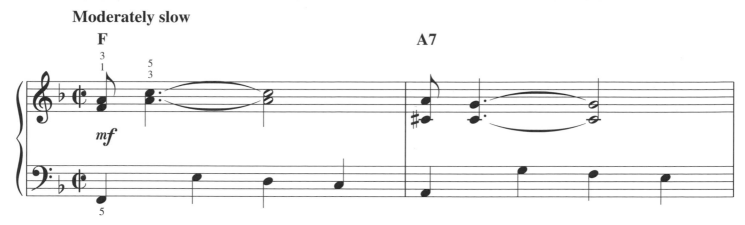

Mel - o - dies   bring   mem - o - ries   that   lin - ger in my

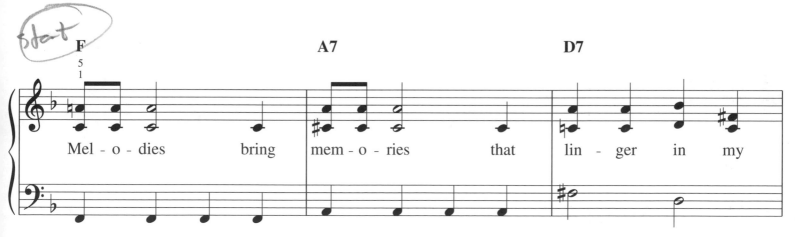

heart. _____   Make me think   of   Geor - gia,   why

68

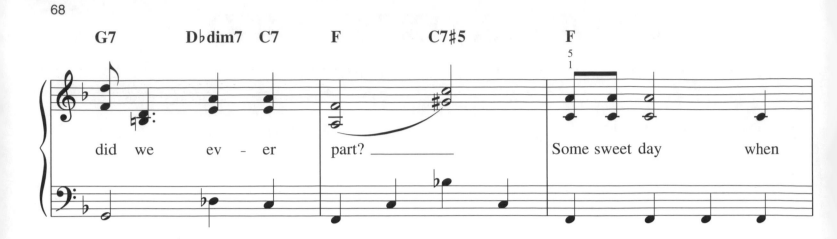

did we ev - er part? _____ Some sweet day when

blos-soms fall and all the world's a song, _____

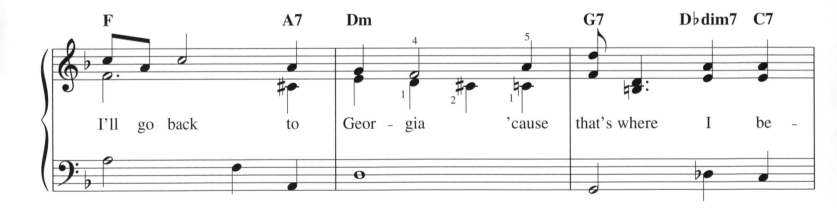

I'll go back to Geor - gia 'cause that's where I be -

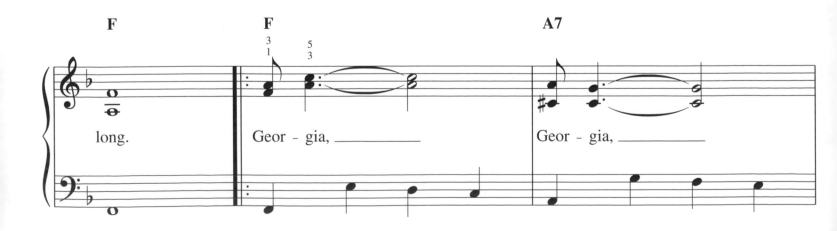

long. Geor - gia, _____ Geor - gia, _____

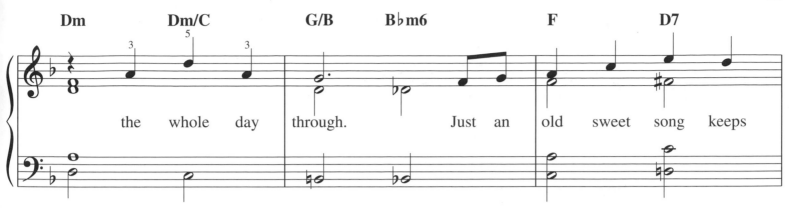

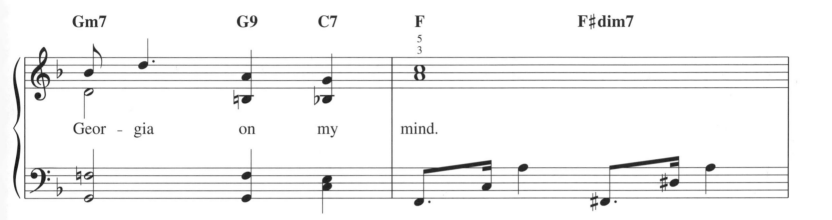

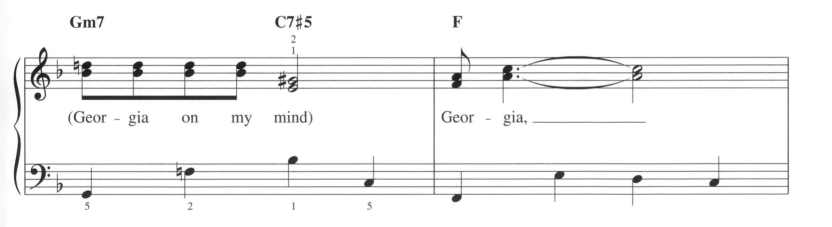

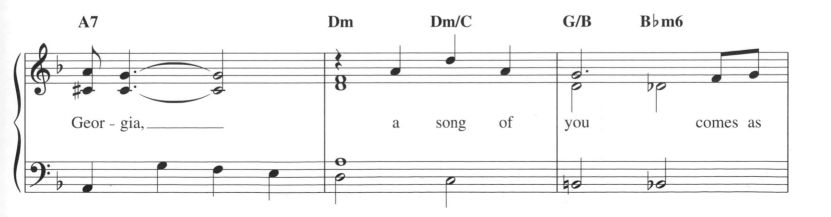

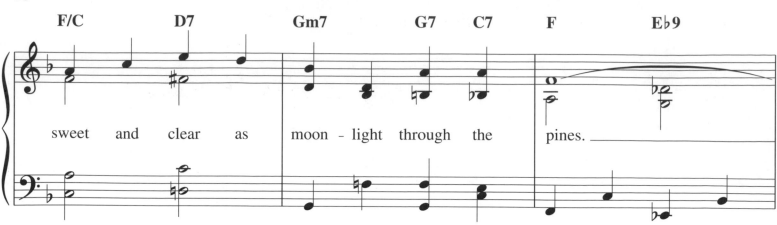

sweet and clear as moon - light through the pines. ____

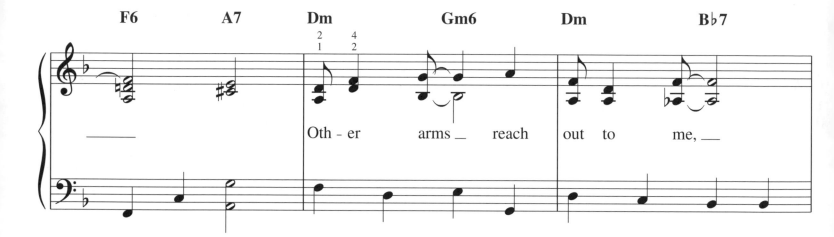

____ Oth - er arms ____ reach out to me, ___

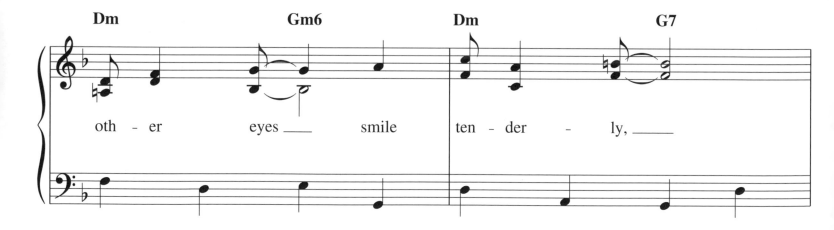

oth - er eyes ____ smile ten - der - ly, ____

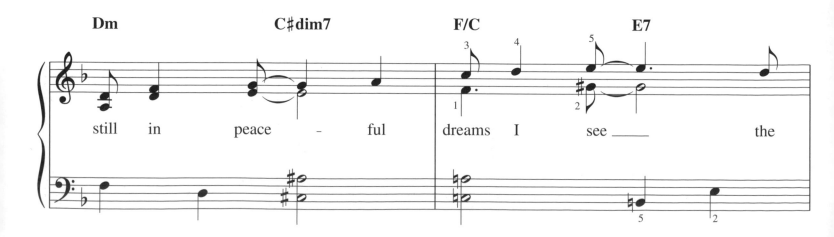

still in peace - ful dreams I see ____ the

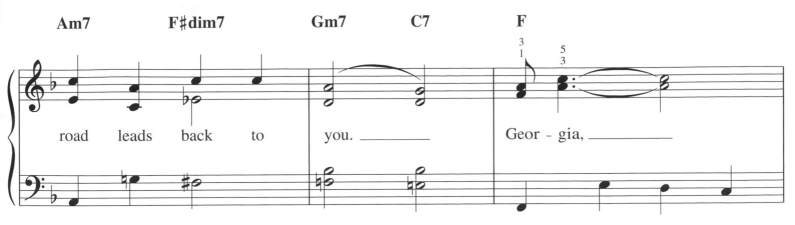

road   leads   back   to   you. _____   Geor - gia, _____

Geor - gia, _____   no   peace   I   find.   Just   an

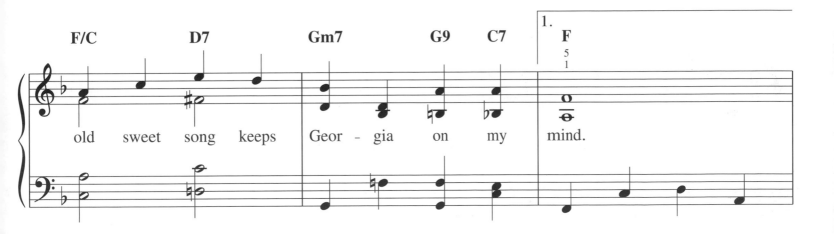

old   sweet   song   keeps   Geor - gia   on   my   mind.

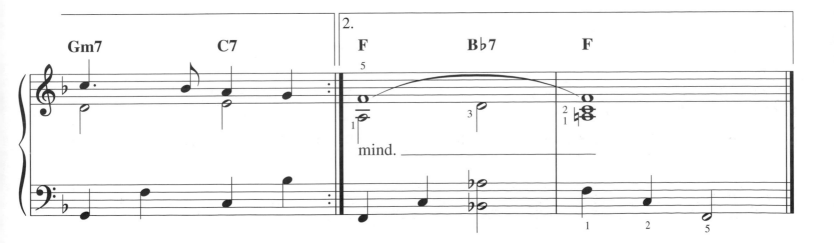

mind. _____

THE GIRL FROM IPANEMA
(Garôta de Ipanema)

Music by ANTONIO CARLOS JOBIM
English Words by NORMAN GIMBEL
Original Words by VINICIUS DE MORAES

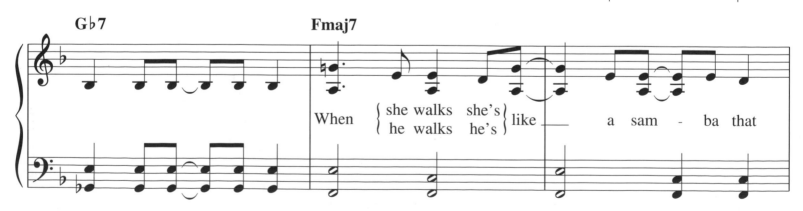

swings   so   cool   and   sways ____   so   gen - tle,   that   when

{ she   pass - es,   each   one ____   she }   pass - es   goes
{ he   pass - es,   each   girl ____   he }

"a-a-h!"   Oh, _____

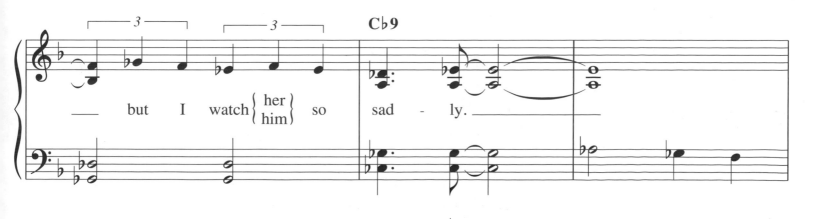

____   but   I   watch { her }   so   sad - ly. _____
                         { him }

74

How _____ can I tell { her / him } I love { her? / him? } _____

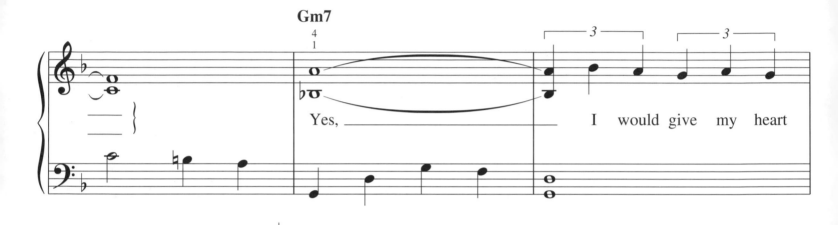

___ { } Yes, _____ I would give my heart

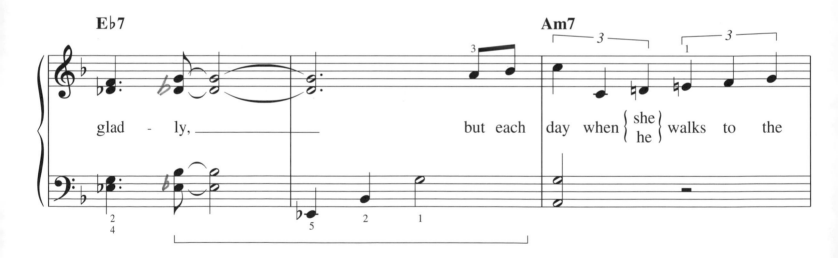

glad - ly, _____ but each day when { she / he } walks to the

sea, { she / he } looks straight a - head not at me.

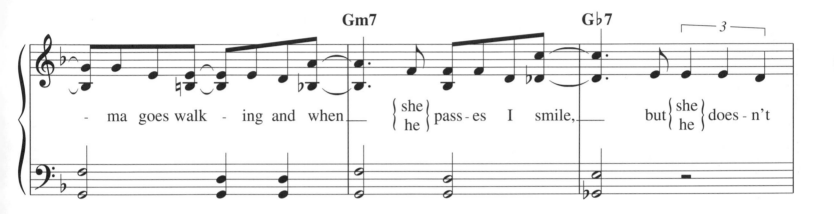

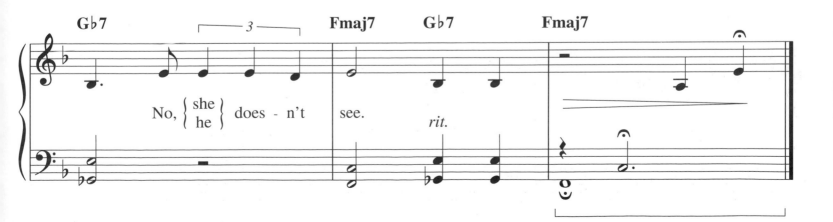

HERE'S THAT RAINY DAY
from CARNIVAL IN FLANDERS

Words by JOHNNY BURKE
Music by JIMMY VAN HEUSEN

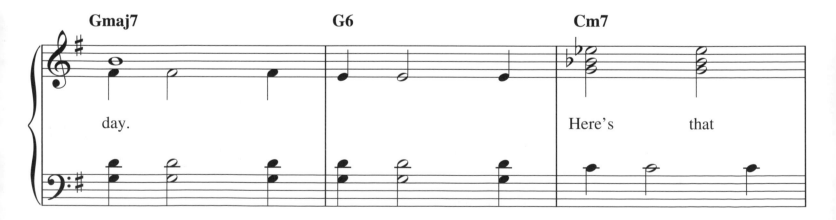

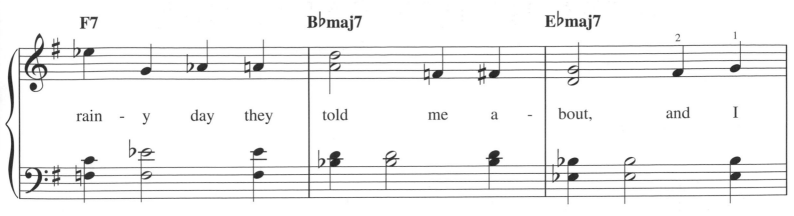

rain - y day they told me a - bout, and I

laughed at the thought that it might turn out this way.

Where is that worn - out wish that

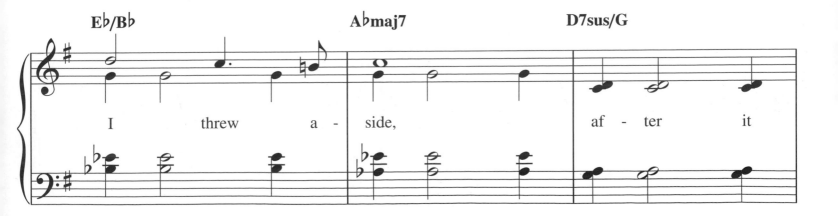

I threw a - side, af - ter it

brought my lov - er near?

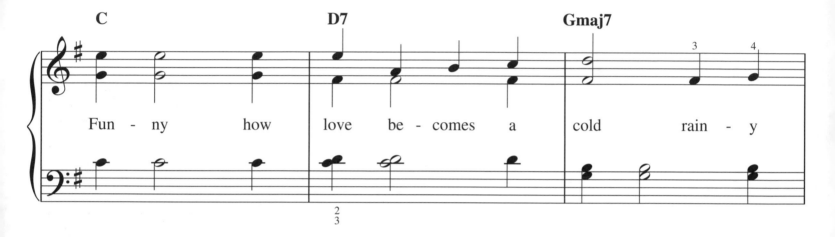

Fun - ny how love be - comes a cold rain - y

day. Fun - ny, that rain - y day is

1.
here.

2.
here.

HOW DEEP IS THE OCEAN
(How High Is the Sky)

Words and Music by
IRVING BERLIN

Moderately

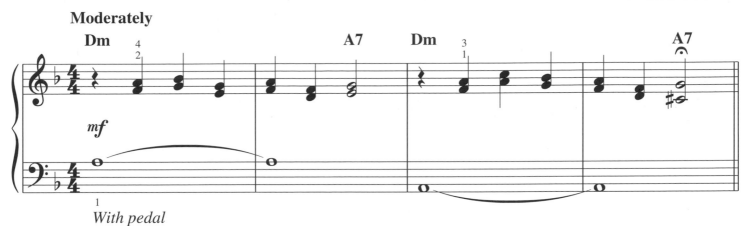

With pedal

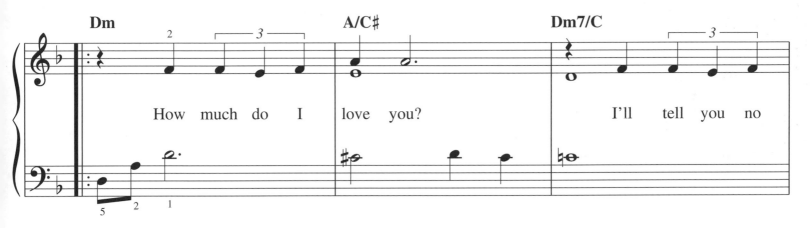

How much do I love you? I'll tell you no

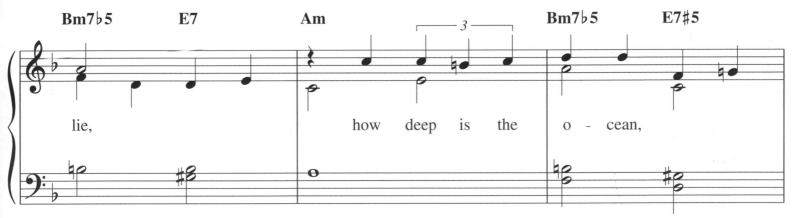

lie, how deep is the o - cean,

how high is the sky? How man - y times a day

____ do I think of you?_____ How man - y

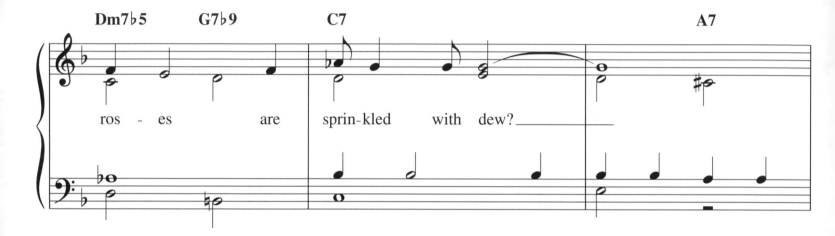

ros - es ____ are ____ sprin-kled with dew?_____

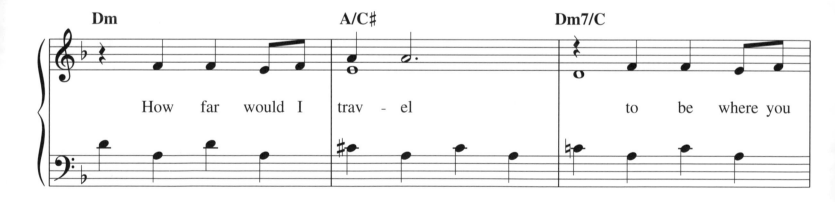

How far would I trav - el ____ to be where you

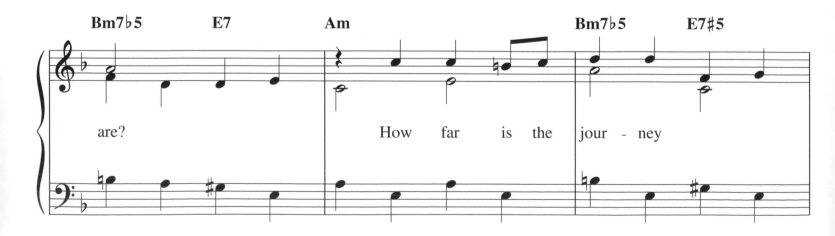

are? ____ How far is the jour - ney

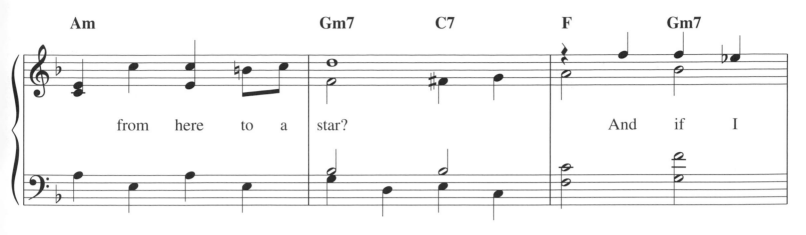

from here to a star? And if I

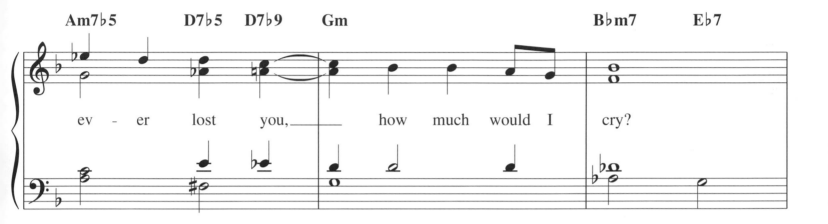

ev - er lost you, ___ how much would I cry?

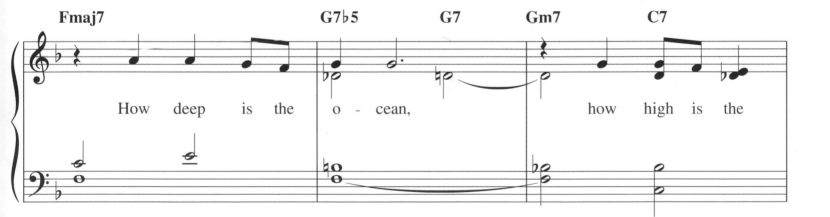

How deep is the o - cean, how high is the

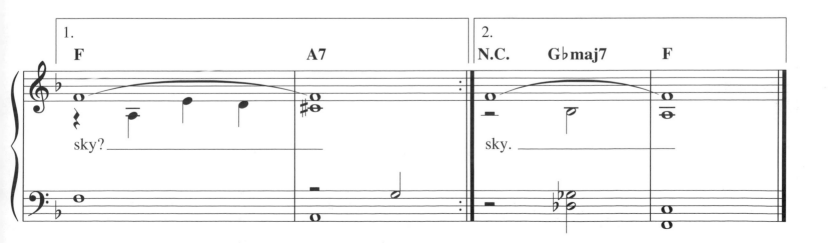

sky? ___ sky. ___

I LEFT MY HEART
IN SAN FRANCISCO

Words by DOUGLASS CROSS
Music by GEORGE CORY

Slow, with a steady beat

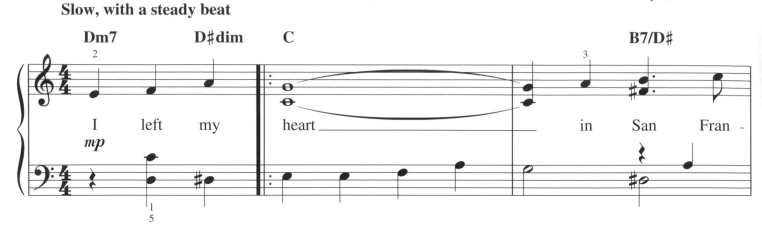

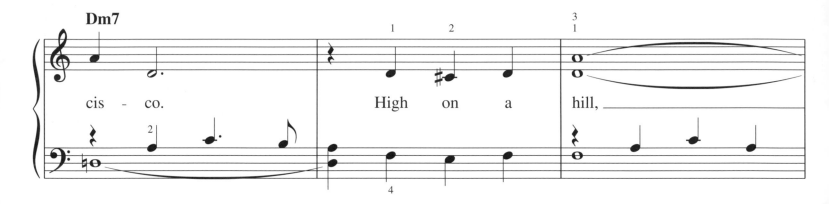

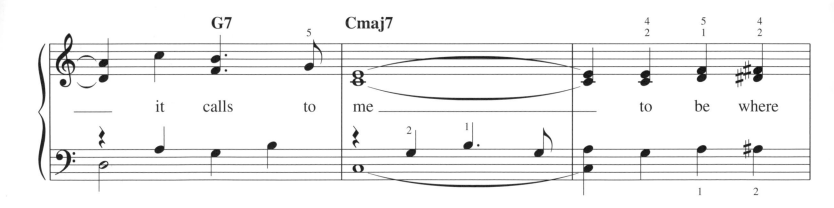

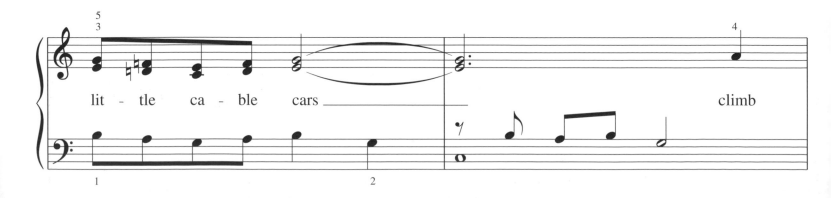

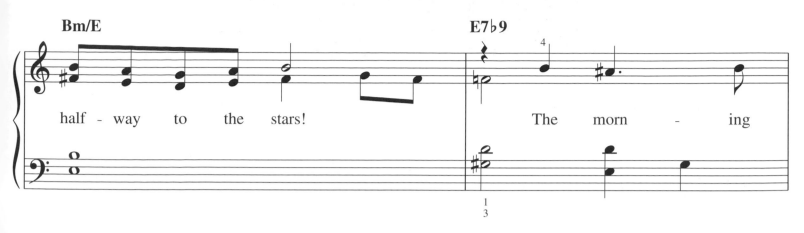

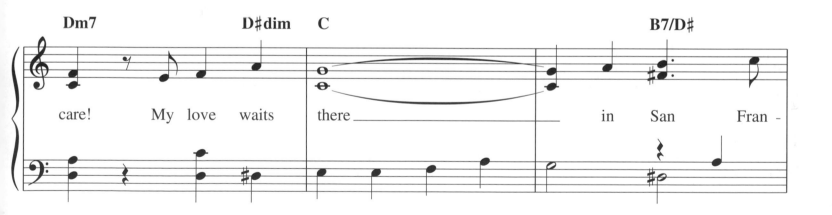

and wind - y sea.   When I come

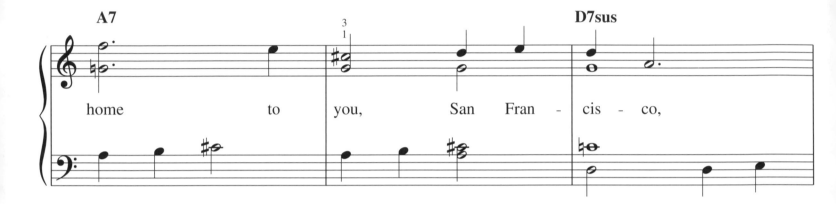

home   to   you,   San Fran - cis - co,

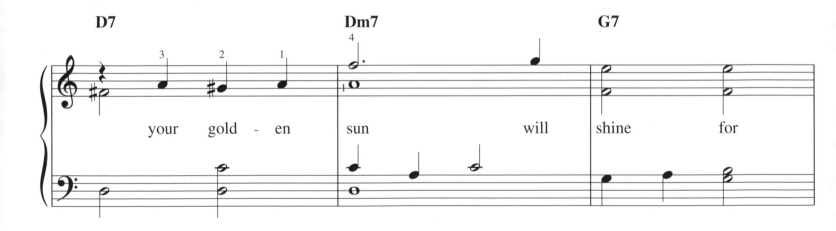

your   gold - en   sun   will   shine   for

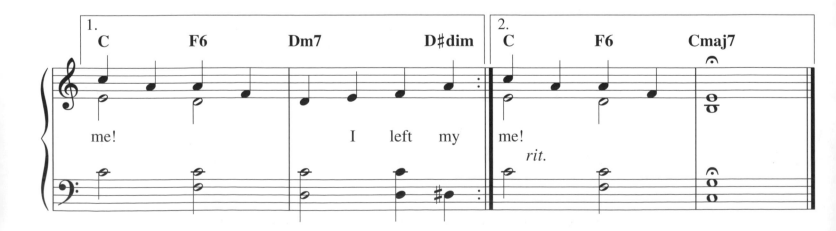

me!   I   left   my   me!

I'LL BE SEEING YOU

from RIGHT THIS WAY

Written by IRVING KAHAL
and SAMMY FAIN

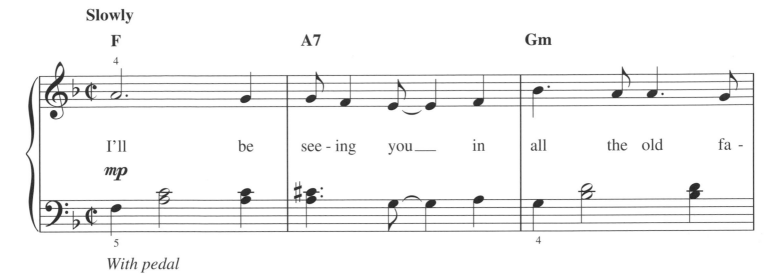

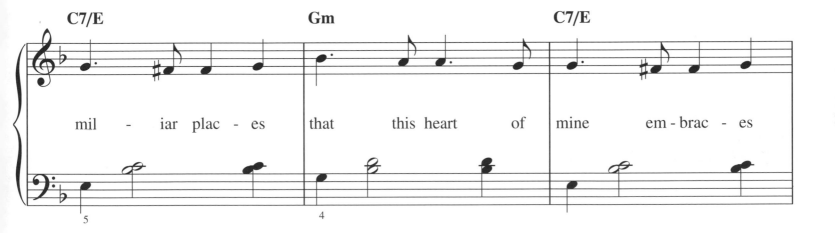

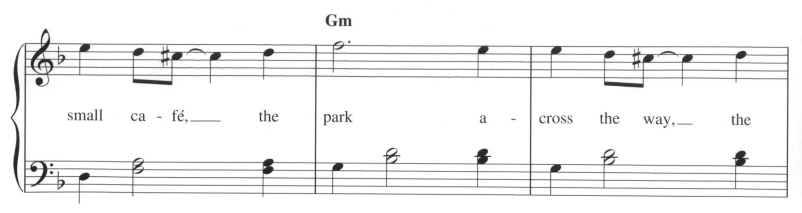

small ca - fé,____ the park a - cross the way,___ the

chil - dren's ca - rou - sel,____ the chest - nut trees,___ the

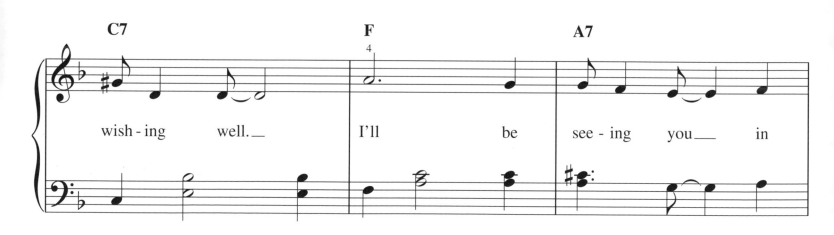

wish - ing well.___ I'll be see - ing you___ in

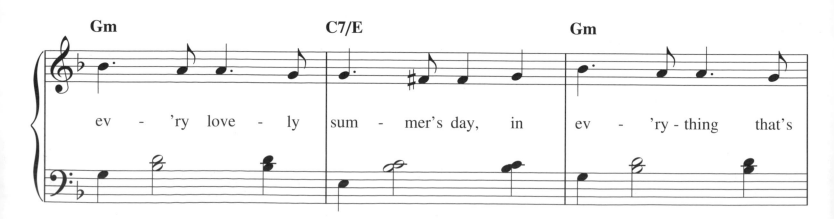

ev - 'ry love - ly sum - mer's day, in ev - 'ry - thing that's

87

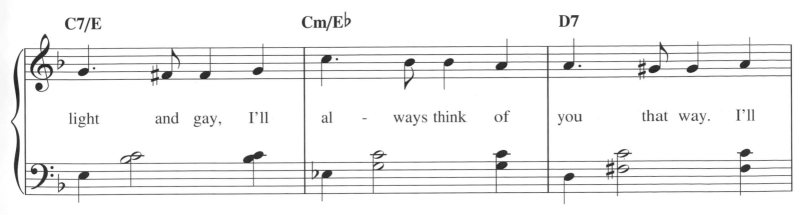

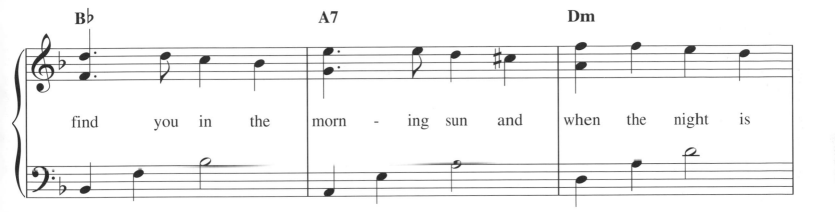

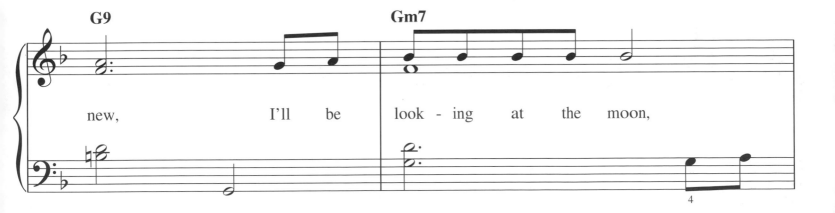

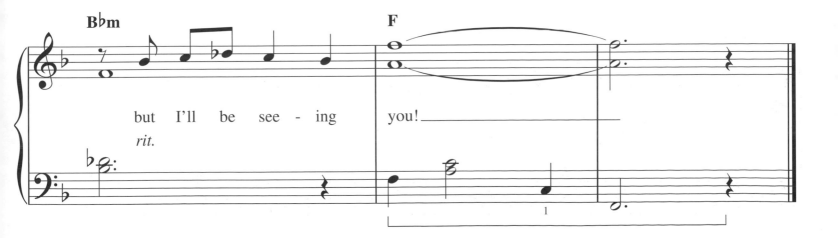

IMAGINE

Words and Music by
JOHN LENNON

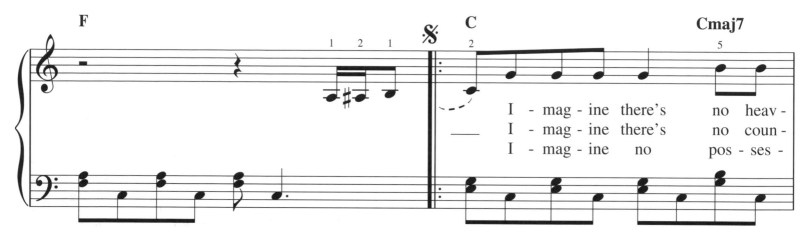

Imagine there's no heaven
Imagine there's no countries
Imagine no possessions

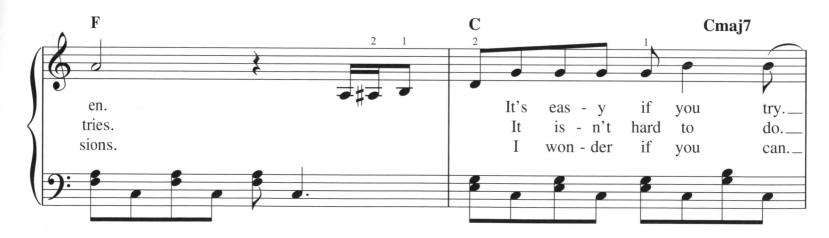

en.
tries.
sions.

It's easy if you try.
It isn't hard to do.
I wonder if you can.

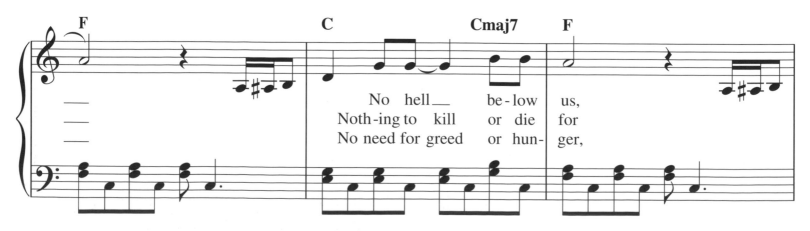

No hell below us,
Nothing to kill or die for
No need for greed or hunger,

89

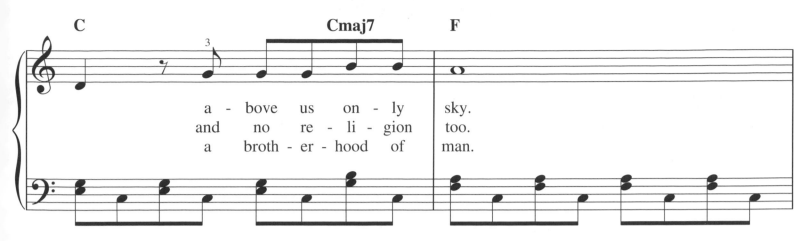

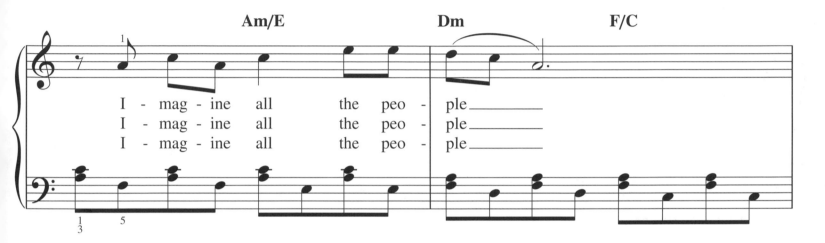

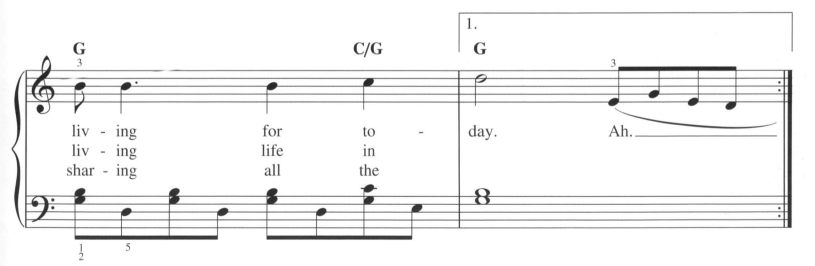

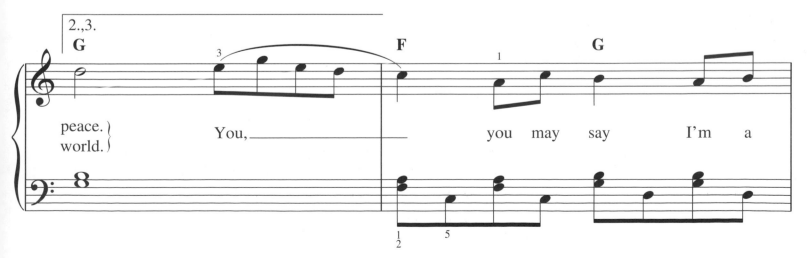

dream - er.   But I'm not the on - ly

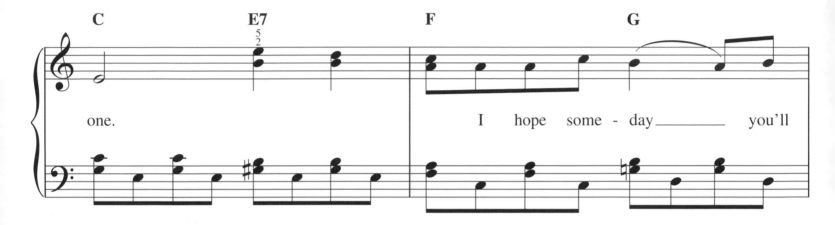

one.   I hope some - day_____ you'll

To Coda   **D.S. al Coda**
(take 2nd ending)

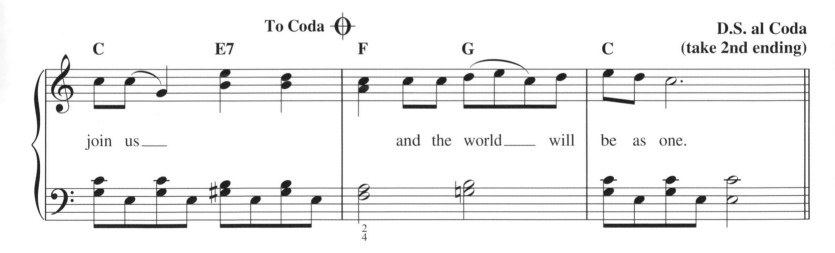

join us____   and the world____ will   be as one.

CODA

rit.   and the world_____ will   be as one.

IT MIGHT AS WELL BE SPRING

from STATE FAIR

Lyrics by OSCAR HAMMERSTEIN II
Music by RICHARD RODGERS

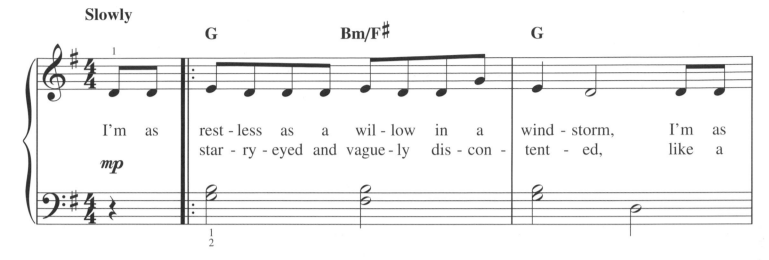

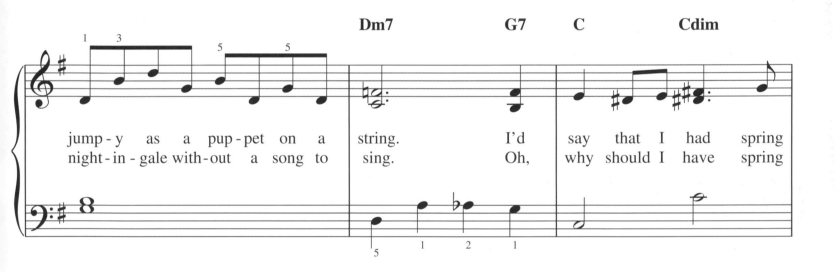

92

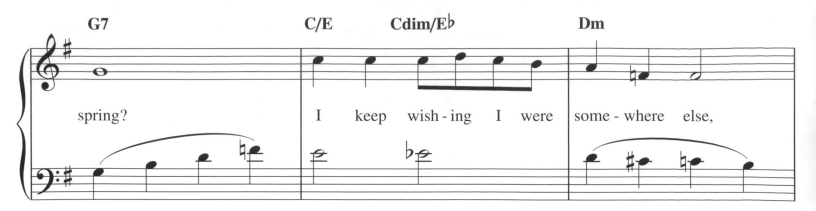

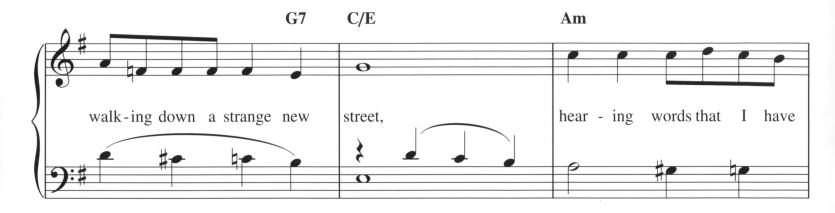

93

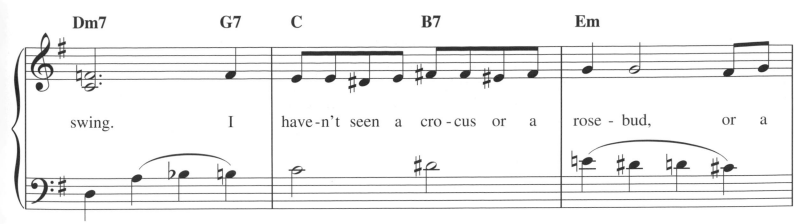

swing.   I   have-n't seen a cro - cus or a   rose - bud,   or a

rob - in   on   the   wing,   but I   feel   so   gay   in a

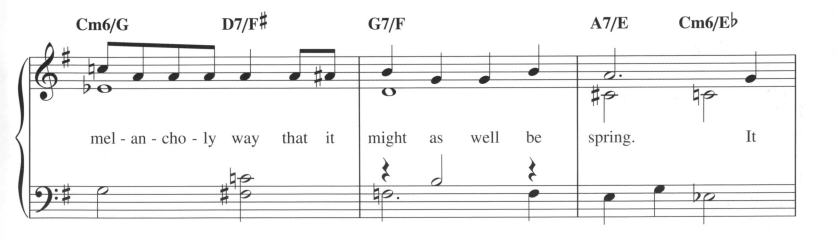

mel - an - cho - ly way that it   might   as   well   be   spring.   It

might___ as   well___ be   spring.

ISN'T IT ROMANTIC?

from the Paramount Picture LOVE ME TONIGHT

Words by LORENZ HART
Music by RICHARD RODGERS

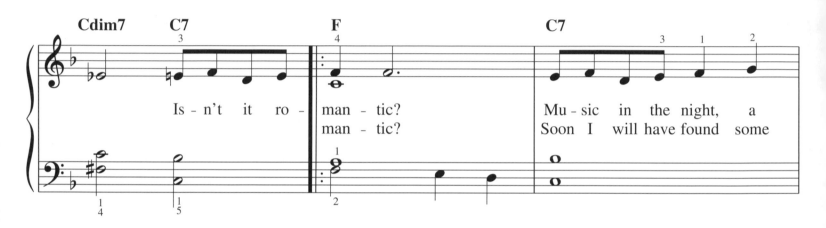

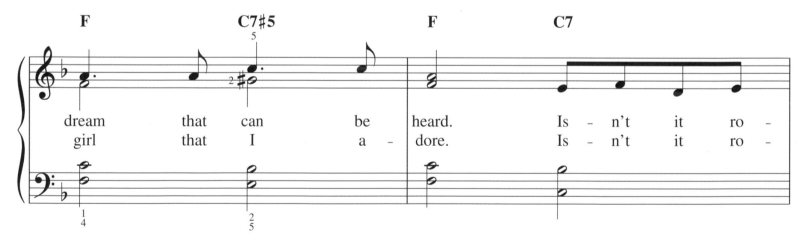

Is - n't it ro- | man - tic?
man - tic?

Mu - sic in the night, a
Soon I will have found some

dream that can be heard.
girl that I a - dore.

Is - n't it ro -
Is - n't it ro -

man - tic?
man - tic?

Mov - ing shad - ows write the
While I sit a - round, my

95

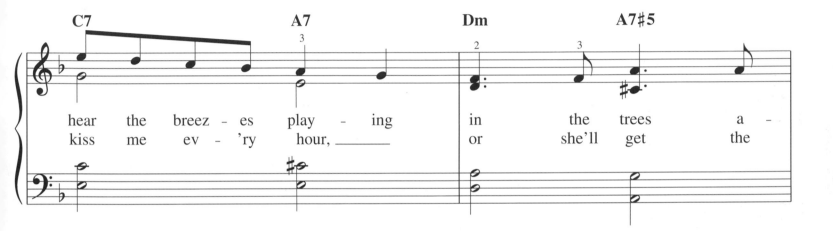

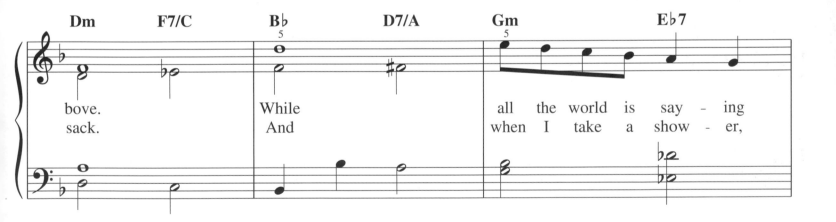

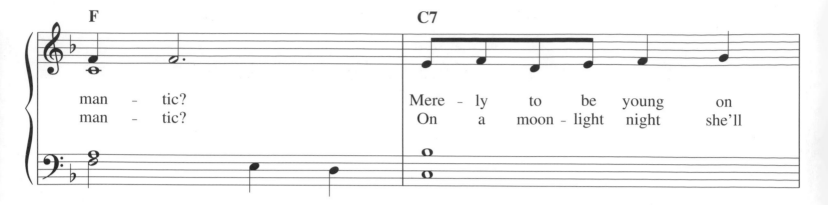

man - tic?
man - tic?

Mere - ly to be young on
On a moon - light night she'll

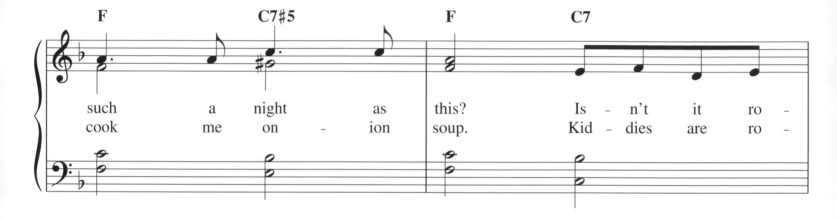

such a night as this?
cook me on - ion soup.

Is - n't it ro -
Kid - dies are ro -

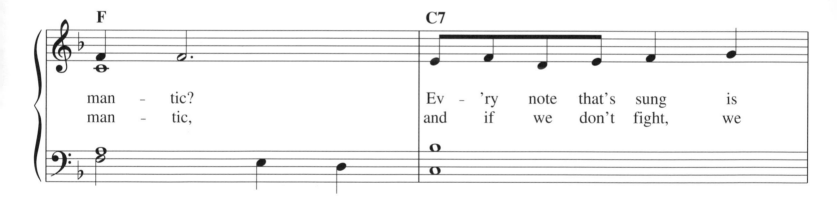

man - tic?
man - tic,

Ev - 'ry note that's sung is
and if we don't fight, we

like a lov - er's kiss.
soon will have a troupe!

Sweet
We'll

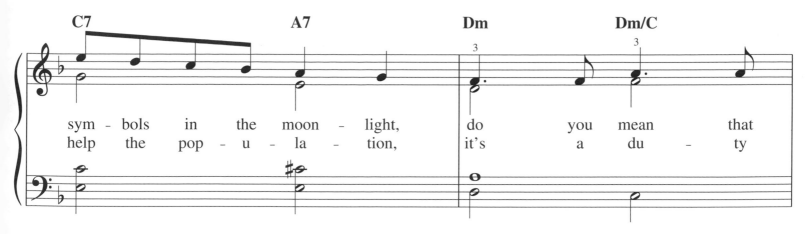

sym - bols in the moon - light, do you mean that
help the pop - u - la - tion, it's a du - ty

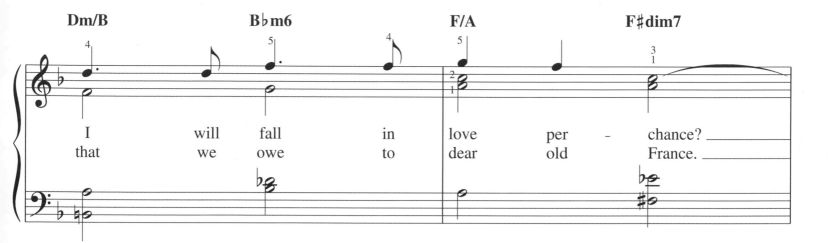

I will fall in love per - chance? ____
that we owe to dear old France. ____

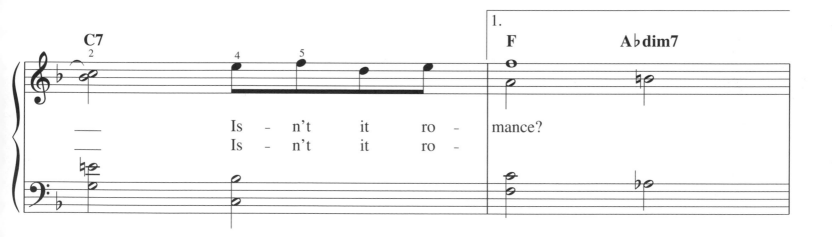

Is - n't it ro - mance?
Is - n't it ro -

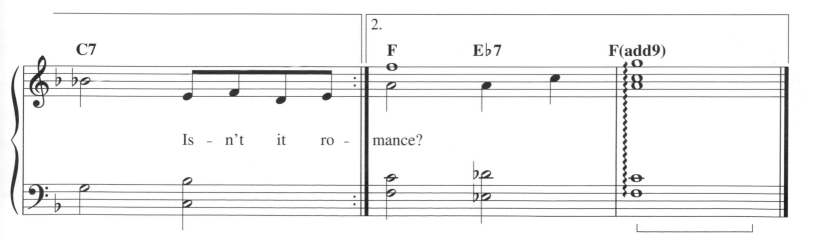

Is - n't it ro - mance?

JUST THE WAY YOU ARE

Words and Music by
BILLY JOEL

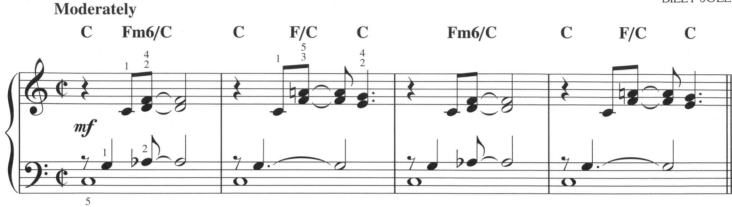

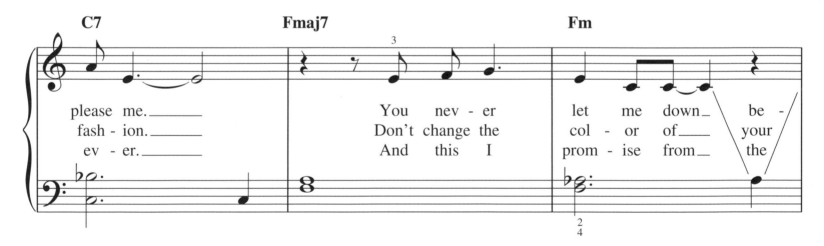

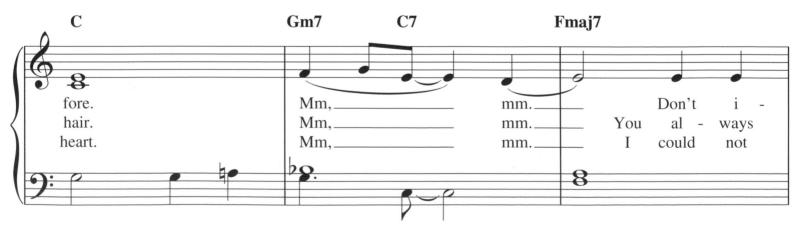

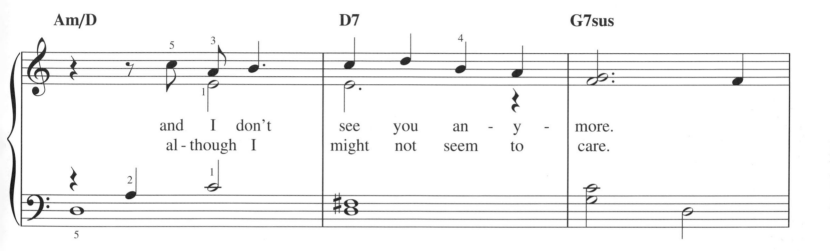

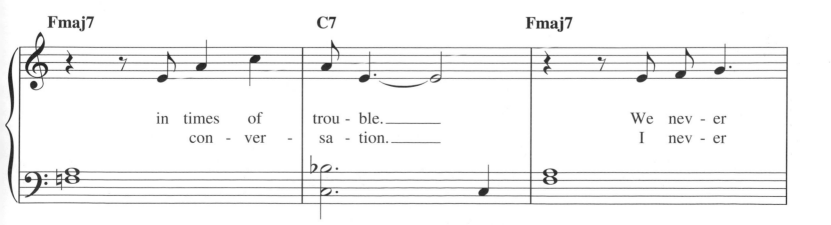

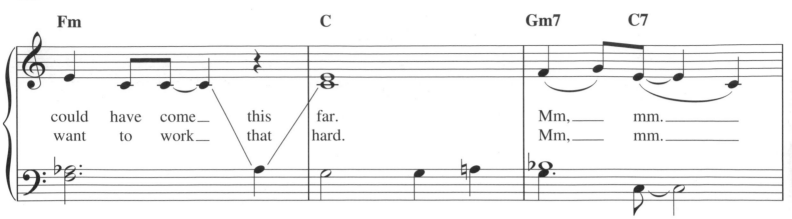

Fm · C · Gm7 · C7

could have come__ this far.
want to work__ that hard.

Mm,____ mm.____
Mm,____ mm.____

Fmaj7 · Fm · C

I took the good times,
I just want some - one

I'll take the
that I can

Am7 · Dm7 · G7

bad times.
talk to.

I'll take you
I want you

just the way__ you
just the way__ you

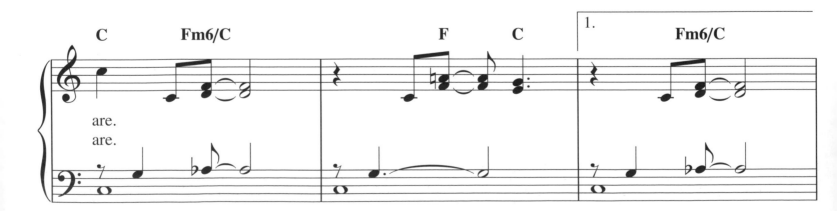

C · Fm6/C · F · C · 1. · Fm6/C

are.
are.

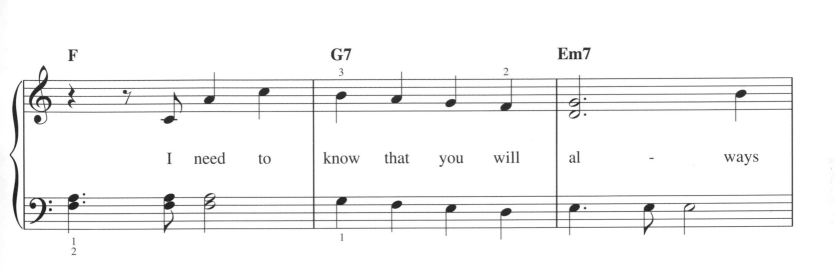

I need to know that you will al - ways

be   the same old   some - one that I

knew.   Oh!   What will it

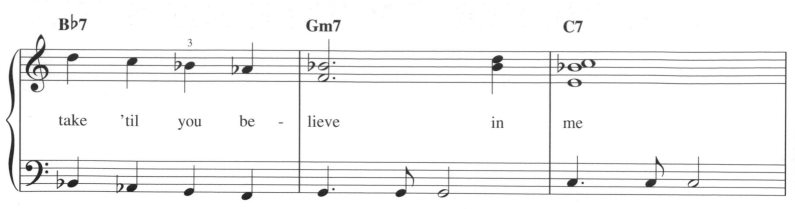

take 'til you be - lieve in me

the way that I be - lieve in you?

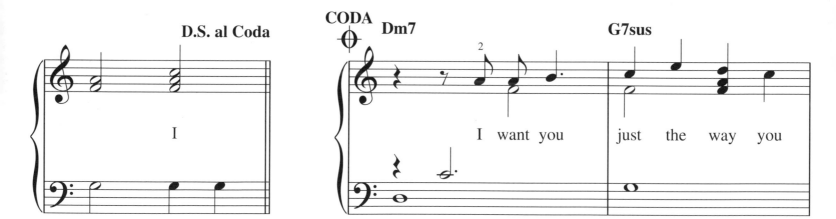

D.S. al Coda

I

CODA

I want you just the way you

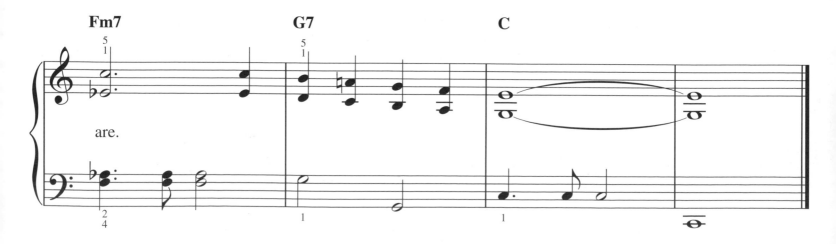

are.

KILLING ME SOFTLY WITH HIS SONG

Words by NORMAN GIMBEL
Music by CHARLES FOX

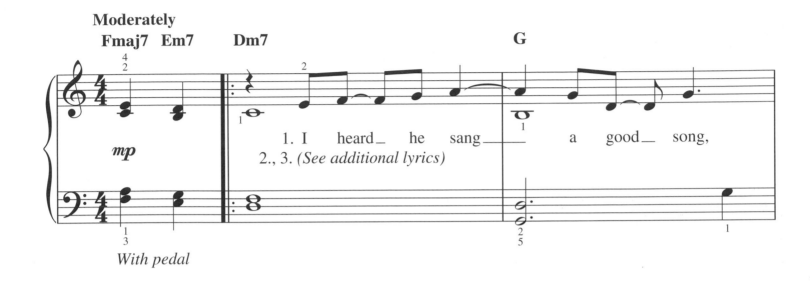

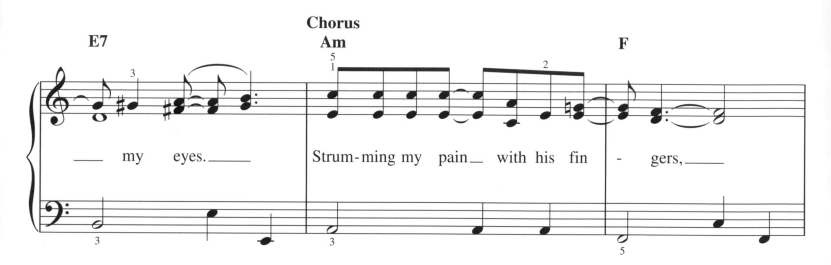

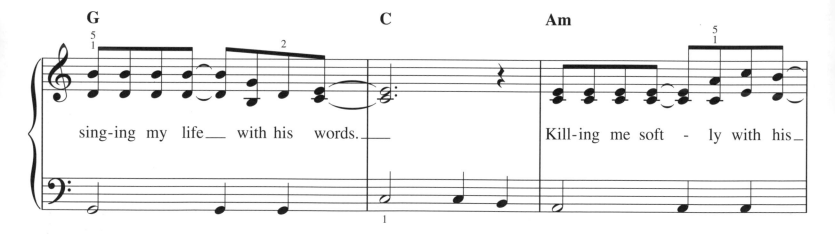

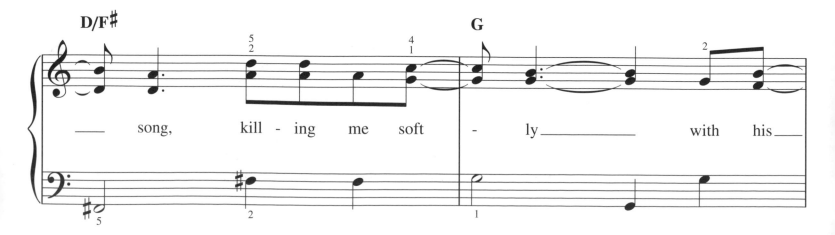

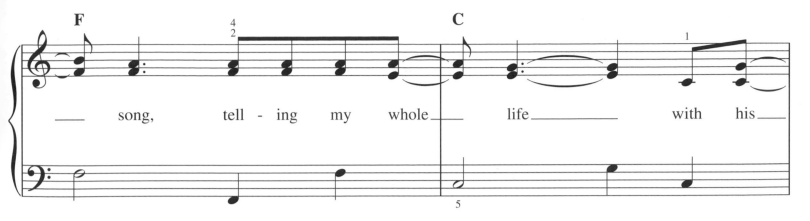

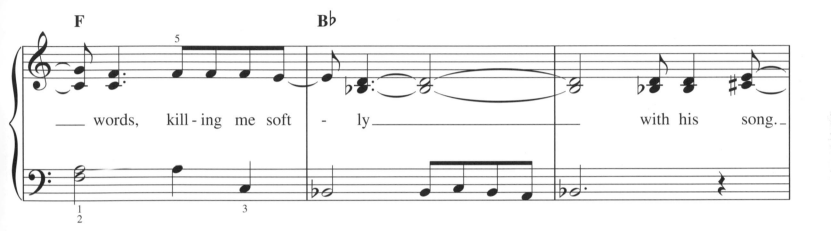

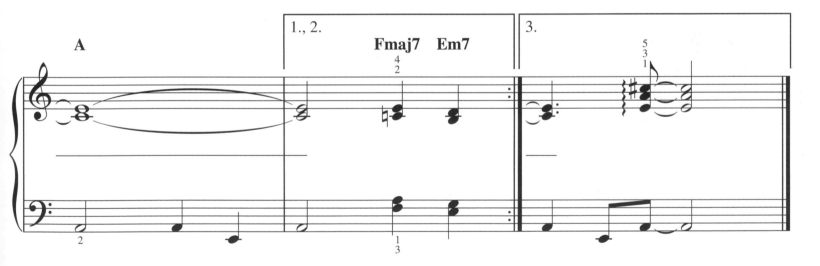

Additional Lyrics

2. I felt all flushed with fever, embarrassed by the crowd,
I felt he found my letters and read each one out loud.
I prayed that he would finish, but he just kept right on.
Chorus

3. He sang as if he knew me, in all my dark despair,
And then he looked right through me, as if I wasn't there.
But he was there, this stranger, singing clear and strong.
Chorus

THE LADY IS A TRAMP

from BABES IN ARMS
from WORDS AND MUSIC

Words by LORENZ HART
Music by RICHARD RODGERS

I get too hun-gry for din-ner at eight,
I don't like crap games with bar-ons and earls,

I like the thea-tre but
Won't go to Har-lem in

nev-er come late,
er-mine and pearls,

I nev-er
Won't dish the

107

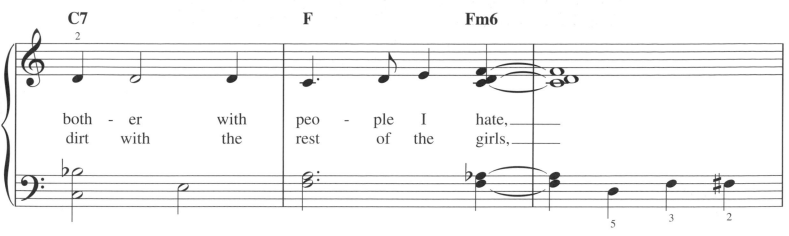

both - er   with   peo - ple I   hate,____
dirt with the   rest   of the girls,____

that's why the   la - dy is   a   tramp.
that's why the   la - dy is   a

tramp.   I   like the free

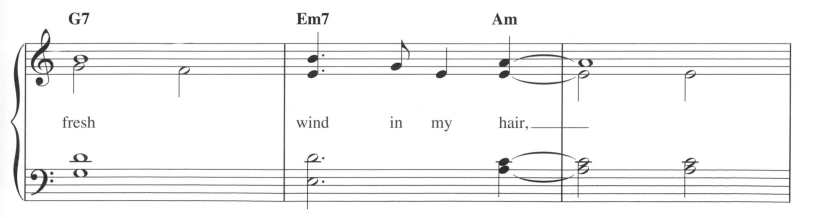

fresh   wind in   my hair,____

108

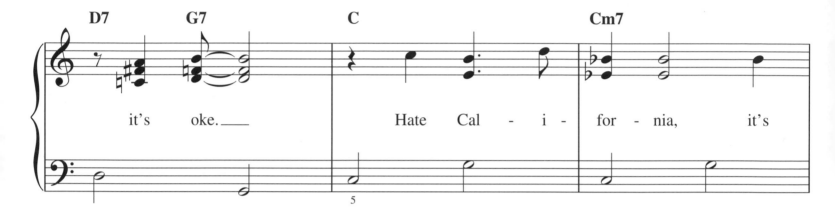

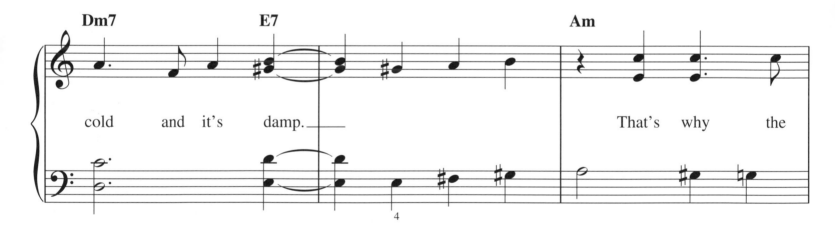

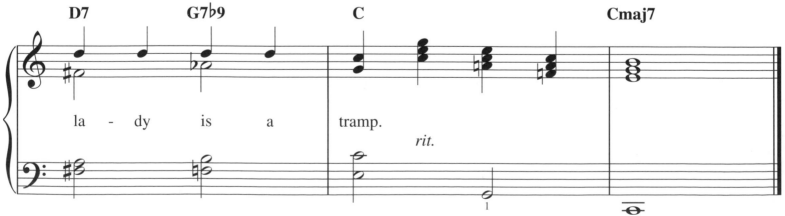

LONG AGO
(And Far Away)
from COVER GIRL

Words by IRA GERSHWIN
Music by JEROME KERN

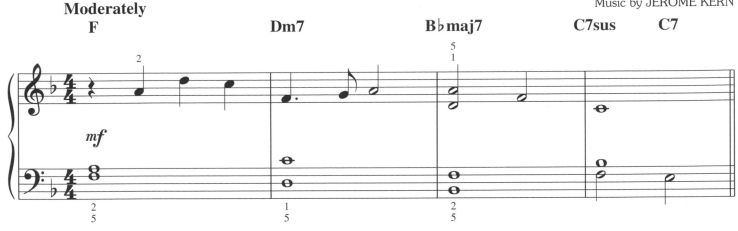

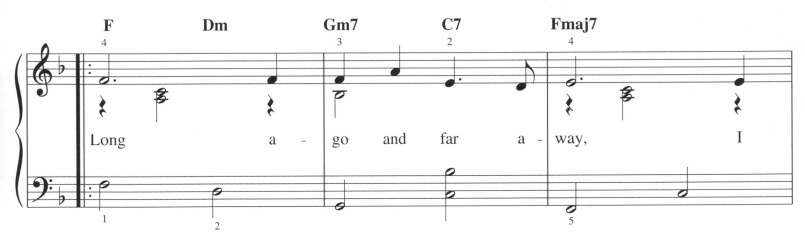

Long a- go and far a- way, I

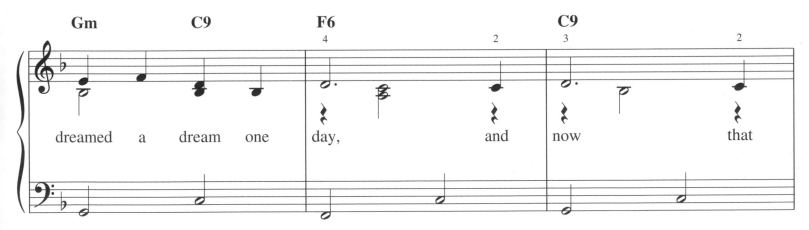

dreamed a dream one day, and now that

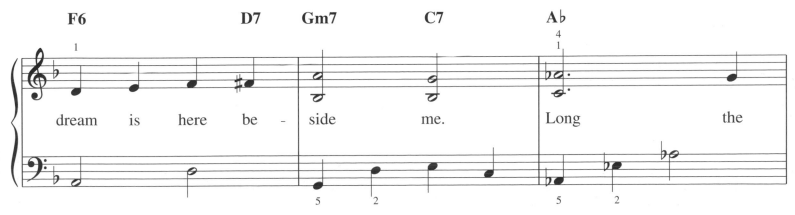

dream is here be- side me. Long the

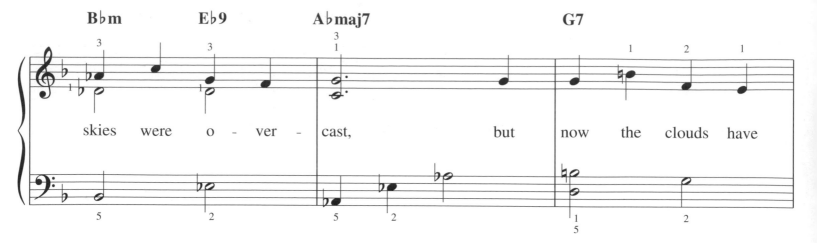

skies were o - ver - cast, but now the clouds have

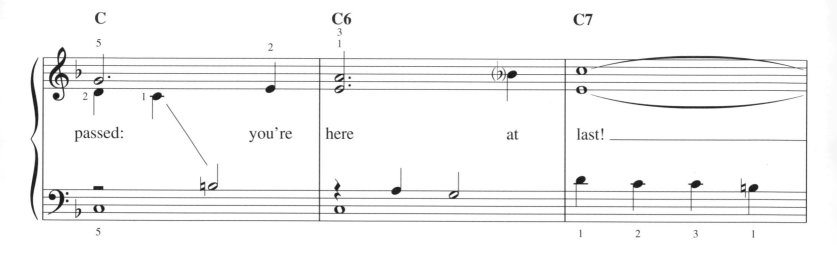

passed: you're here at last! _____

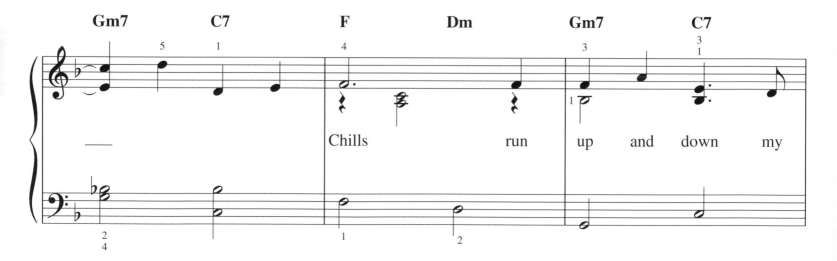

_____ Chills run up and down my

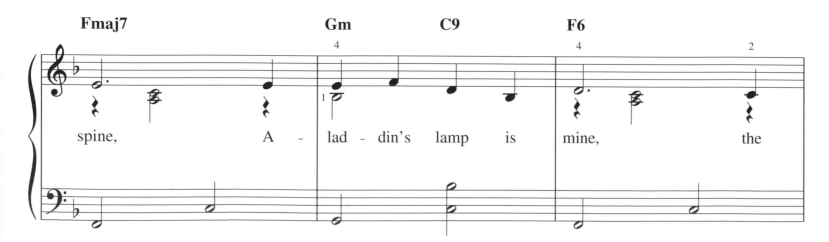

spine, A - lad - din's lamp is mine, the

C9   **F6**   **D7**   **Gm7**   **C7**

dream   I   dreamed was   not   de - nied   me.

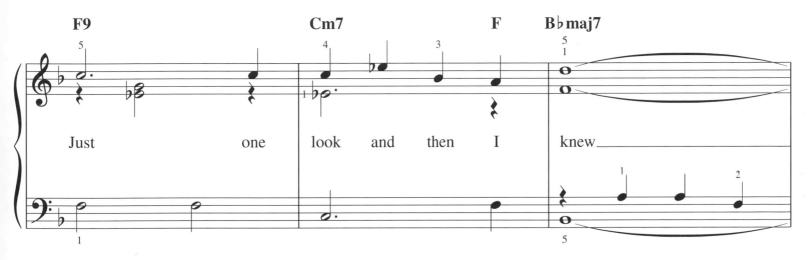

F9   **Cm7**   **F**   **B♭maj7**

Just   one   look   and   then   I   knew _____

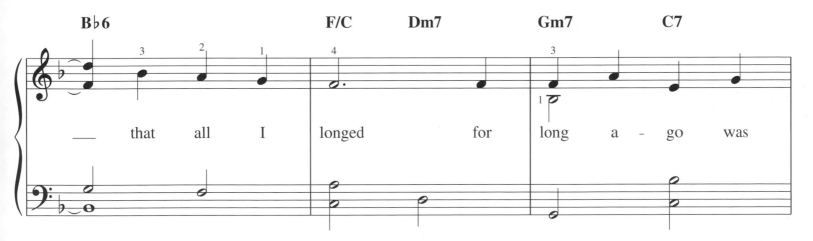

B♭6   **F/C**   **Dm7**   **Gm7**   **C7**

___ that   all   I   longed   for   long   a - go   was

1.   **F6**   **Gm**   **C7sus**   **C7**   2.   **F6**

you.   you.

p

8vb

LET IT BE

Words and Music by JOHN LENNON
and PAUL McCARTNEY

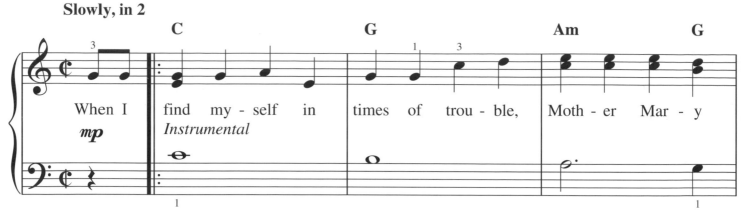

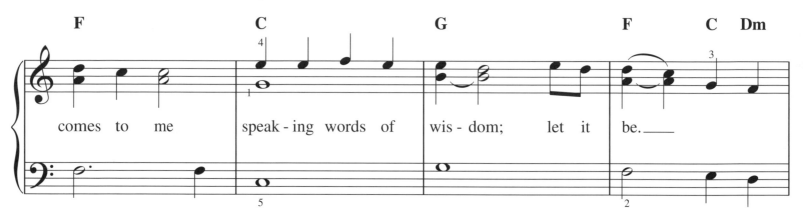

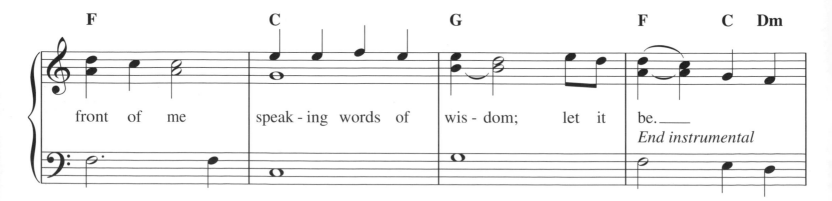

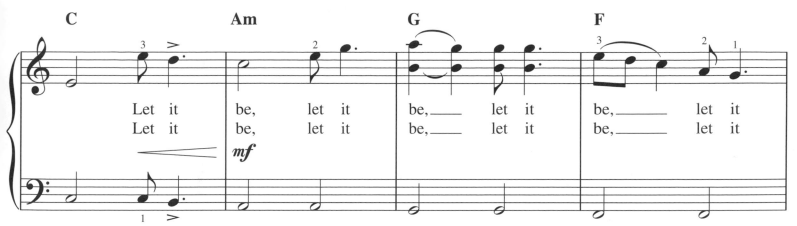

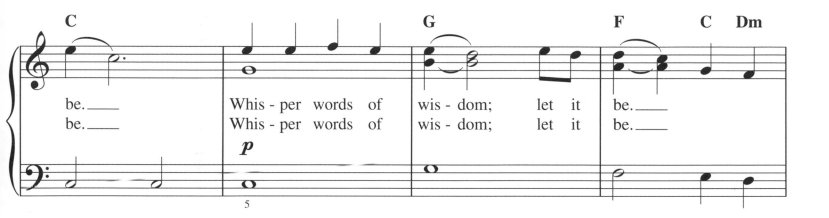

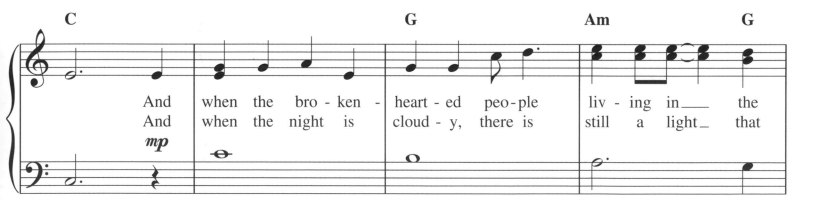

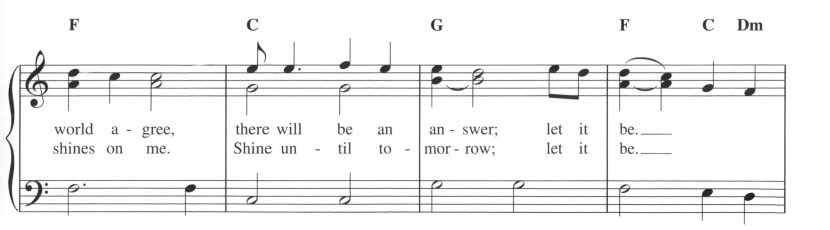

C   **G**

For | though they may be | part - ed, there is
I | wake up to the | sound of mu - sic,

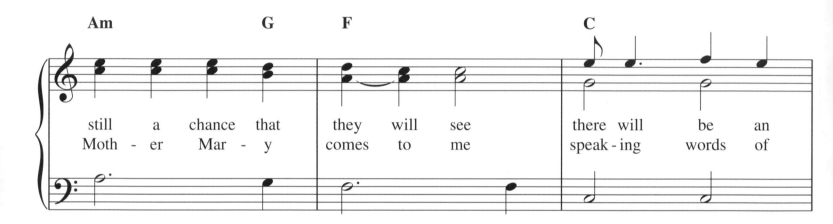

Am   **G**   **F**   **C**

still a chance that | they will see | there will be an
Moth - er Mar - y | comes to me | speak - ing words of

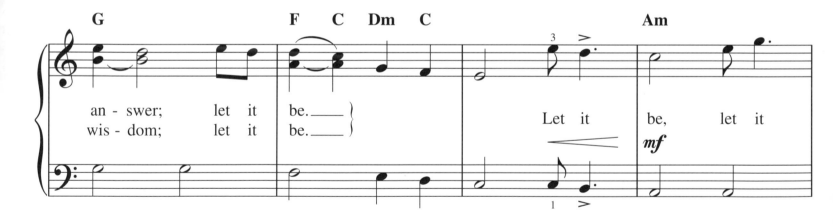

G   **F** **C** **Dm** **C**   **Am**

an - swer; let it | be. __ | Let it be, let it
wis - dom; let it | be. __ |

mf

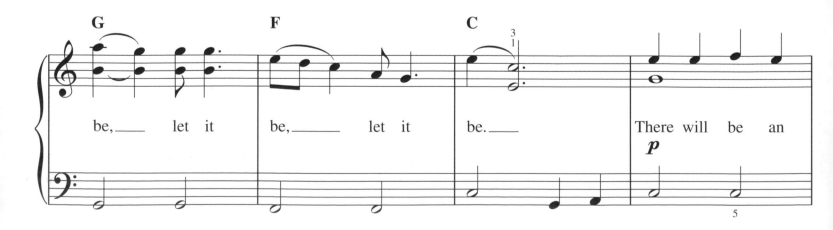

G   **F**   **C**

be, __ let it | be, __ let it | be. __ | There will be an

p

5

an - swer;   let it   be.____   Let it   be,   let it

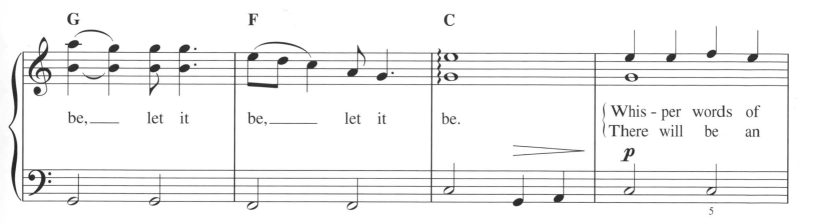

be,____   let it   be,____   let it   be.   Whis - per words of

There will be an

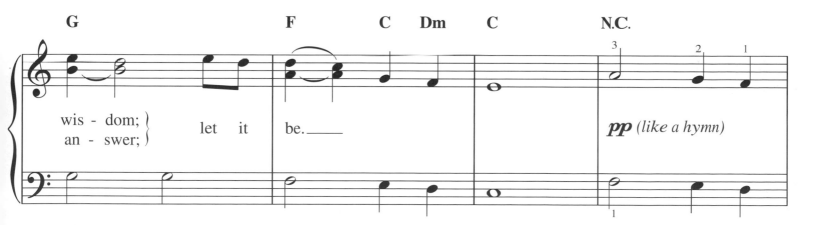

wis - dom;   let it   be.____

an - swer;

pp (like a hymn)

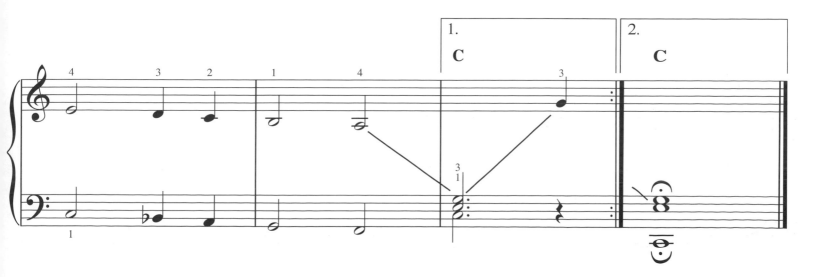

1.   C

2.   C

LOVE ME TENDER

from LOVE ME TENDER

Words and Music by ELVIS PRESLEY
and VERA MATSON

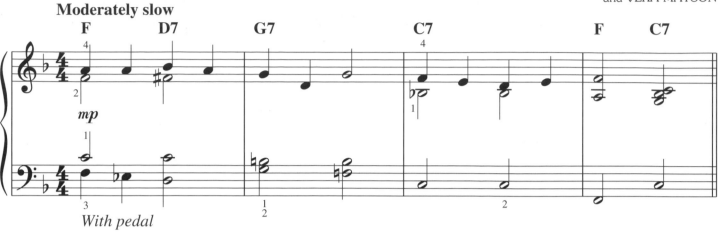

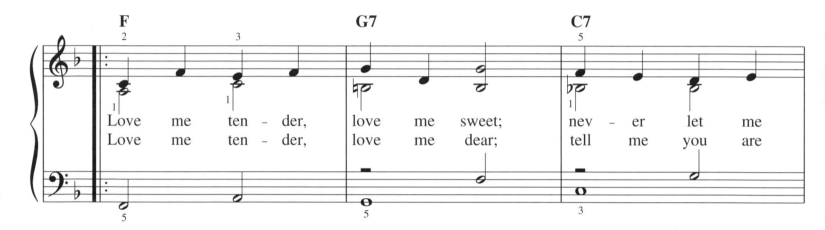

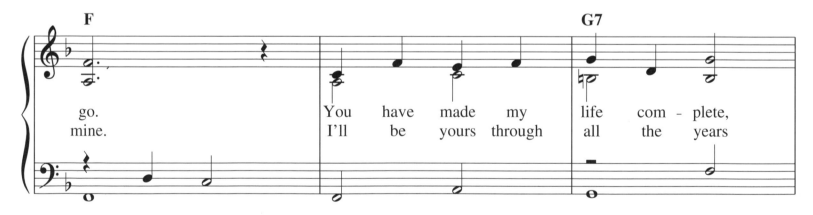

love me true, all my dreams ful - fill.

For, my dar - lin', I love you, and I al - ways will.

Love me ten - der, love me long; take me to your
When at last my dreams come true, dar - ling, this I

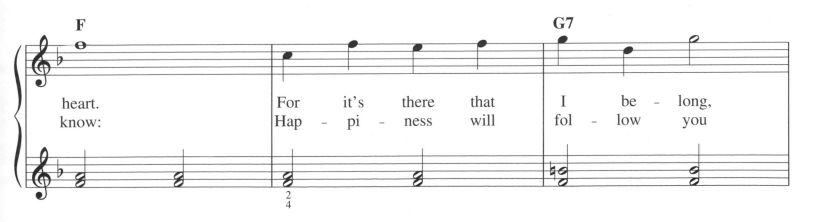

heart. For it's there that I be - long,
know: Hap - pi - ness will fol - low you

and we'll nev - er part. }
ev - 'ry - where you go. }

Love me ten - der,

love me true,

all my dreams ful - fill.

For, my dar - lin', I love you, and I al - ways

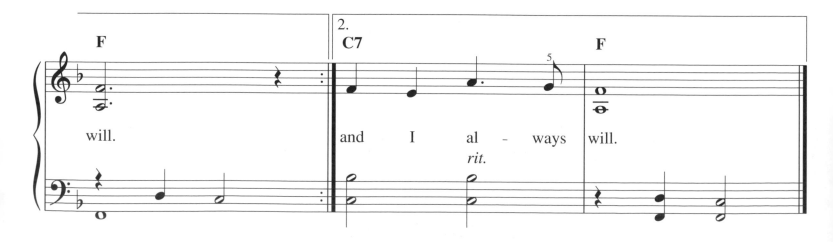

will.

and I al - ways will.

rit.

MONA LISA

from the Paramount Picture CAPTAIN CAREY, U.S.A.

Words and Music by JAY LIVINGSTON
and RAY EVANS

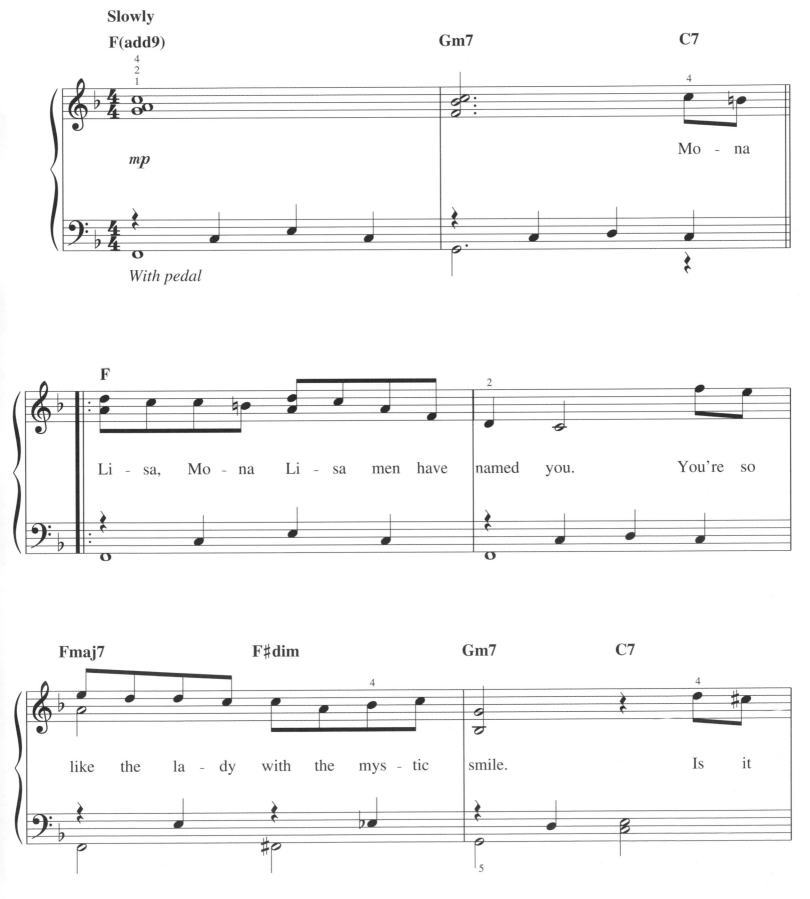

B♭m   **F**   **F♯dim**

dreams have been brought to your door - step. They just

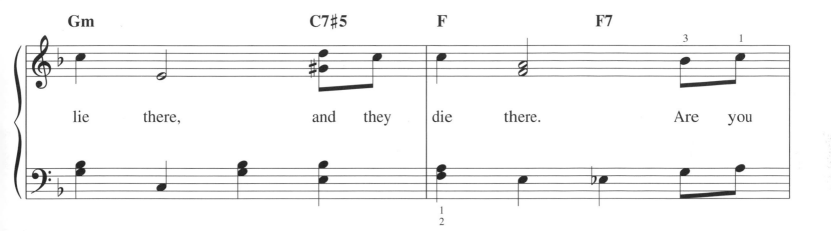

Gm   **C7♯5**   **F**   **F7**

lie there, and they die there. Are you

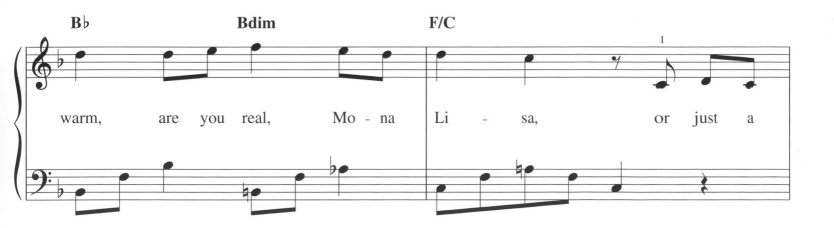

B♭   **Bdim**   **F/C**

warm, are you real, Mo - na Li - sa, or just a

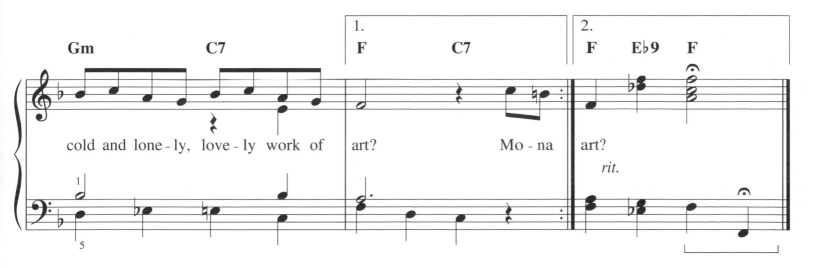

Gm   **C7**   **1.** **F**   **C7**   **2.** **F** **E♭9** **F**

cold and lone - ly, love - ly work of art? Mo - na art?

rit.

MEMORY
from CATS

Music by ANDREW LLOYD WEBBER
Text by TREVOR NUNN after T.S. ELIOT

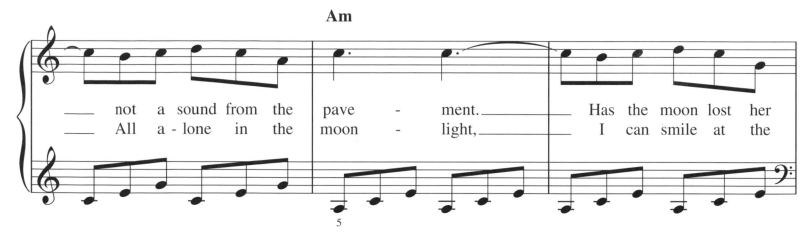

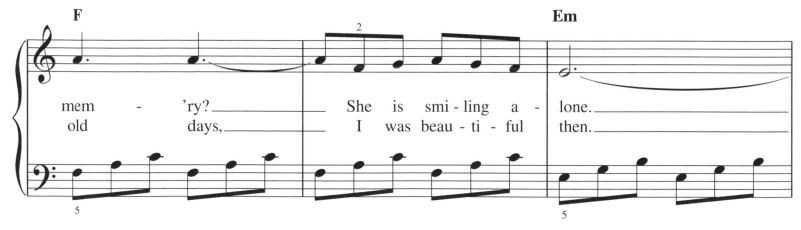

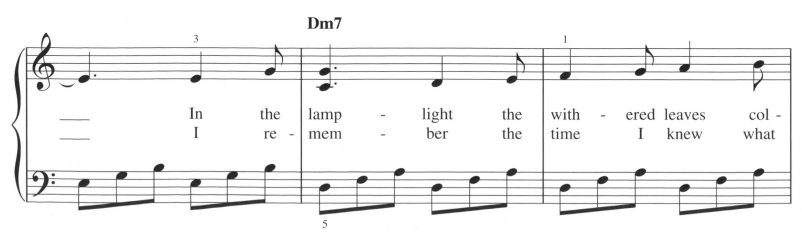

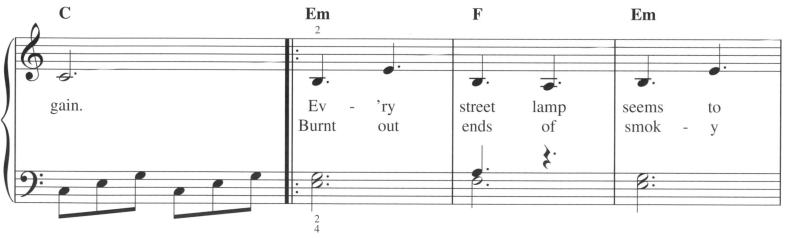

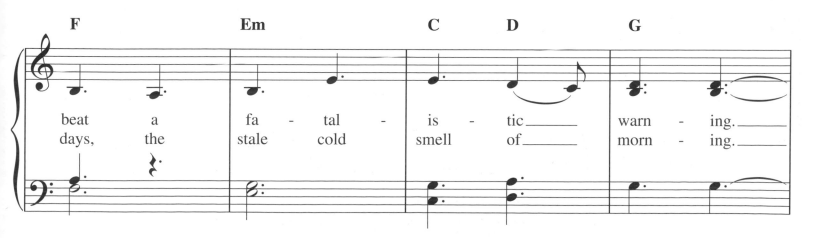

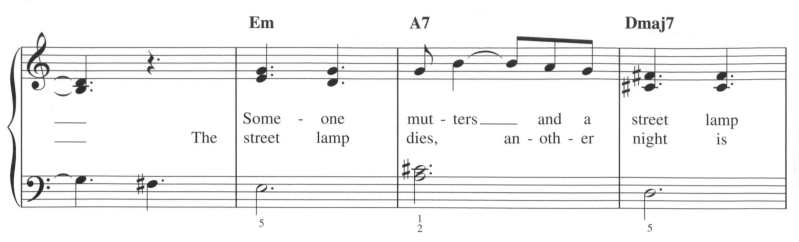

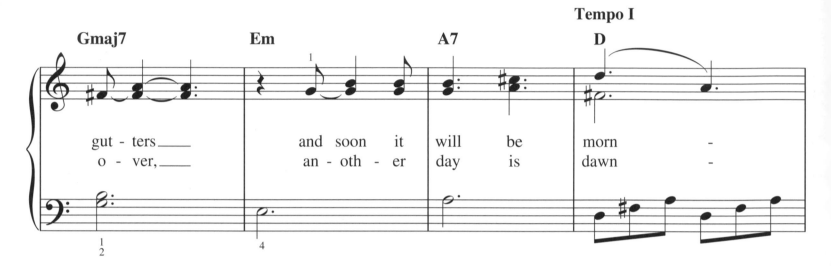

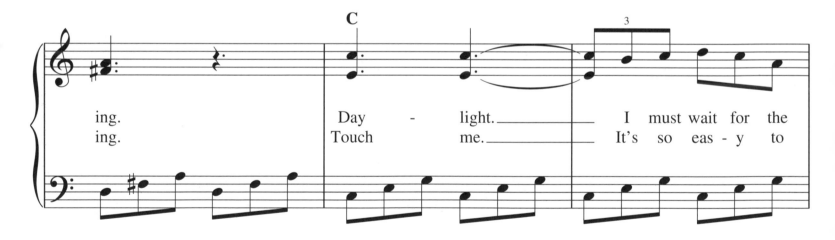

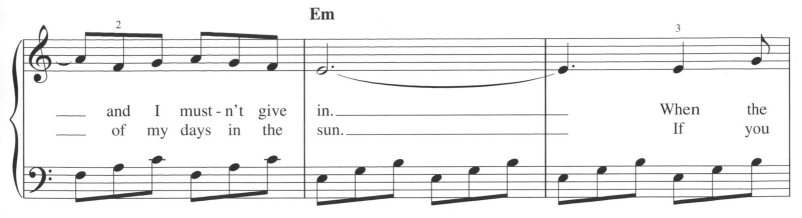

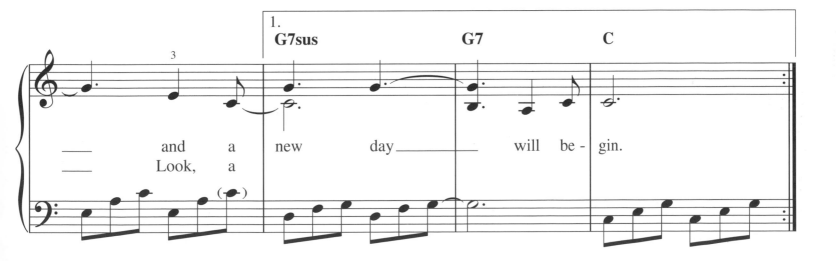

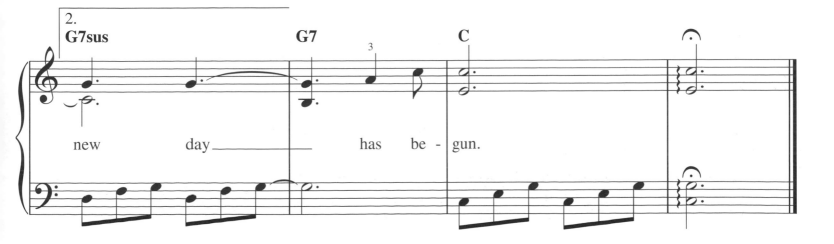

MOOD INDIGO

from SOPHISTICATED LADIES

Words and Music by DUKE ELLINGTON,
IRVING MILLS and ALBANY BIGARD

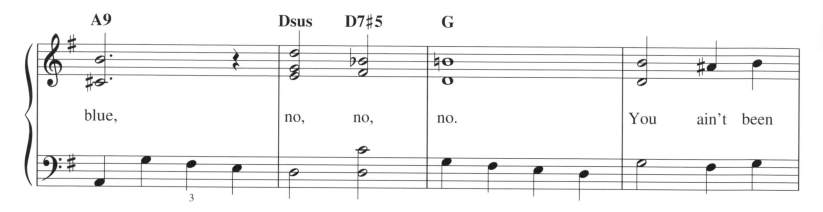

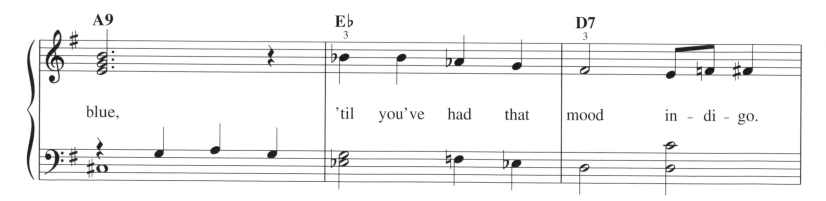

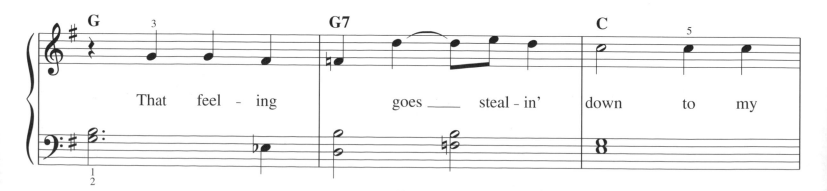

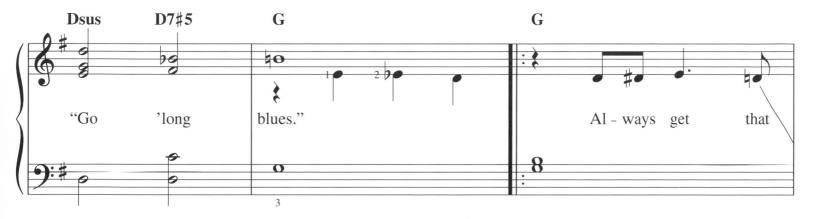

cry.

'Cause there's no-bod-y who cares a-bout me, —

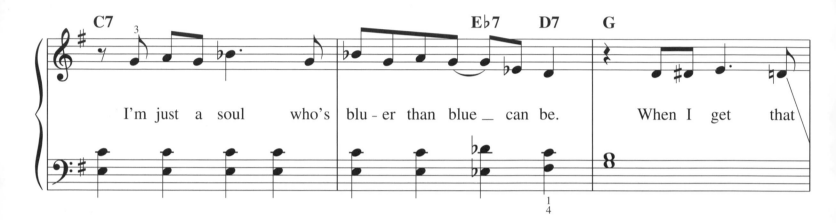

I'm just a soul who's blu-er than blue — can be.

When I get that

mood / in - di - go, —

I could lay me down and die.

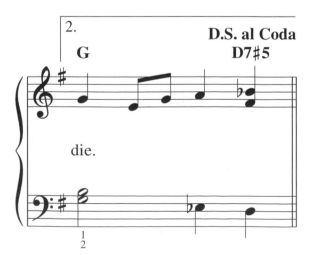

die.

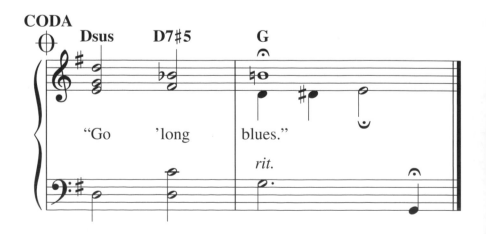

"Go 'long blues."

rit.

MOON RIVER

from the Paramount Picture BREAKFAST AT TIFFANY'S

Words by JOHNNY MERCER
Music by HENRY MANCINI

Slowly and expressively

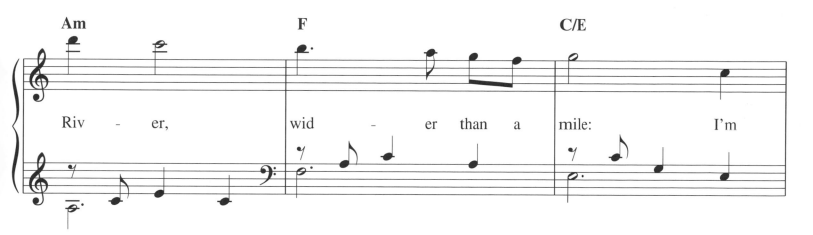

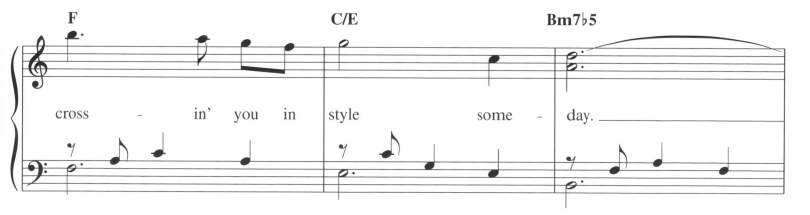

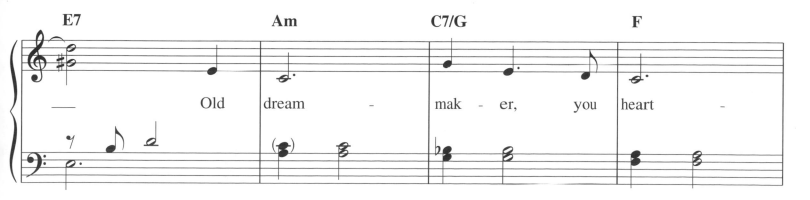

breaker, wher - ev - er you're go - in', I'm go - in' your

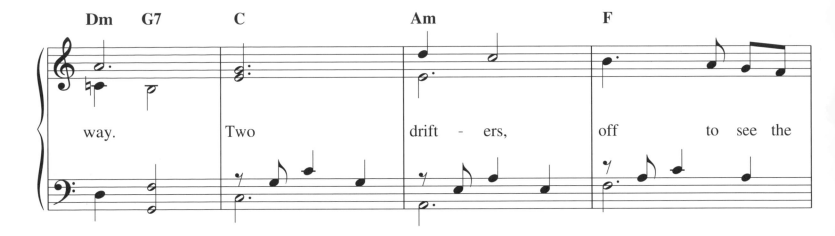

way. Two drift - ers, off to see the

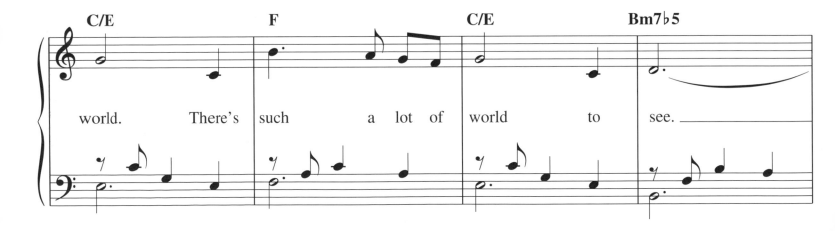

world. There's such a lot of world to see.

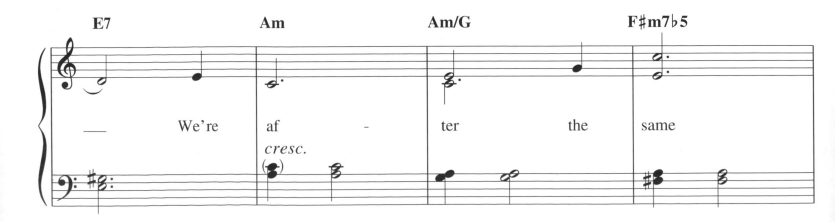

We're af - ter the same

cresc.

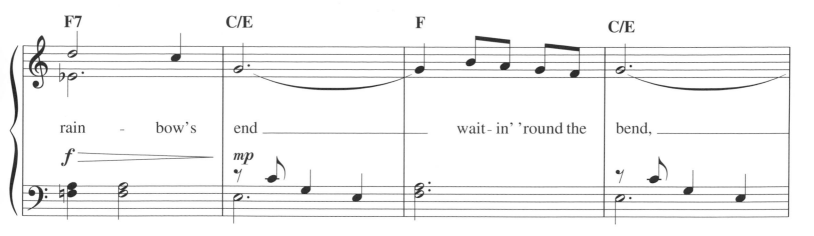

rain - bow's end _____ wait- in' 'round the bend, _____

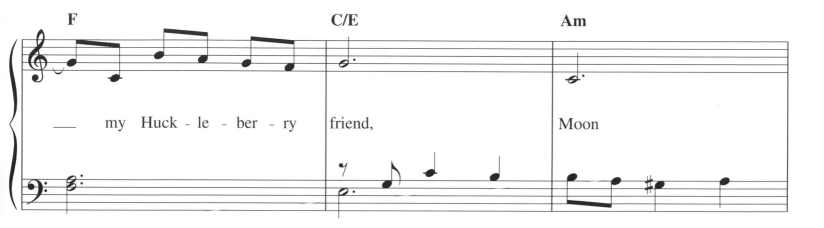

_____ my Huck - le - ber - ry friend, Moon

Riv - er _____ and me.

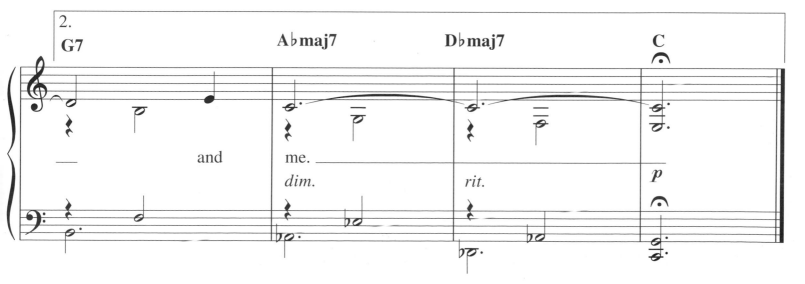

_____ and me. _____

dim. *rit.*

MOONGLOW

Words and Music by WILL HUDSON,
EDDIE DE LANGE and IRVING MILLS

Easy Swing

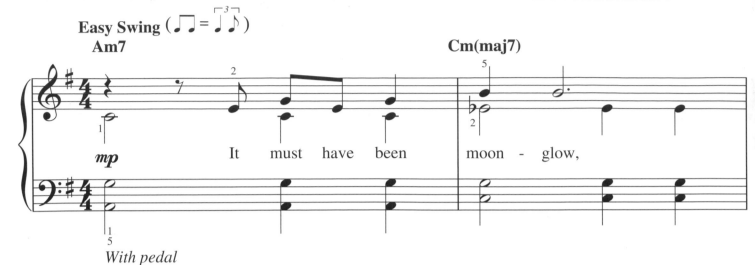

It must have been moon - glow,

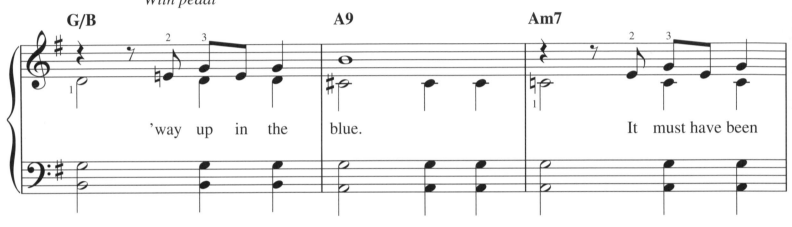

'way up in the blue. It must have been

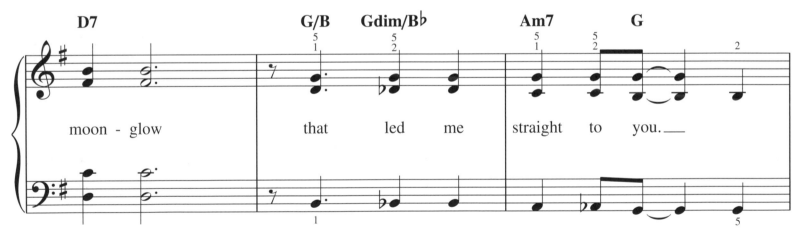

moon - glow that led me straight to you.___

I still hear you say - ing, "Dear one, hold me

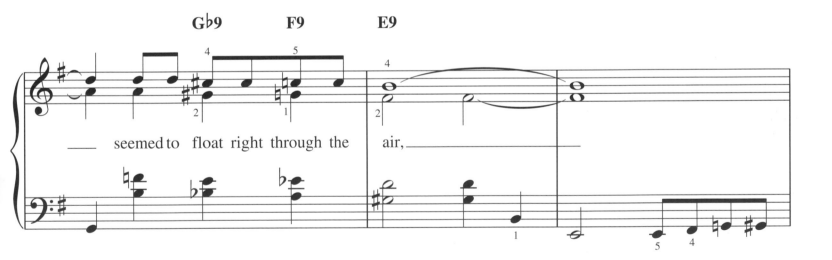

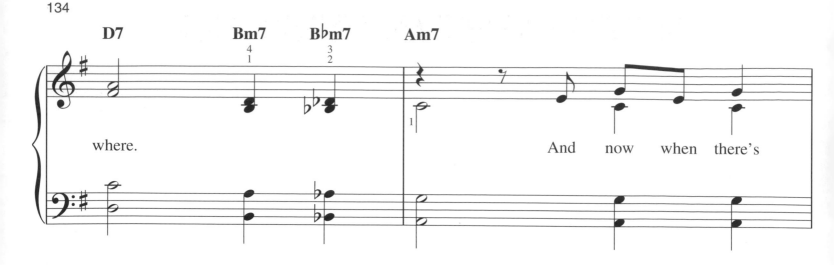

where.   And   now   when   there's

moon - glow   way   up   in   the   blue,

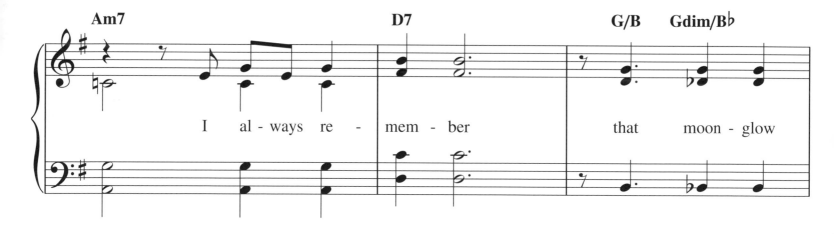

I   al - ways   re - mem - ber   that   moon - glow

gave   me   you.

8vb

MOONLIGHT IN VERMONT

Words and Music by JOHN BLACKBURN
and KARL SUESSDORF

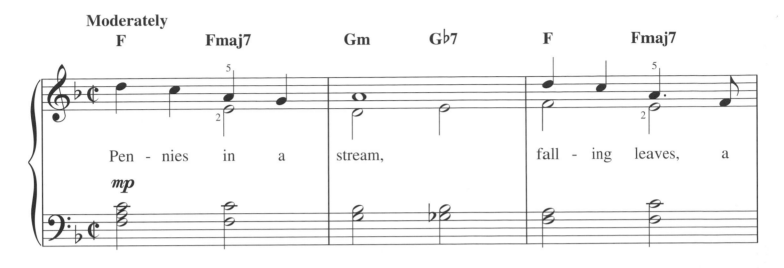

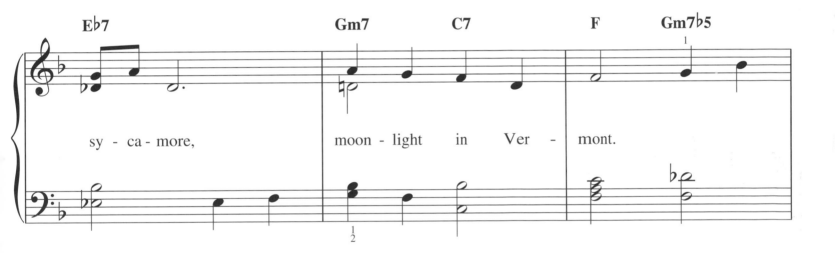

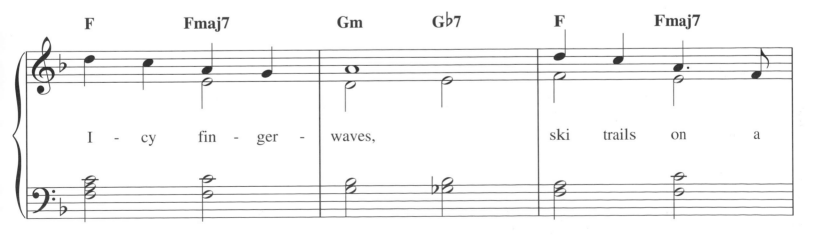

mountain-side, moonlight in Ver - mont.

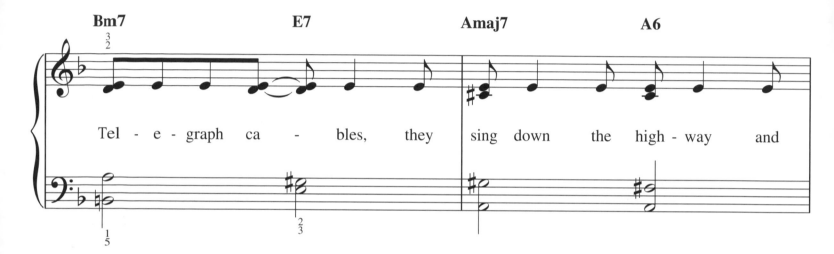

Tel - e - graph ca - bles, they sing down the high-way and

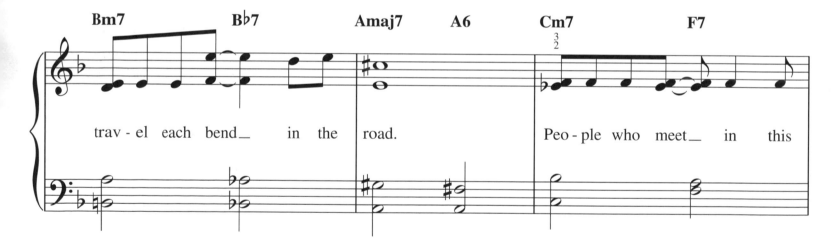

trav - el each bend___ in the road. Peo - ple who meet___ in this

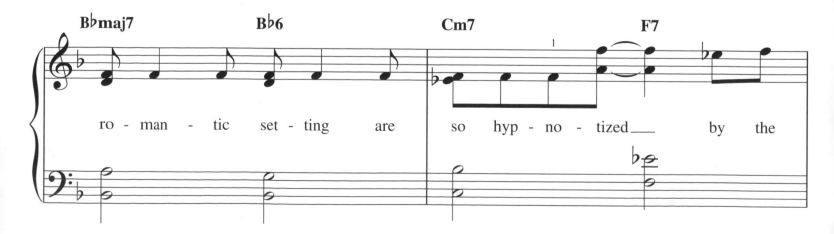

ro - man - tic set - ting are so hyp - no - tized___ by the

137

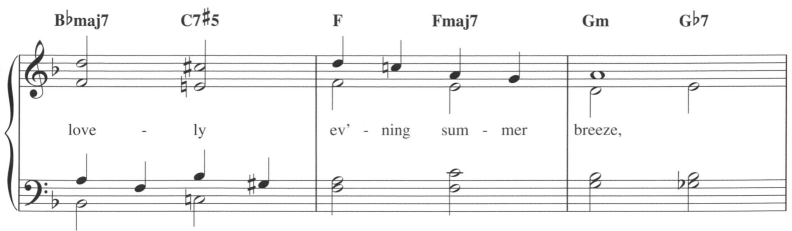

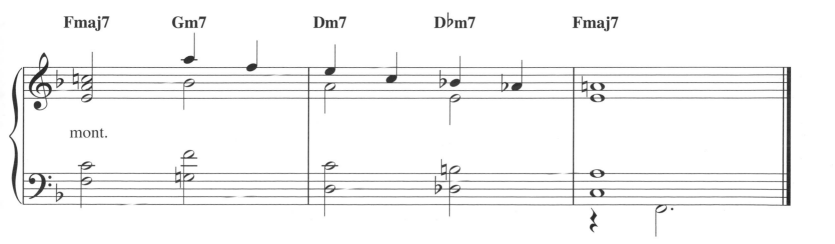

MORE

(Ti Guarderò Nel Cuore)

from the Film MONDO CANE

Music by NINO OLIVIERO and RIZ ORTOLANI
Italian Lyrics by MARCELLO CIORCIOLINI
English Lyrics by NORMAN NEWELL

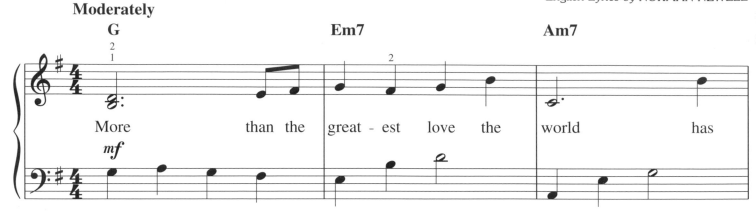

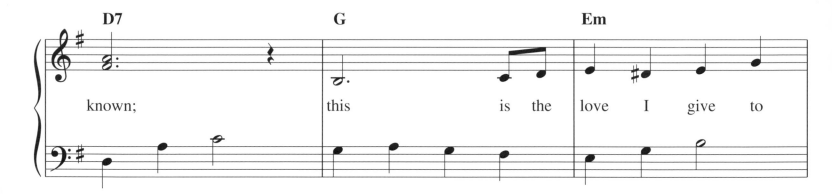

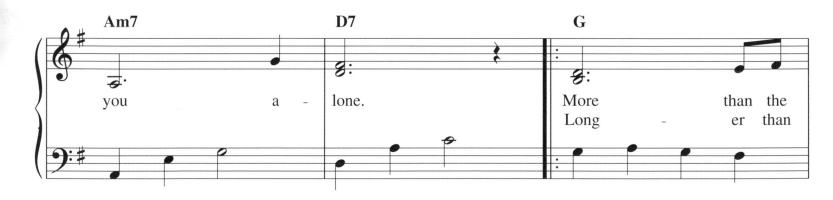

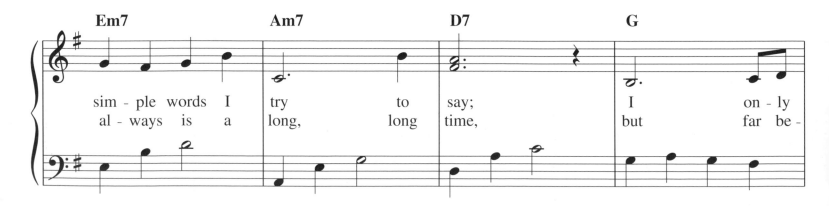

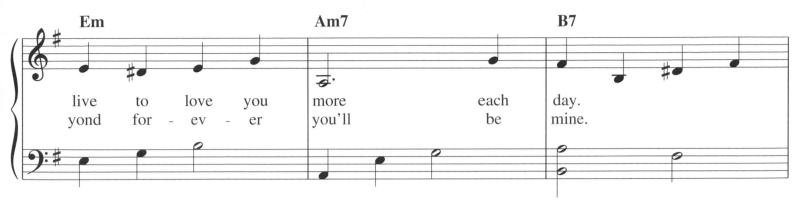

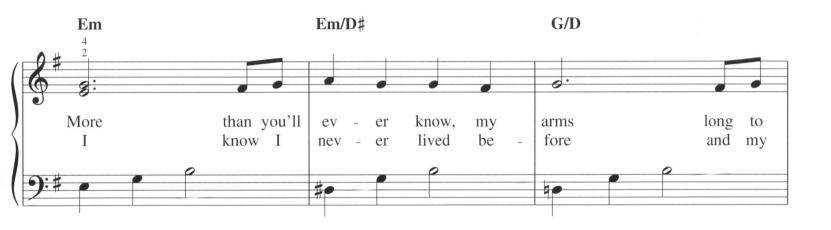

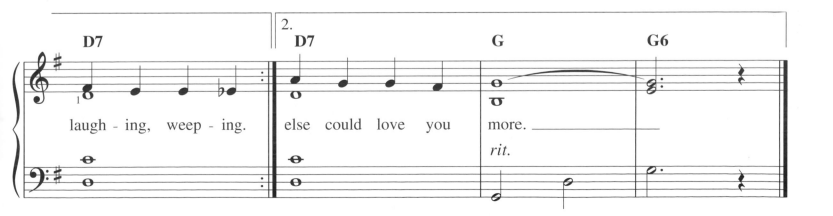

MY FAVORITE THINGS
from THE SOUND OF MUSIC

Lyrics by OSCAR HAMMERSTEIN II
Music by RICHARD RODGERS

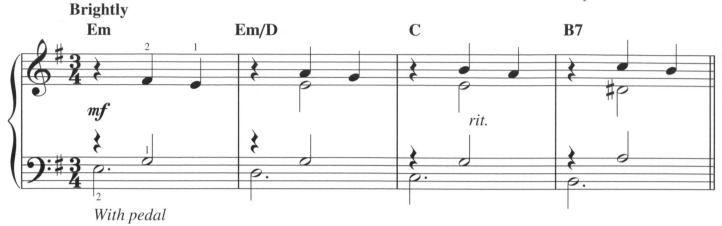

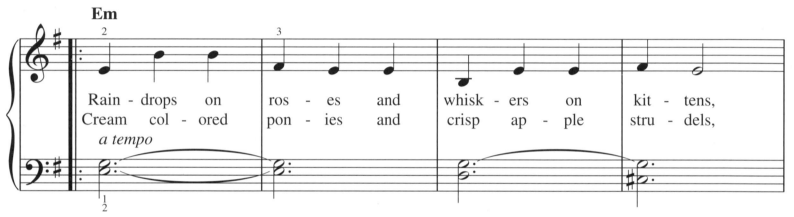

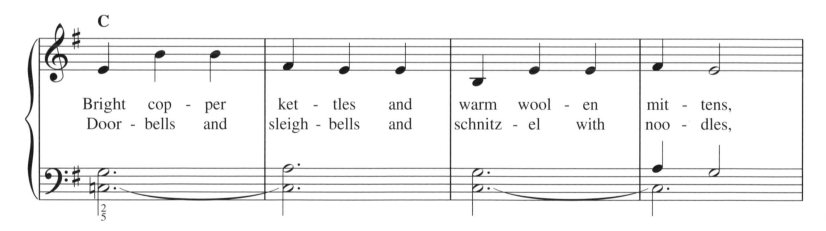

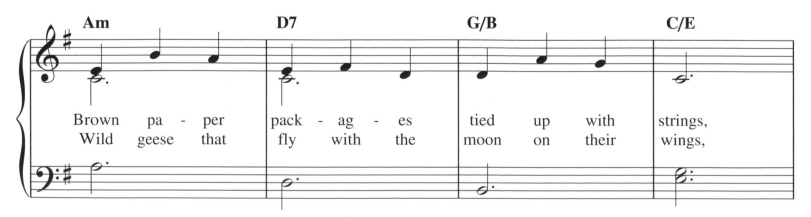

141

These are a few of my fa - vor - ite things.
These are a few of my fa - vor - ite things.

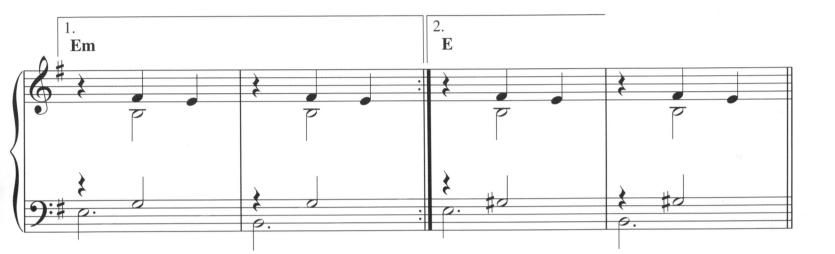

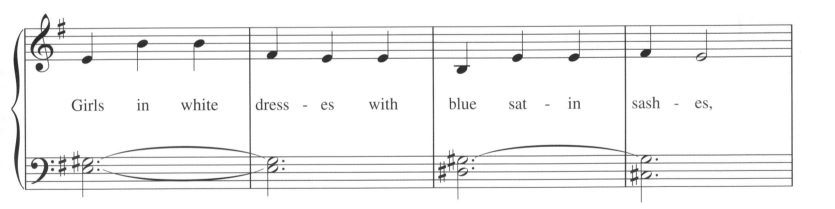

Girls in white dress - es with blue sat - in sash - es,

Snow - flakes that stay on my nose and eye - lash - es,

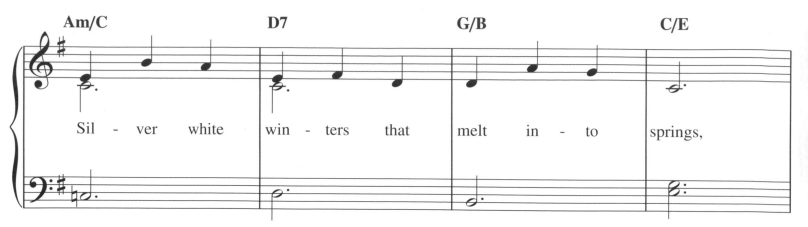

Sil - ver white win - ters that melt in - to springs,

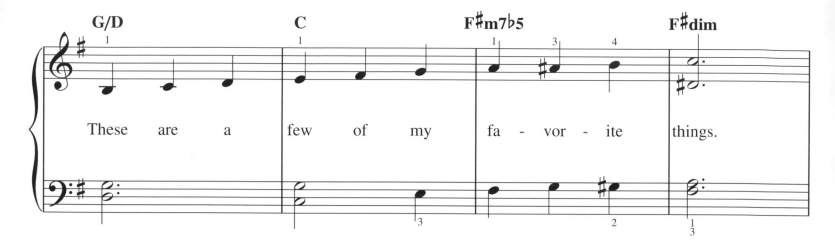

These are a few of my fa - vor - ite things.

When the dog bites, When the bee stings,

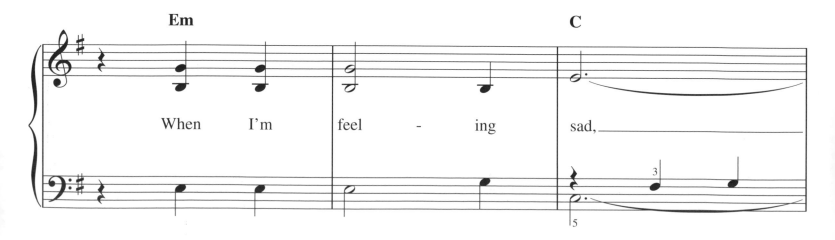

When I'm feel - ing sad,

143

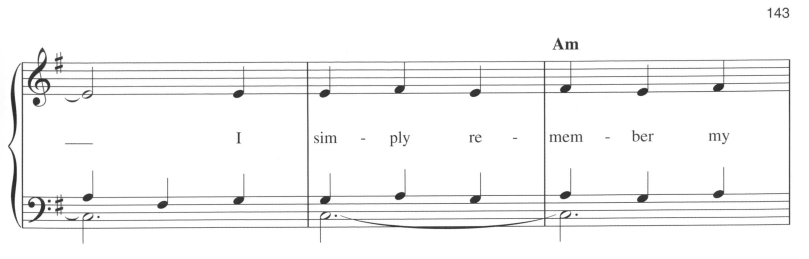

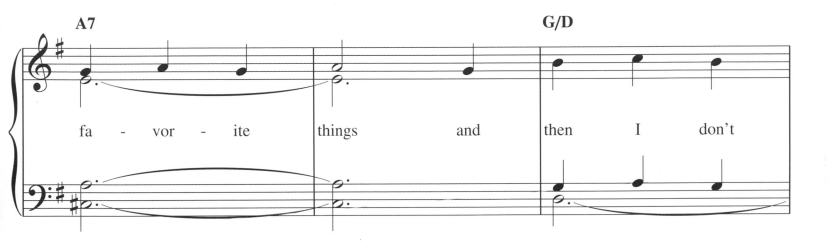

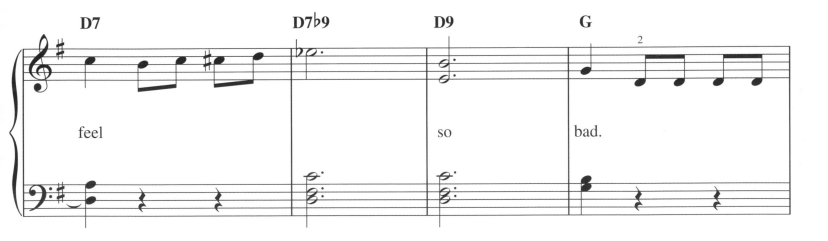

MY FUNNY VALENTINE
from BABES IN ARMS

Words by LORENZ HART
Music by RICHARD RODGERS

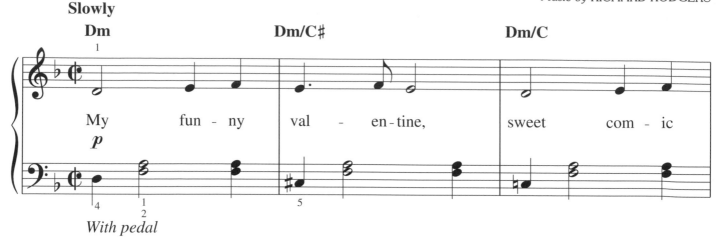

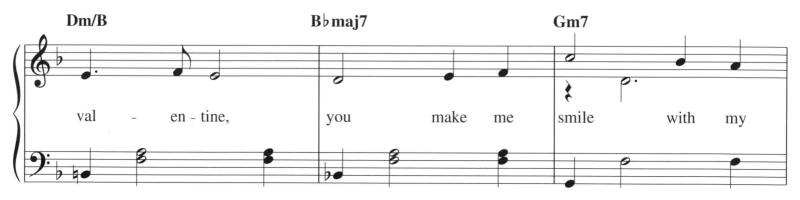

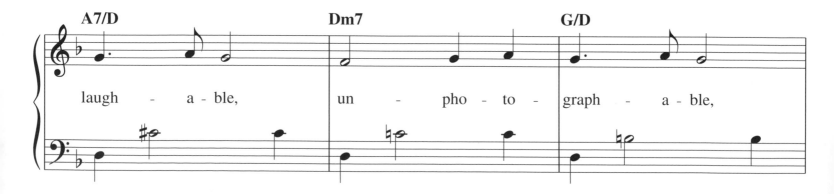

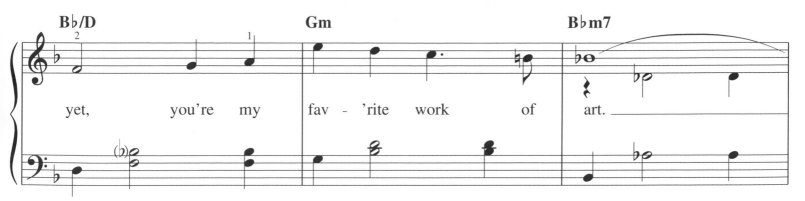

yet,   you're   my   fav - 'rite   work   of   art. _____

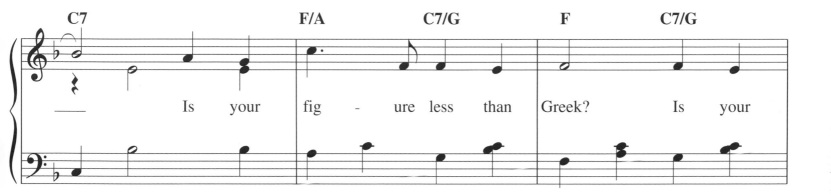

_____   Is   your   fig - ure less than   Greek?   Is   your

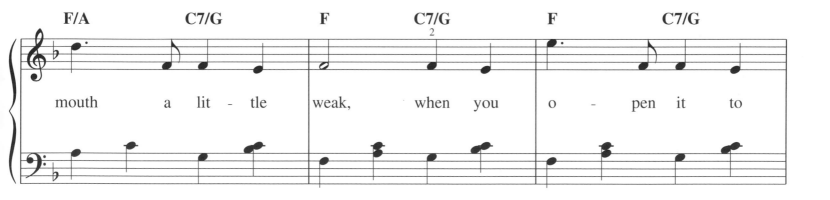

mouth   a   lit - tle   weak,   when you   o - pen it to

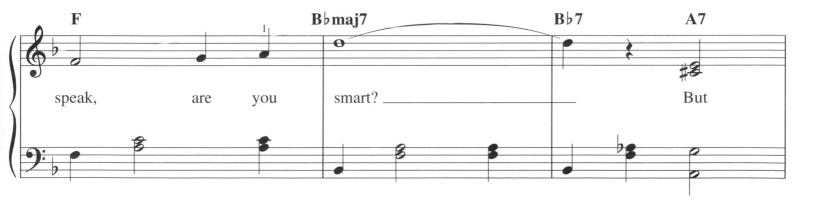

speak,   are   you   smart? _____   But

don't   change   a   hair   for   me,   not   if   you

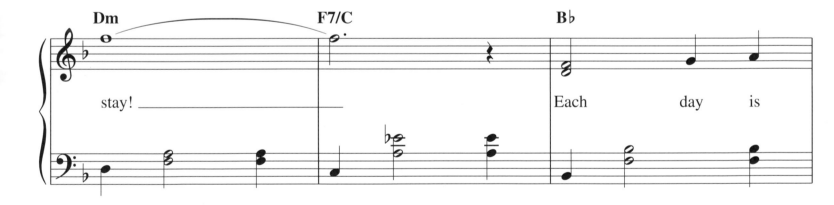

care   for   me,   stay,   lit - tle   val - en - tine

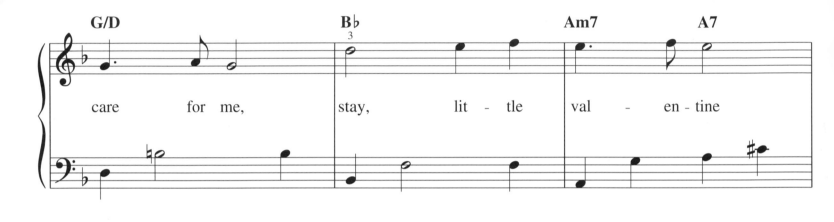

stay! _____   Each   day   is

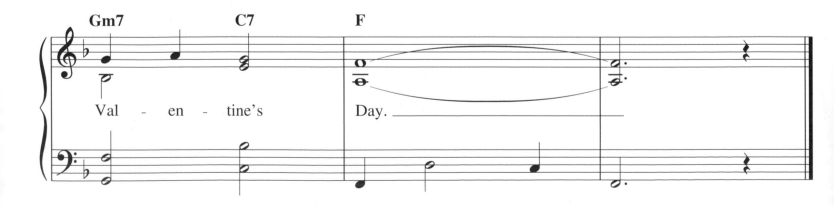

Val - en - tine's   Day. _____

PIANO MAN

Words and Music by
BILLY JOEL

Moderately

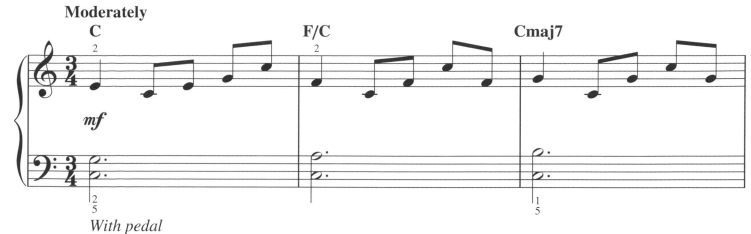

With pedal

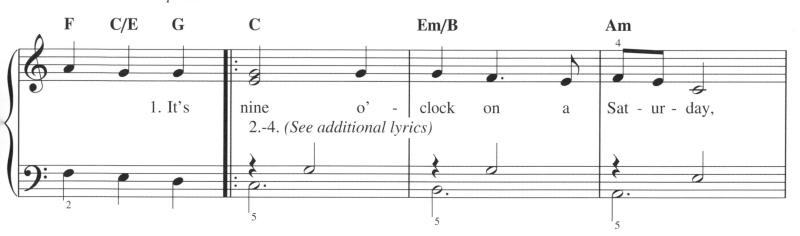

1. It's nine o' - clock on a Sat - ur - day,
2.-4. *(See additional lyrics)*

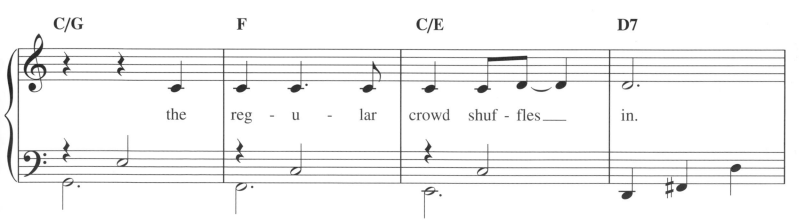

the reg - u - lar crowd shuf - fles___ in.

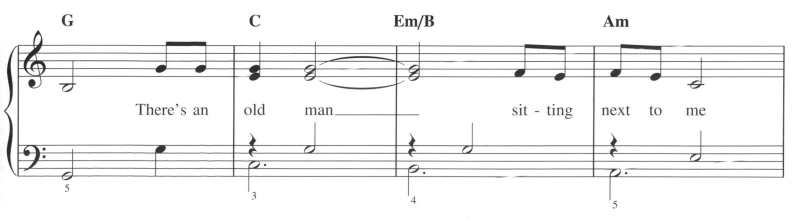

There's an old man___ sit - ting next to me

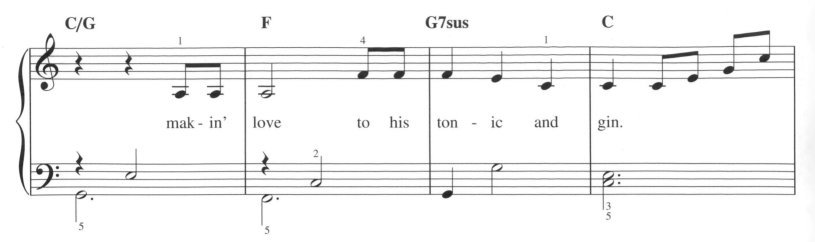

mak - in' love   to his   ton - ic and   gin.

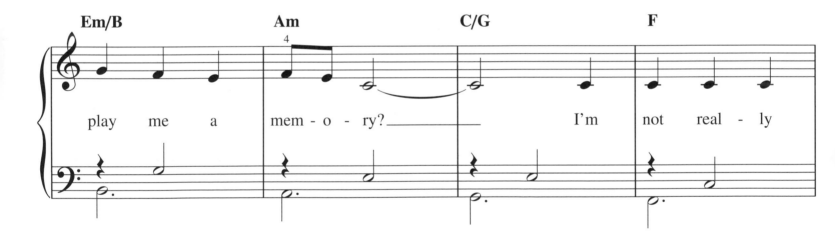

He says,   "Son, can you

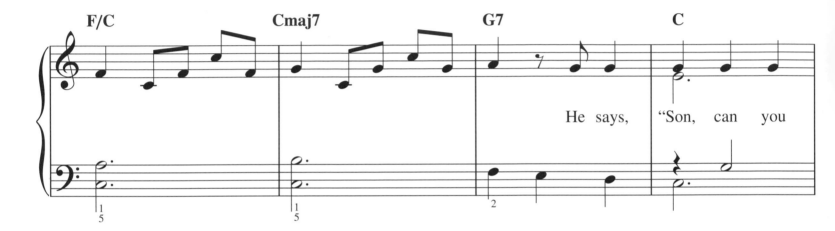

play   me   a   mem - o - ry?_____   I'm   not   real - ly

sure   how   it   goes,   but it's   sad   and   it's

149

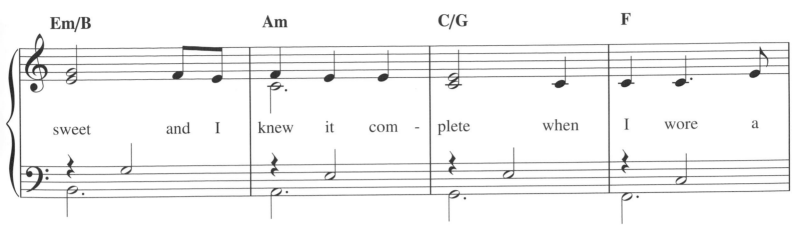

sweet and I knew it com - plete when I wore a

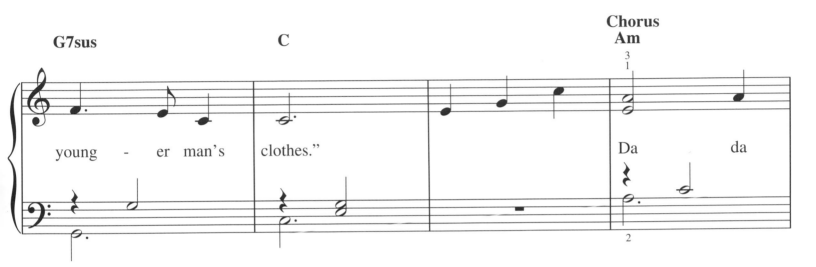

young - er man's clothes." **Chorus** Da da

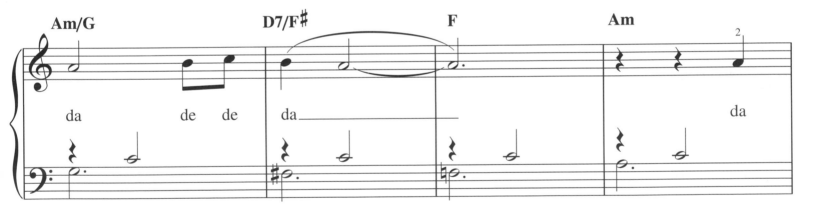

da de de da da

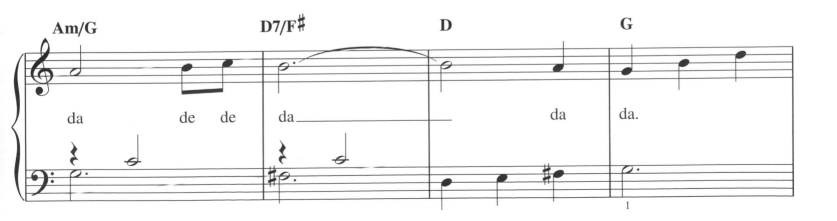

da de de da da da.

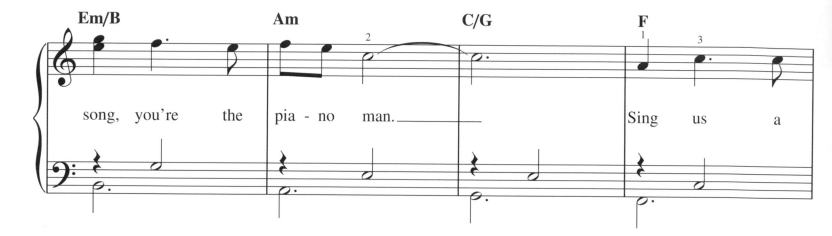

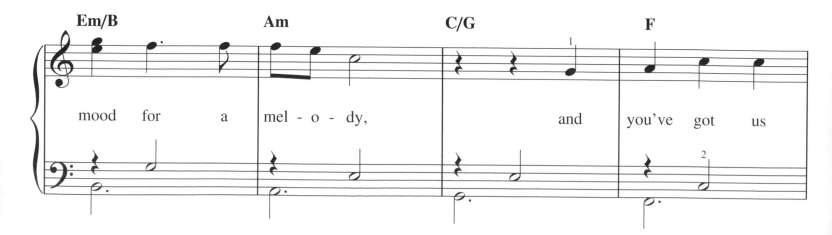

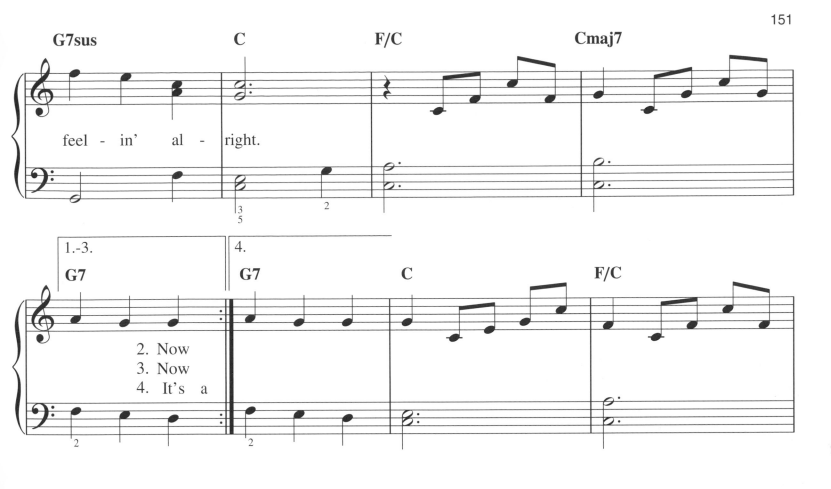

feel - in' al - right.

rit.

Additional Lyrics

2. Now John at the bar is a friend of mine,
   He gets me my drinks for free,
   And he's quick with a joke or to light up your smoke,
   But there's someplace that he'd rather be.
   He says, "Bill, I believe this is killing me,"
   As a smile ran away from his face.
   "Well, I'm sure that I could be a movie star
   If I could get out of this place.
   Chorus

3. Now Paul is a real estate novelist
   Who never had time for a wife,
   And he's talkin' with Davy who's still in the Navy
   And probably will be for life.
   And the waitress is practicing politics
   As the businessmen slowly get stoned.
   Yes, they're sharing a drink they call loneliness,
   But it's better than drinkin' alone.
   Chorus

4. It's a pretty good crowd for a Saturday,
   And the manager gives me a smile
   'Cause he knows that it's me they've been comin' to see
   To forget about life for a while.
   And the piano sounds like a carnival,
   And the microphone smells like a beer,
   And they sit at the bar and put bread in my jar
   And say, "Man, what are you doin' here?"
   Chorus

MY WAY

English Words by PAUL ANKA
Original French Words by GILLES THIBAULT
Music by JACQUES REVAUX and CLAUDE FRANCOIS

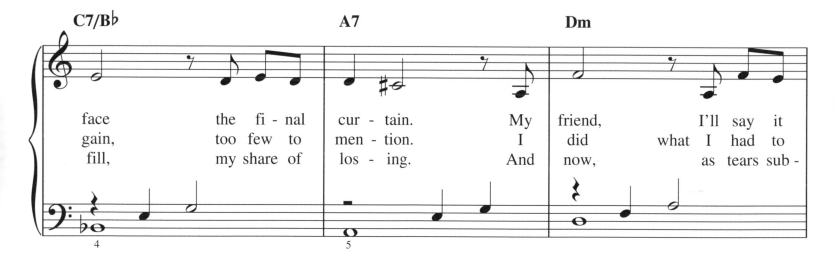

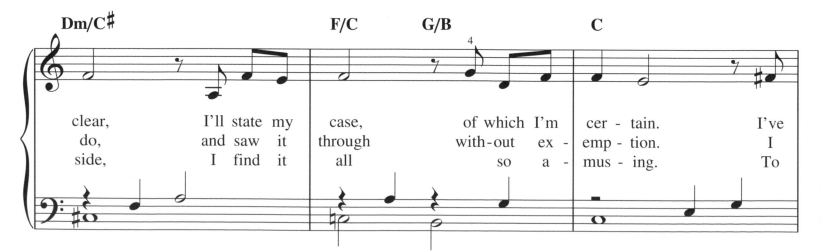

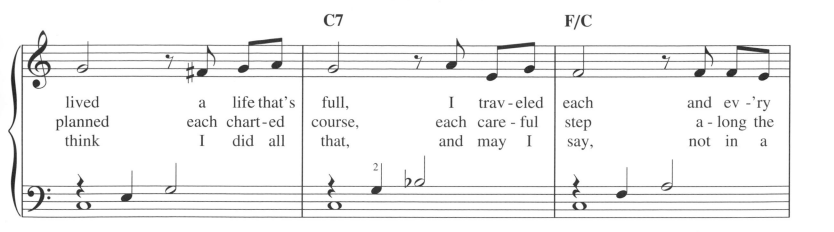

lived   a   life that's   full,   I   trav-eled   each   and ev-'ry
planned   each chart-ed   course,   each care-ful   step   a-long the
think   I did all   that,   and may I   say,   not in a

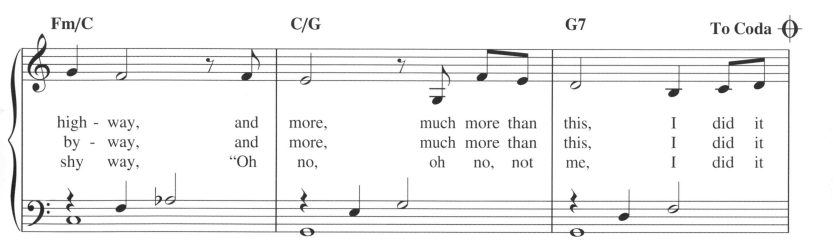

high-way,   and   more,   much more than   this,   I   did   it
by-way,   and   more,   much more than   this,   I   did   it
shy way,   "Oh   no,   oh no, not   me,   I   did   it

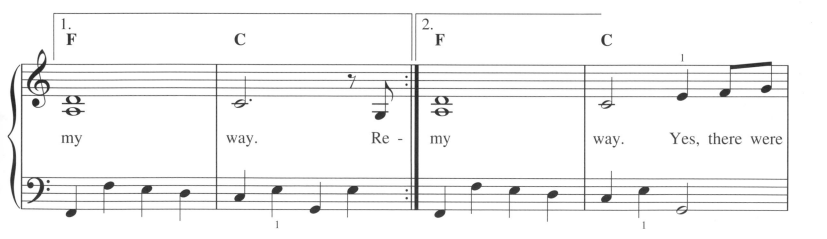

my   way.   Re-   my   way.   Yes, there were

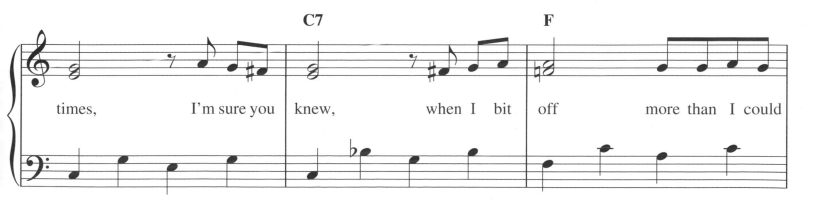

times,   I'm sure you   knew,   when I bit   off   more than I could

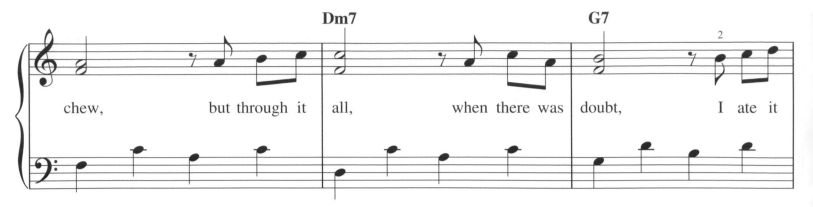

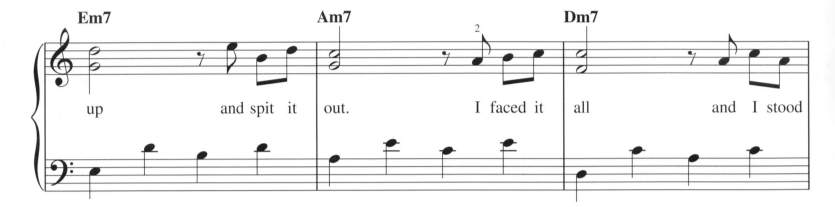

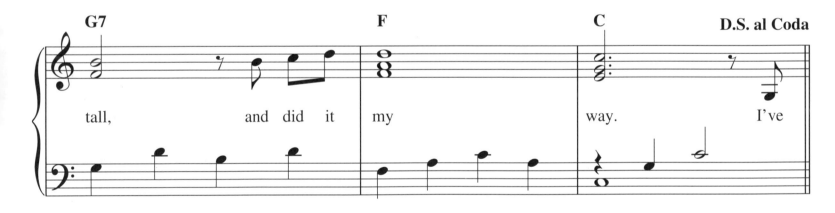

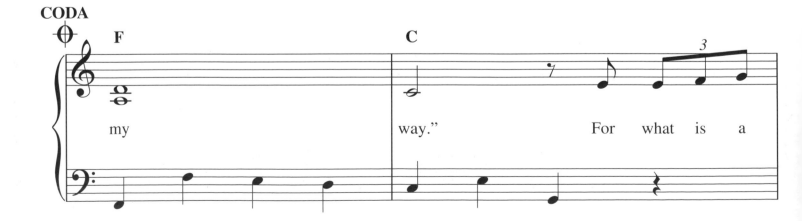

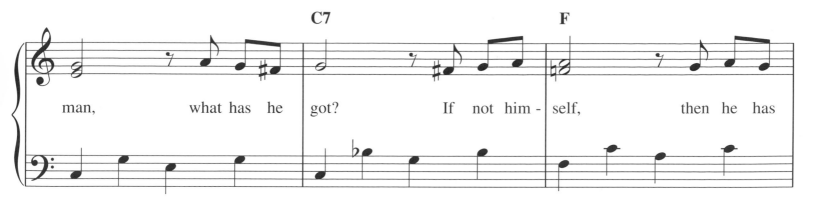

man, what has he got? If not him - self, then he has

naught. To say the things he tru - ly feels, and not the

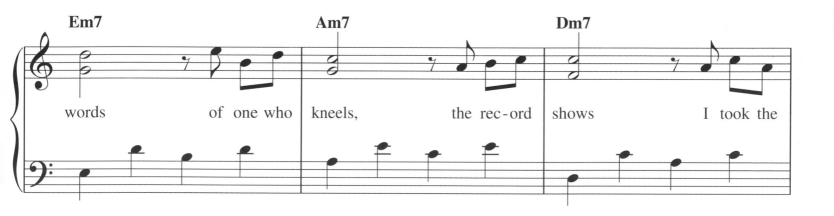

words of one who kneels, the rec - ord shows I took the

blows, and did it my way.

OL' MAN RIVER
from SHOW BOAT

Lyrics by OSCAR HAMMERSTEIN II
Music by JEROME KERN

Slowly, in 2

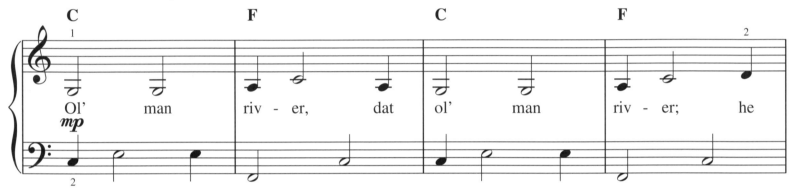

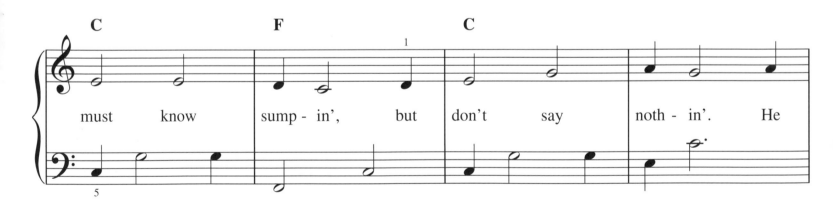

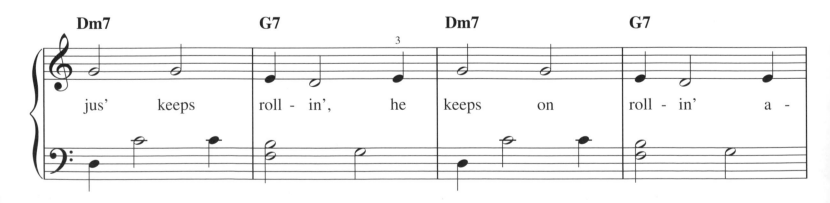

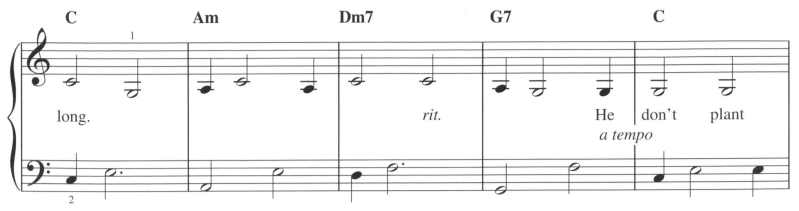

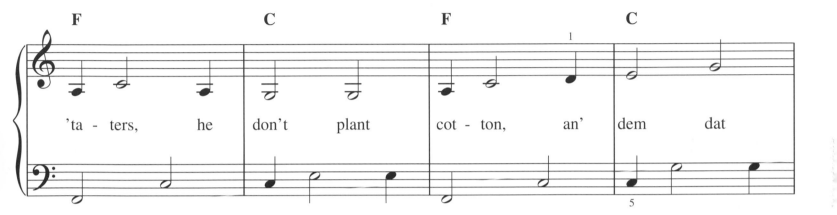

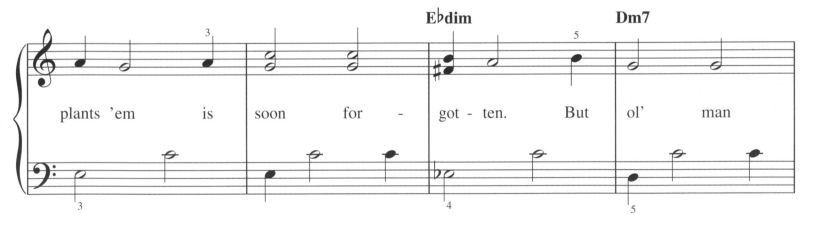

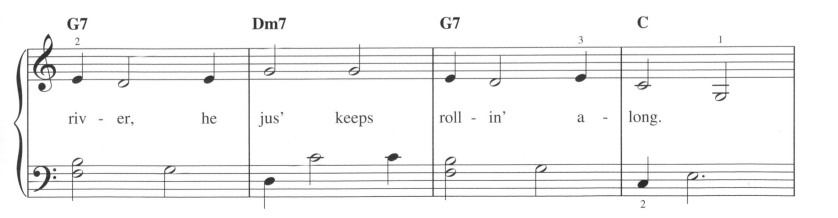

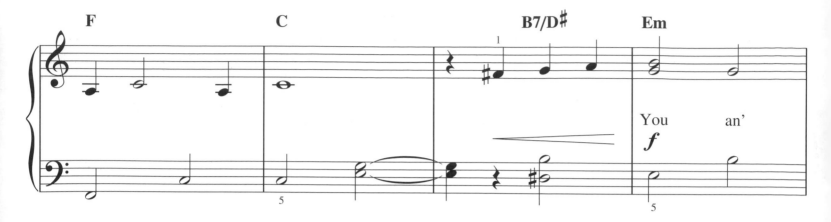

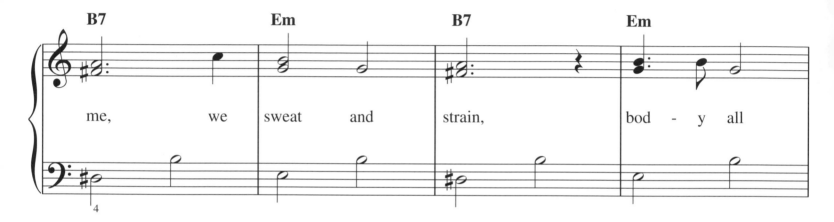

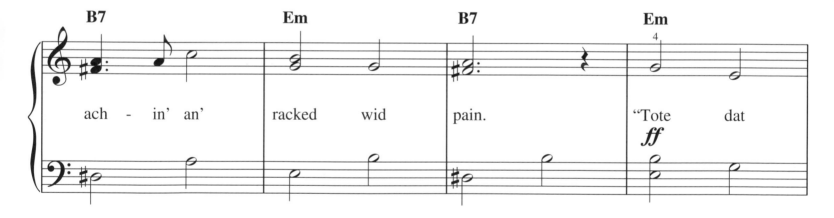

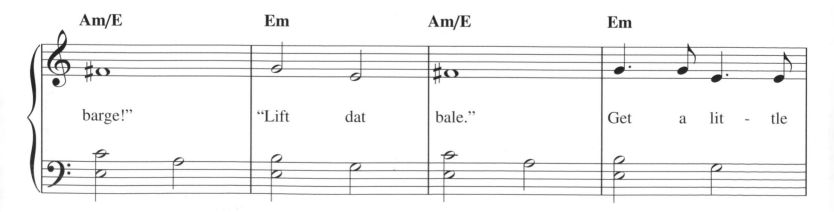

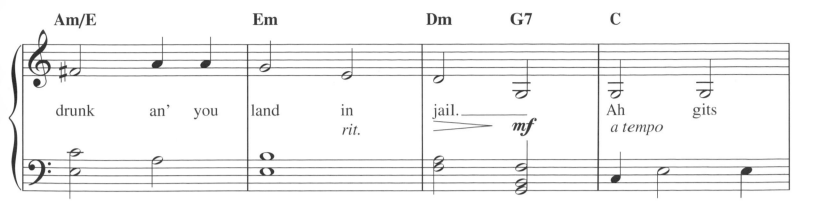

drunk an' you land in jail. Ah gits

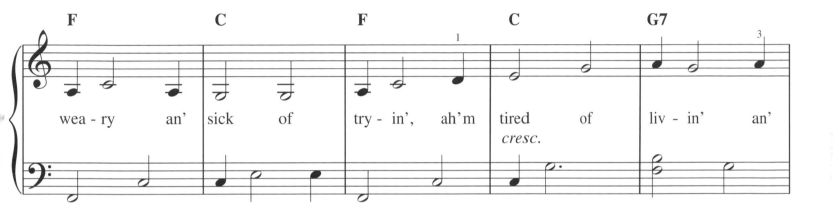

wea - ry an' sick of try - in', ah'm tired of liv - in' an'

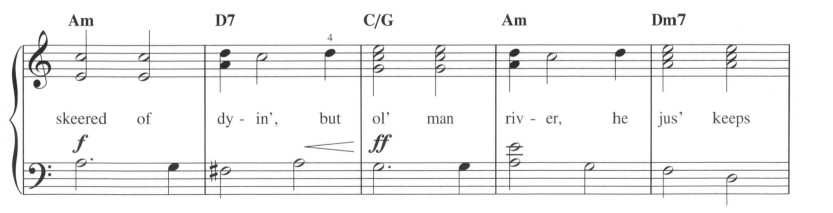

skeered of dy - in', but ol' man riv - er, he jus' keeps

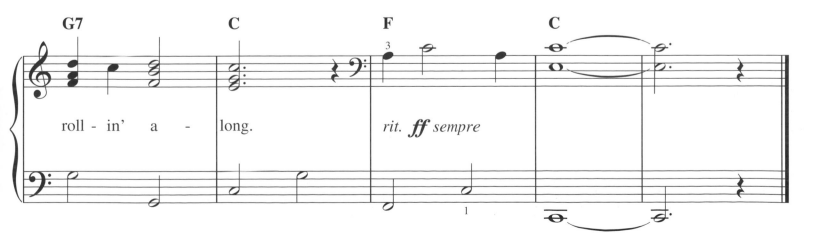

roll - in' a - long. *rit.* **ff** *sempre*

ON THE STREET WHERE YOU LIVE

from MY FAIR LADY

Words by ALAN JAY LERNER
Music by FREDERICK LOEWE

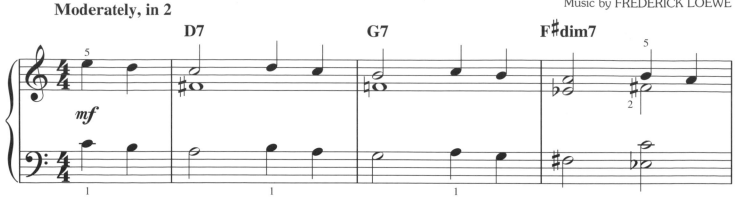

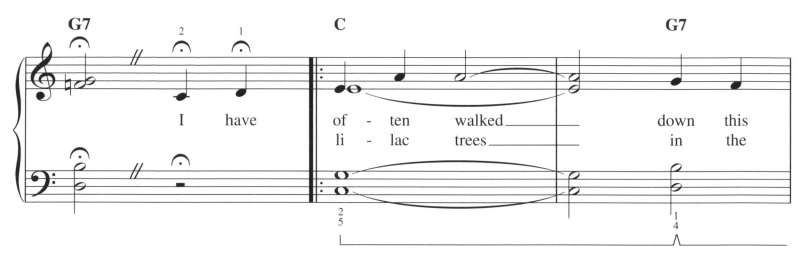

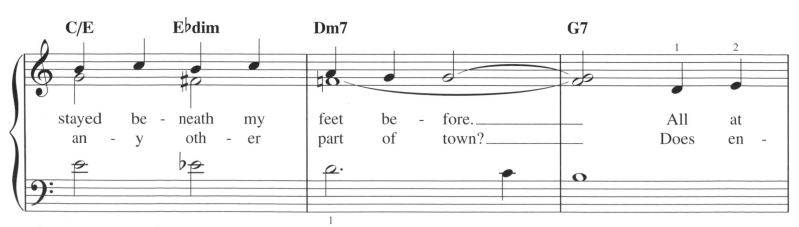

161

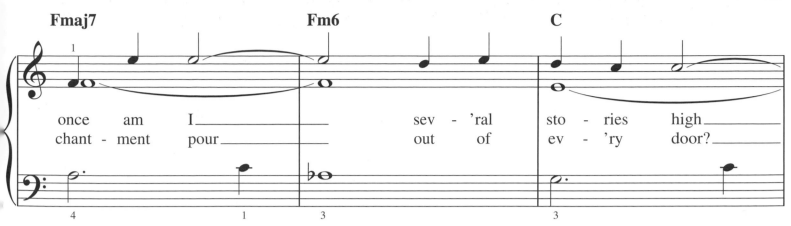

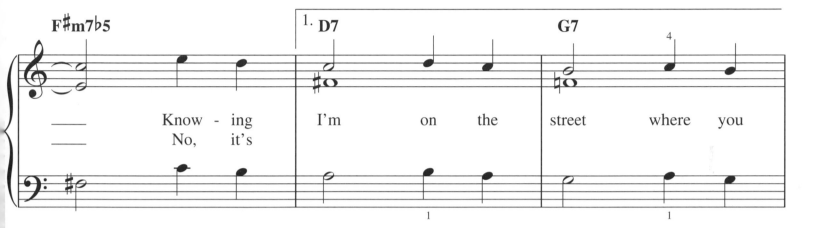

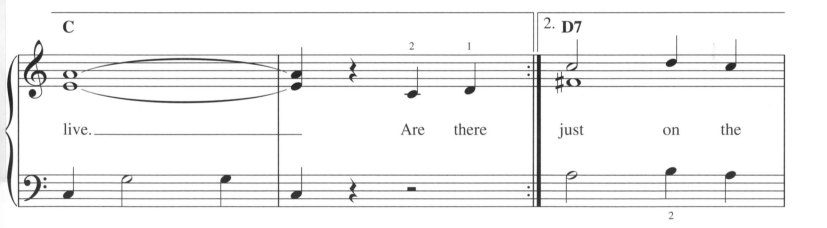

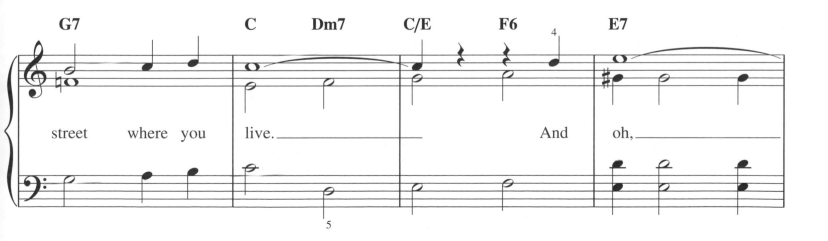

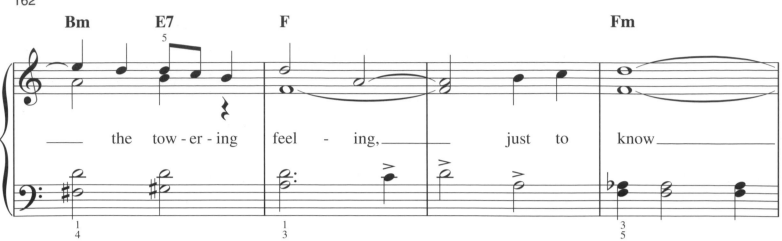

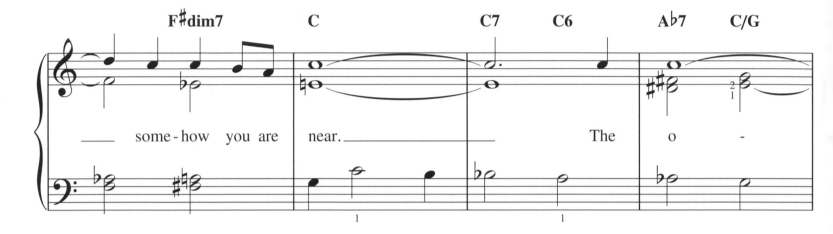

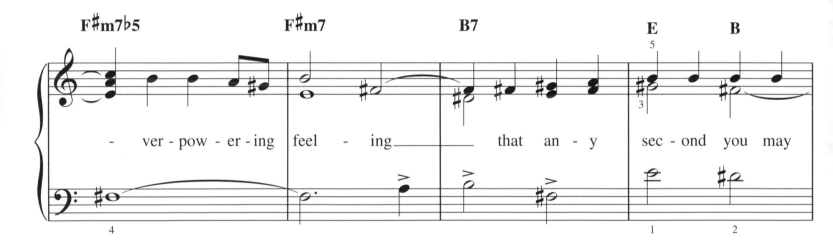

they don't both-er me,_____ For there's no-where else on

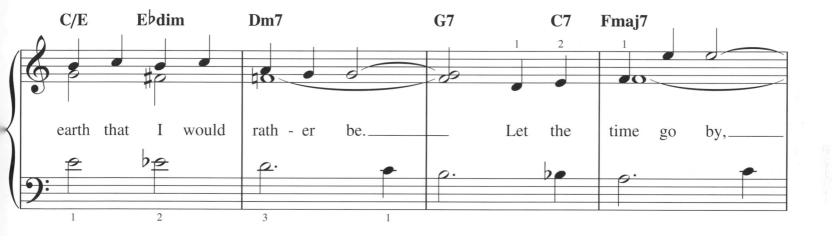

earth that I would rath-er be._____ Let the time go by,_____

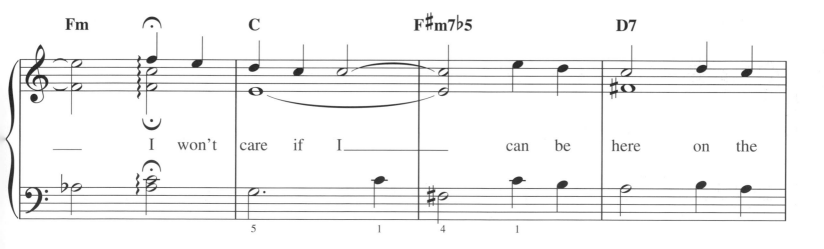

_____ I won't care if I_____ can be here on the

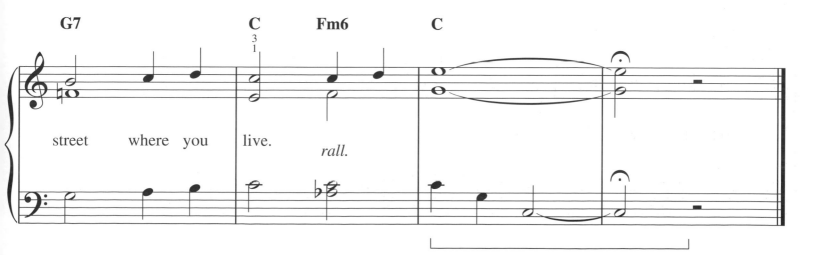

street where you live. *rall.*

PEOPLE
from FUNNY GIRL

Words by BOB MERRILL
Music by JULE STYNE

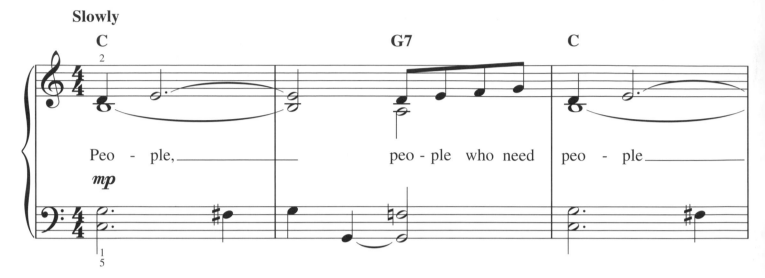

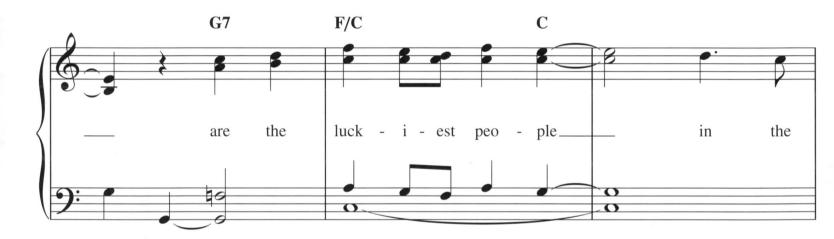

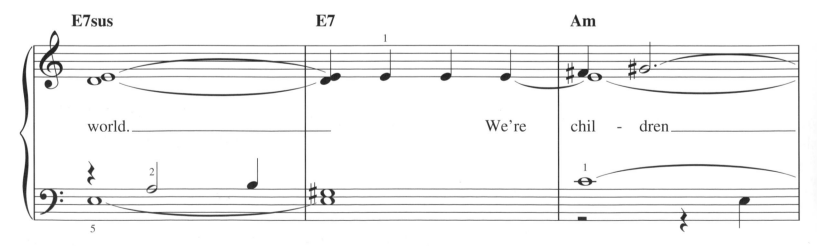

need - ing oth - er chil - dren, _____ and yet

let - ting our grown - up pride hide all the need in -

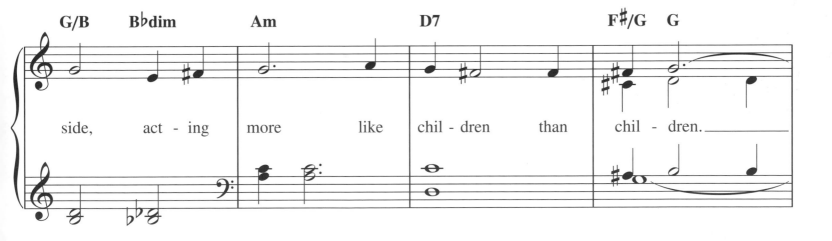

side, act - ing more like chil - dren than chil - dren. _____

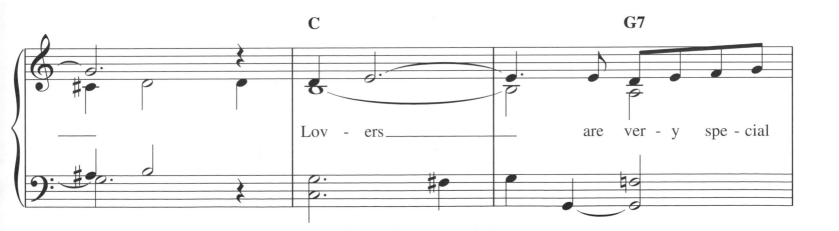

Lov - ers _____ are ver - y spe - cial

peo - ple,_____ they're the luck - i - est peo - ple_____

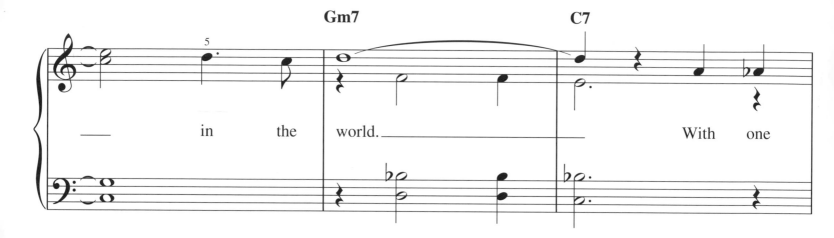

_____ in the world._____ With one

per - son,_____ one ver - y spe - cial per - son,_____

_____ a feel - ing deep in your soul_____ says, "you were

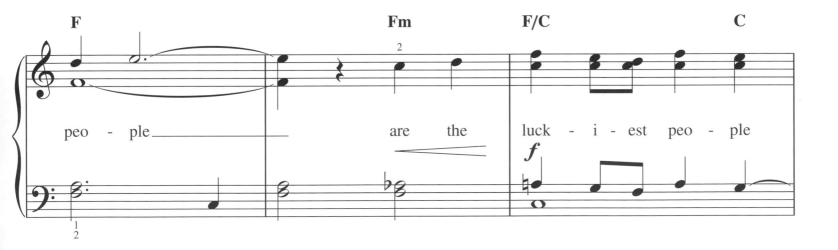

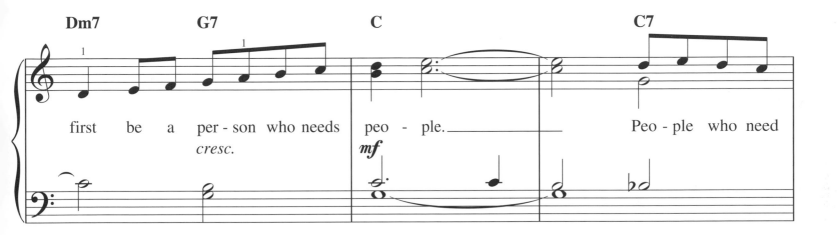

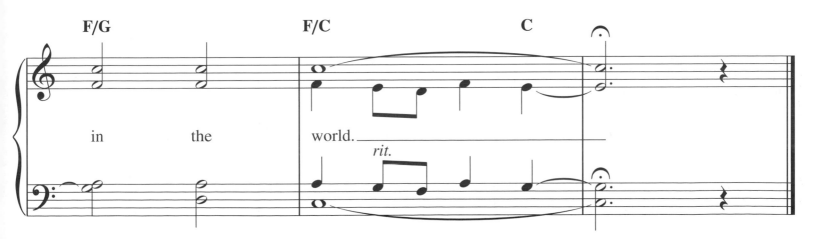

THE RAINBOW CONNECTION
from THE MUPPET MOVIE

Words and Music by PAUL WILLIAMS
and KENNETH L. ASCHER

Flowing Waltz

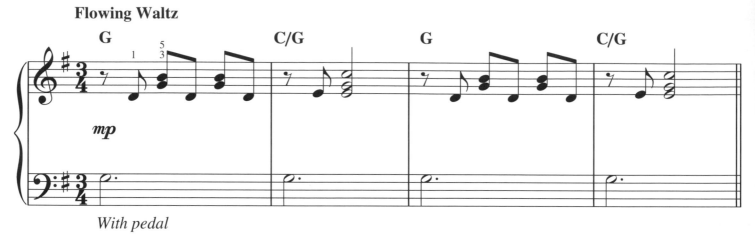

With pedal

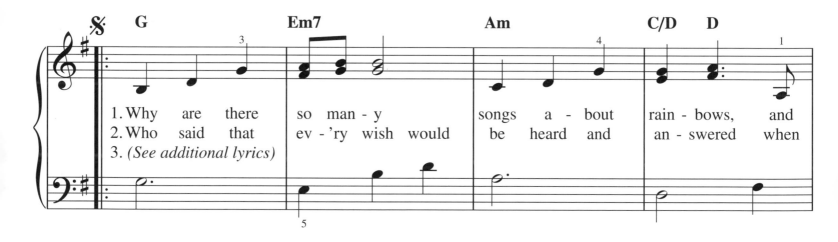

1. Why are there so man - y songs a - bout rain - bows, and
2. Who said that ev - 'ry wish would be heard and an - swered when
3. *(See additional lyrics)*

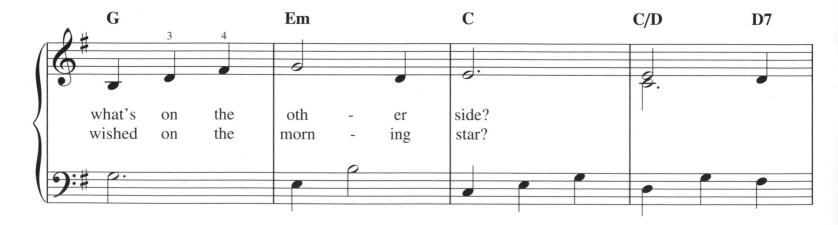

what's on the oth - er side?
wished on the morn - ing star?

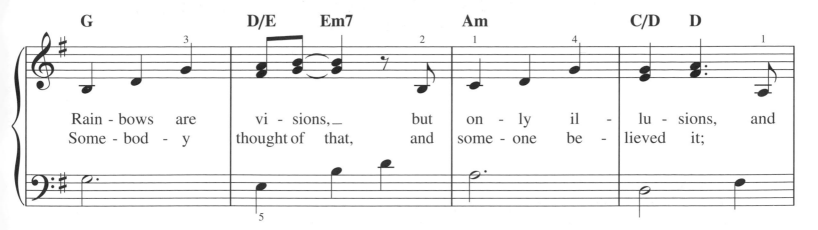

Rain - bows are | vi - sions,_ but | on - ly il - lu - sions, and
Some - bod - y | thought of that, and | some - one be - lieved it;

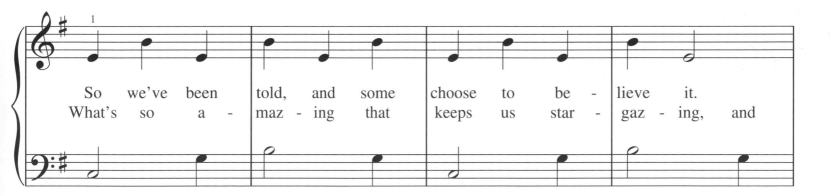

rain - bows have | noth - ing to | hide.
look what it's | done_ so | far.

So we've been | told, and some | choose to be - lieve it.
What's so a - | maz - ing that | keeps us star - gaz - ing, and

I know they're | wrong; wait and | see._____
what do we | think we might | see?_____

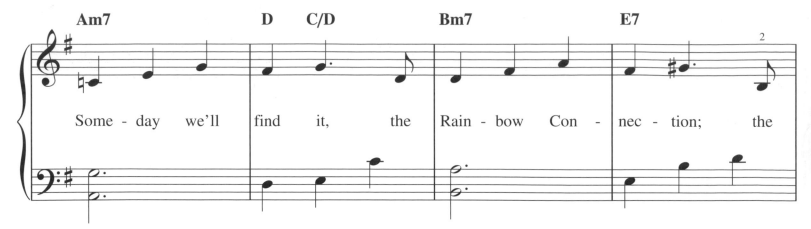

Some - day we'll find it, the Rain - bow Con - nec - tion; the

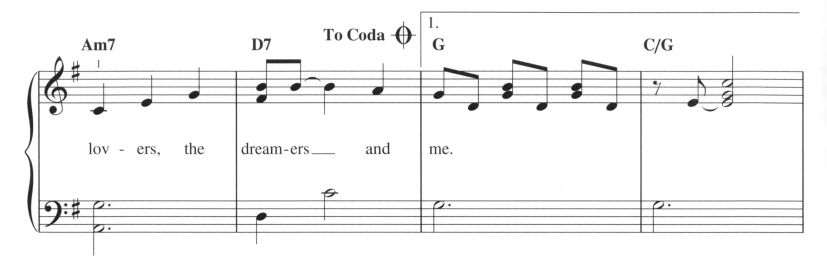

lov - ers, the dream-ers ___ and me.

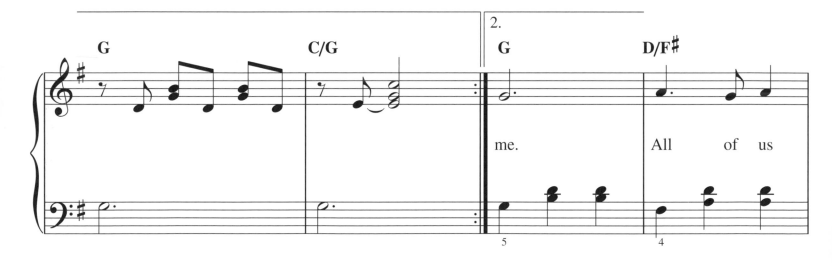

me.   All   of   us

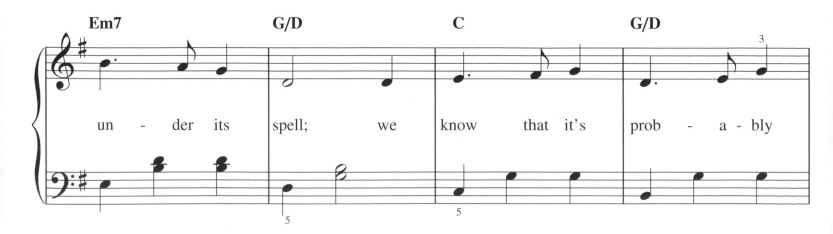

un - der its spell; we know that it's prob - a - bly

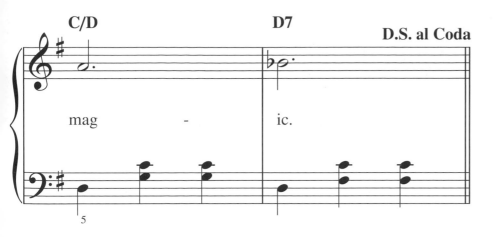

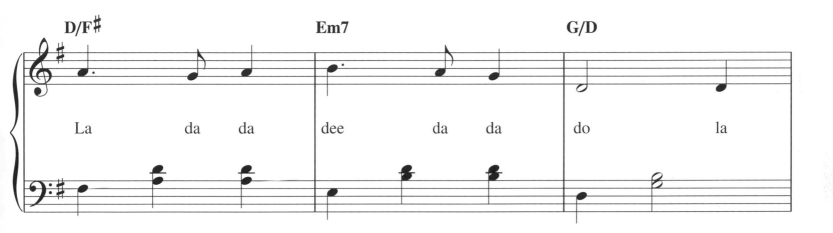

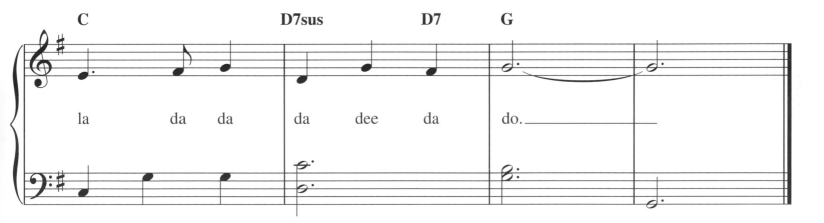

Additional Lyrics

3. Have you been half asleep and have you heard voices?
   I've heard them calling my name.
   Is this the sweet sound that calls the young sailors?
   The voice might be one and the same.
   I've heard it too many times to ignore it.
   It's something that I'm s'posed to be.
   Someday we'll find it,
   The Rainbow Connection;
   The lovers, the dreamers and me.

SATIN DOLL

from SOPHISTICATED LADIES

Words by JOHNNY MERCER and BILLY STRAYHORN
Music by DUKE ELLINGTON

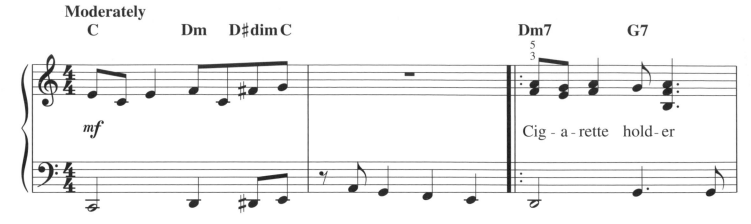

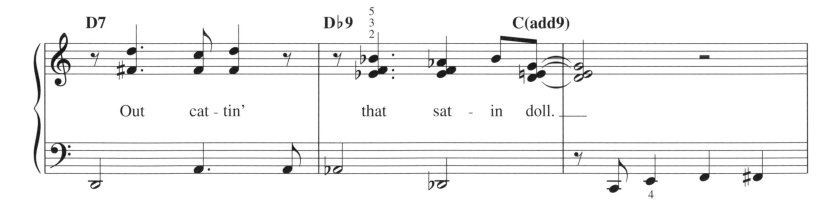

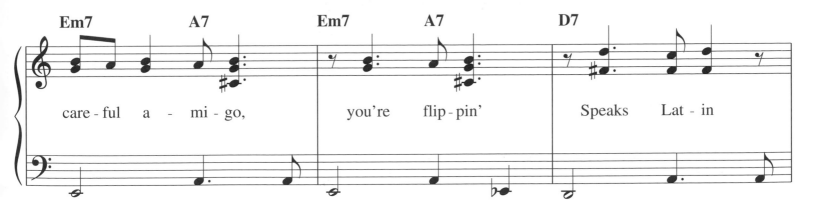

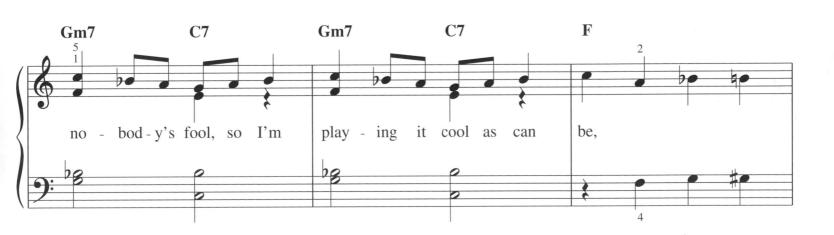

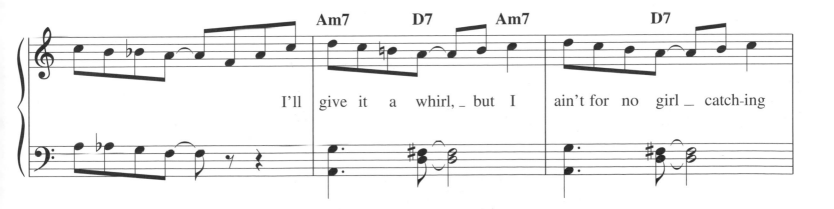

174

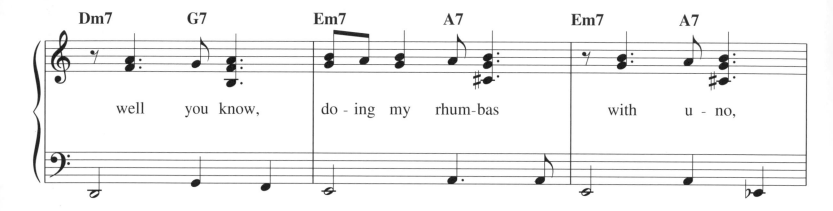

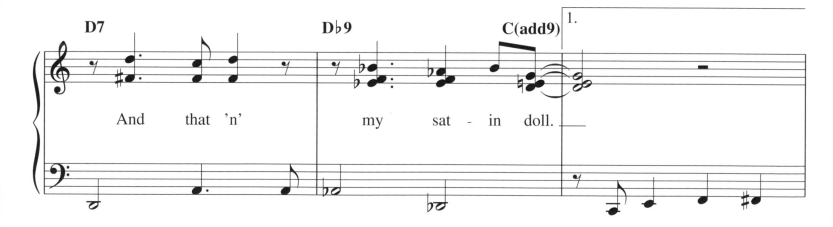

SOME DAY MY PRINCE WILL COME

Words by LARRY MOREY
Music by FRANK CHURCHILL

Slow Waltz

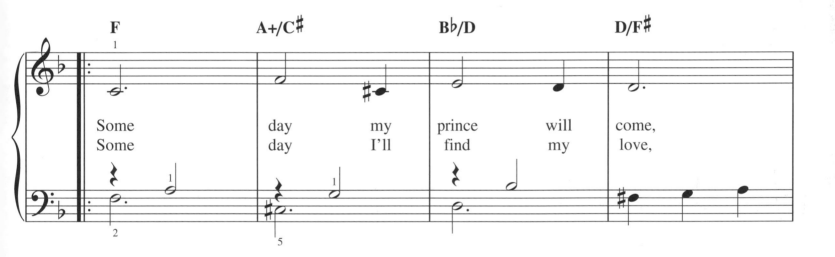

Some day my prince will come,
Some day I'll find my love,

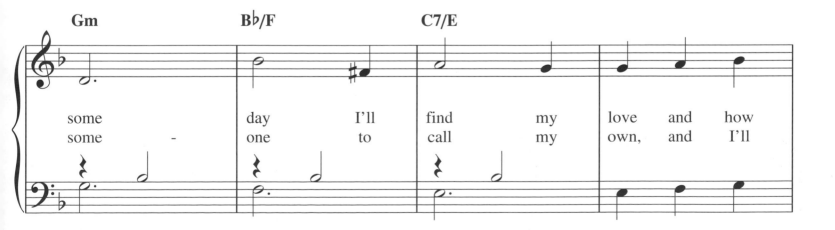

some day I'll find my love and how
some - one to call my own, and how I'll

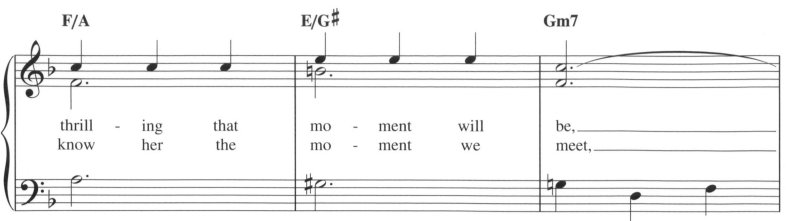

thrill - ing that   mo - ment will   be,_____
know her the   mo - ment we   meet,_____

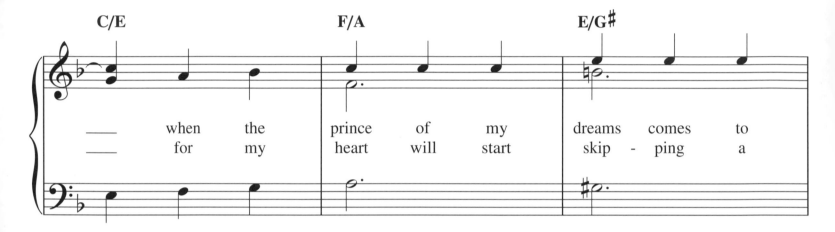

_____ when the   prince of my   dreams comes to
_____ for my   heart will start   skip - ping a

me._____   He'll   whis - per
beat._____   Some day   we'll

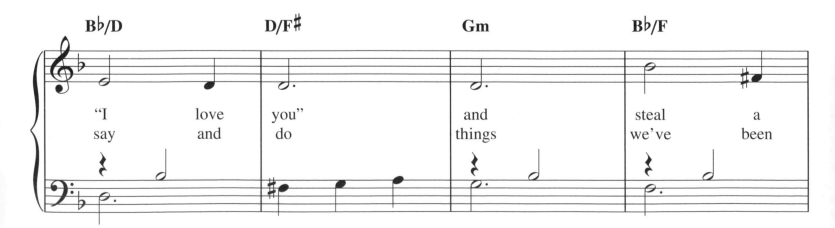

"I love   you"   and   steal a
say and   do   things   we've been

kiss   or   two. Though he's
long -   ing   to. Though she's far   a - way,   I'll

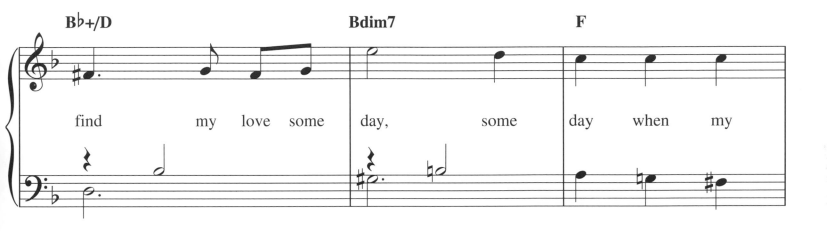

find   my love some   day,   some   day when   my

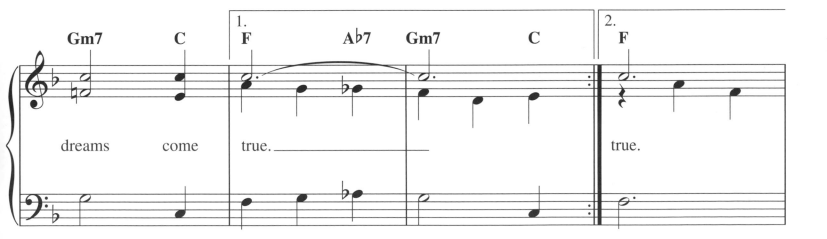

dreams   come   true._____   true.

rit.

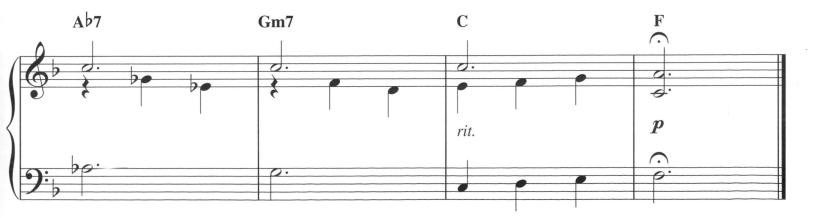

p

SEPTEMBER SONG
from the Musical Play KNICKERBOCKER HOLIDAY

Words by MAXWELL ANDERSON
Music by KURT WEILL

Moderately

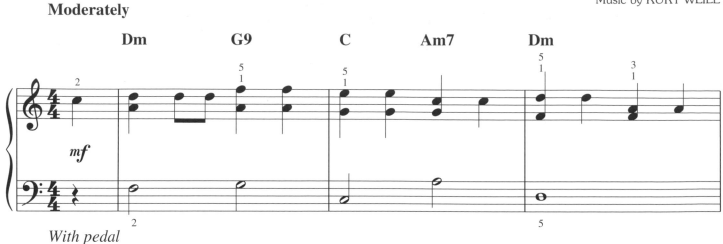

With pedal

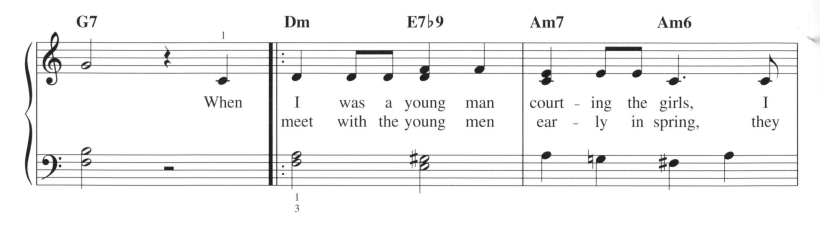

When
meet

I was a young man court - ing the girls, I
with the young men ear - ly in spring, they

played me a wait - ing game. If a maid re - fused me with
court you in song and rhyme. They woo you with words and a

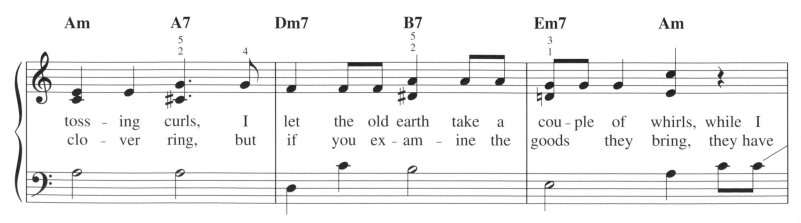

toss - ing curls, I let the old earth take a cou - ple of whirls, while I
clo - ver ring, but if you ex - am - ine the goods they bring, they have

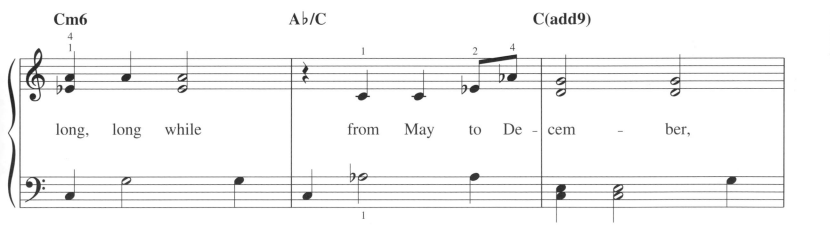

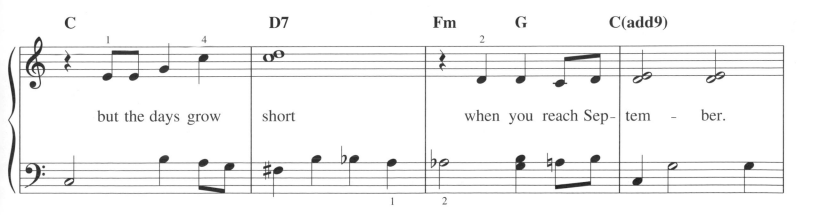

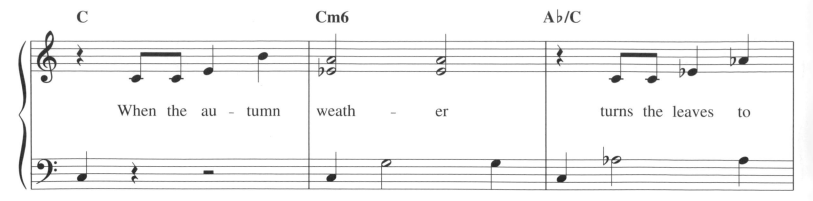

When the au - tumn weath – er turns the leaves to

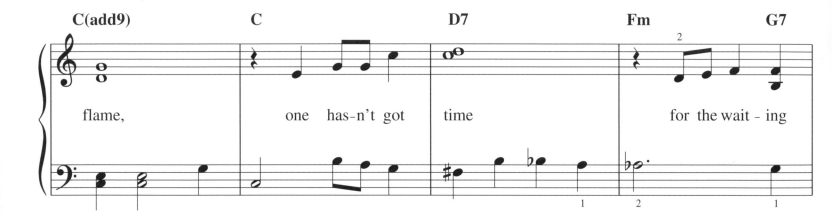

flame, one has-n't got time for the wait - ing

game. Oh, the days dwin-dle down ___ to a

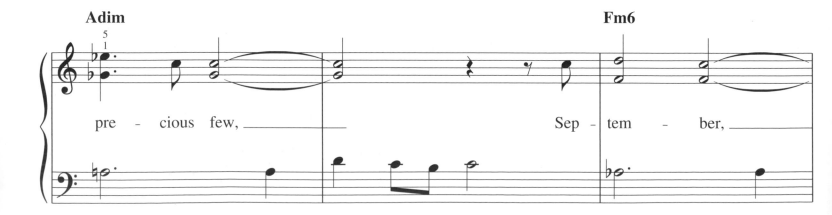

pre - cious few, ___ Sep - tem - ber, ___

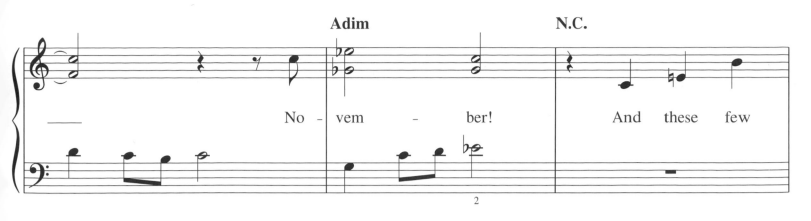

No - vem - ber! And these few

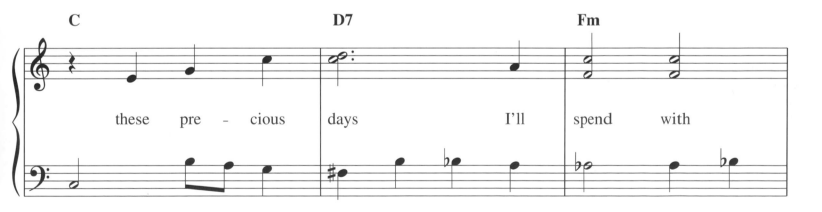

pre - cious days I'll spend with you,

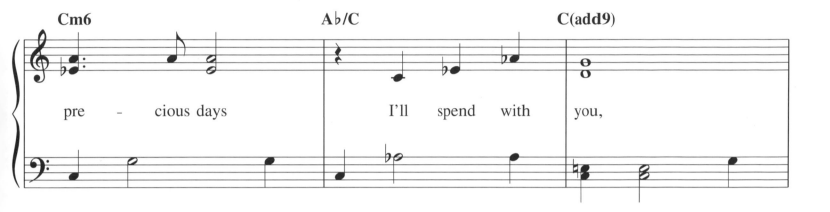

these pre - cious days I'll spend with

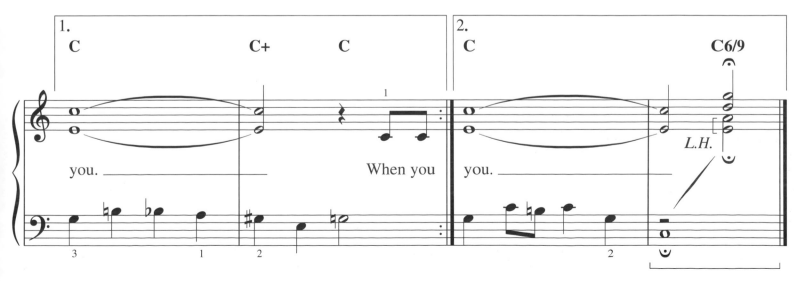

you. _____ When you you. _____

THE SOUND OF MUSIC
from THE SOUND OF MUSIC

Lyrics by OSCAR HAMMERSTEIN II
Music by RICHARD RODGERS

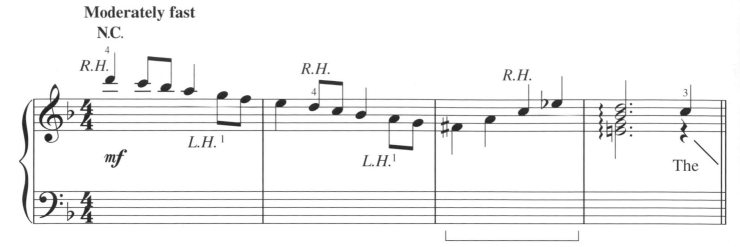

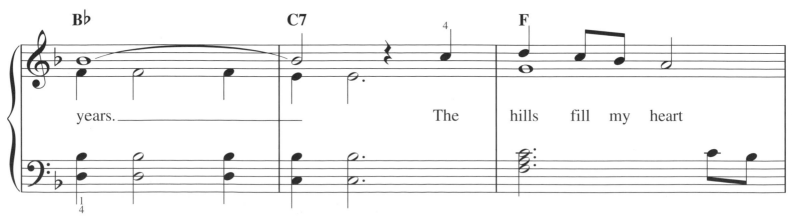

183

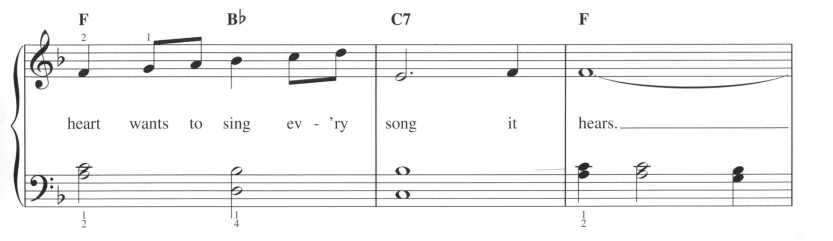

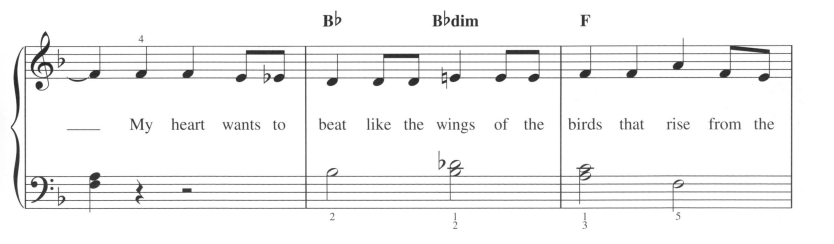

chime that flies from a | church on a breeze, To | laugh like a brook when it

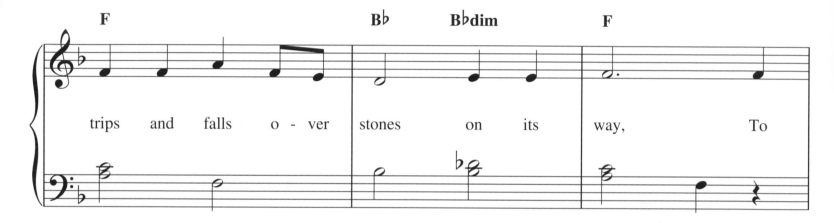

trips and falls o - ver | stones on its way, To

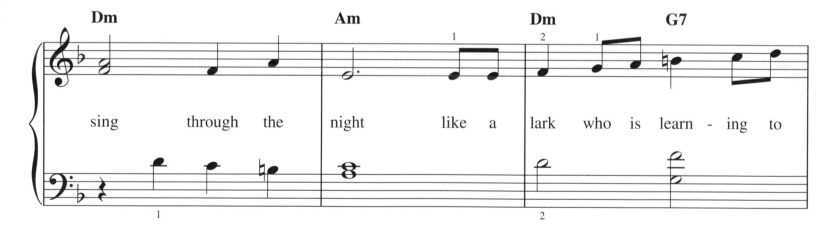

sing through the | night like a | lark who is learn - ing to

pray. I | go to the hills | when my heart is

185

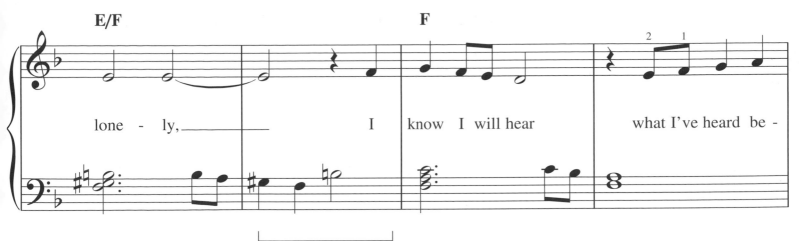

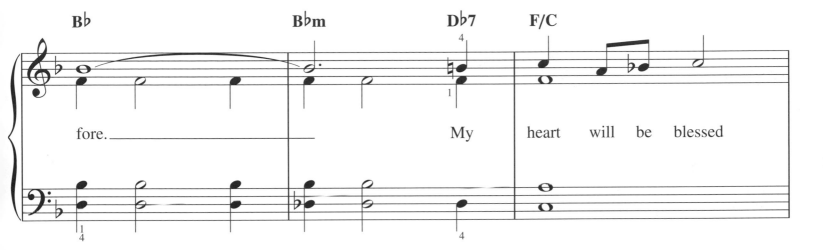

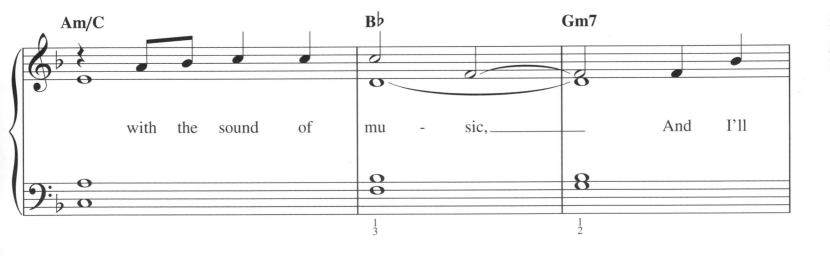

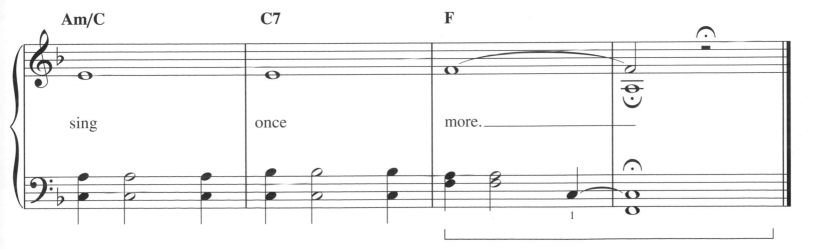

SPANISH EYES

Words by CHARLES SINGLETON and EDDIE SNYDER
Music by BERT KAEMPFERT

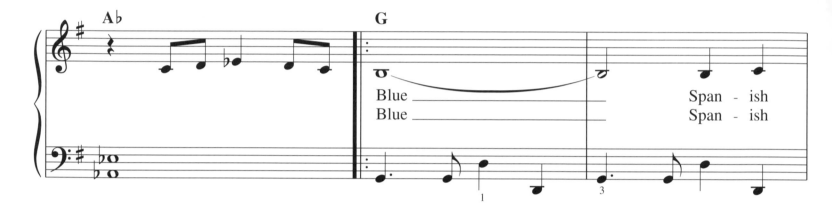

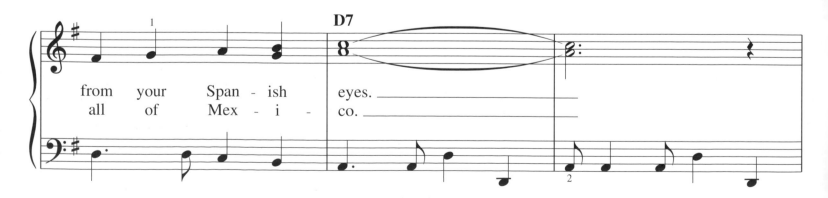

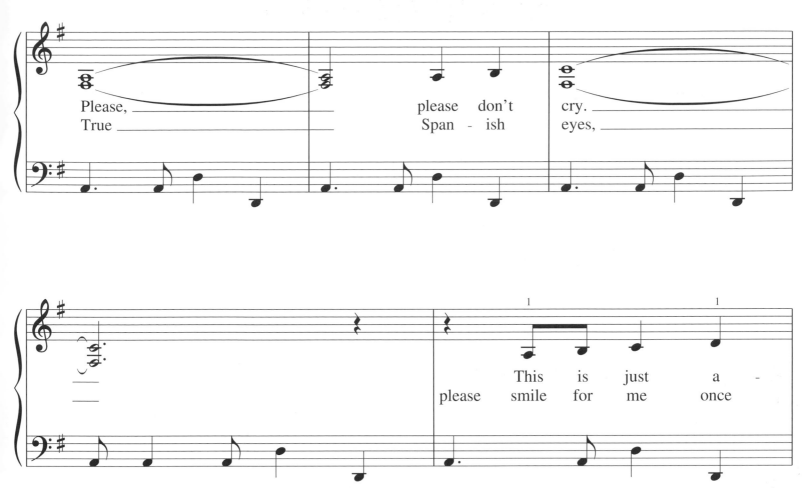

Please, _____ please don't cry. _____
True _____ Span - ish eyes, _____

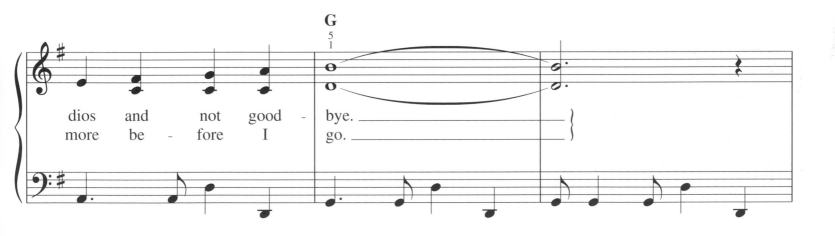

This is just a -
please smile for me once

dios and not good - bye. _____
more be - fore I go. _____

Soon _____ I'll re - turn, _____

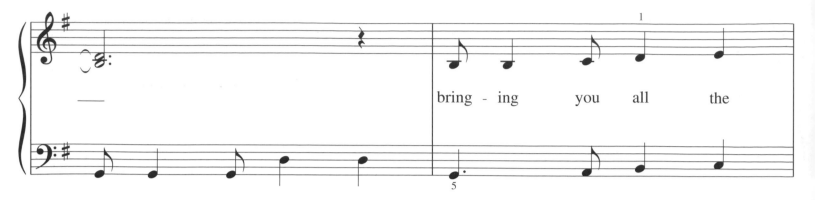

bring - ing   you   all   the

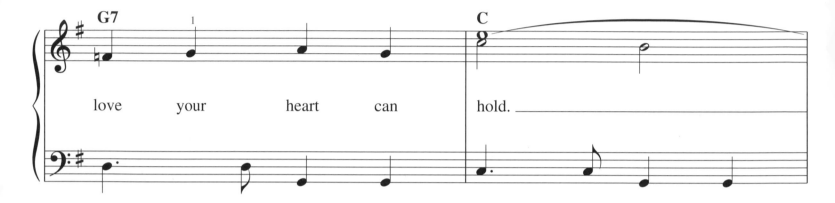

G7   love   your   heart   can   **C** hold. _____

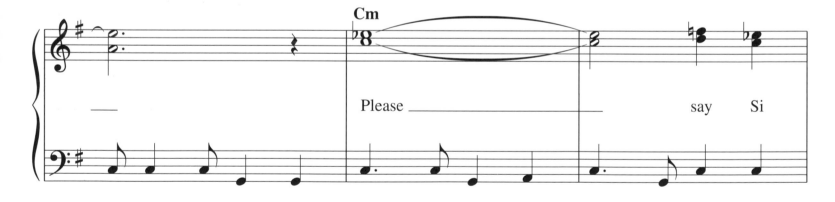

_____   **Cm** Please _____   say   Si

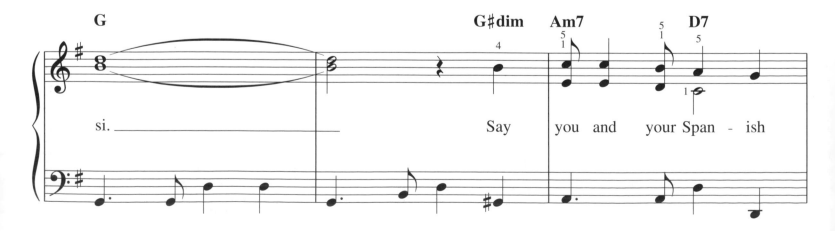

G si. _____   **G♯dim** **Am7** Say   you   and   your **D7** Span - ish

189

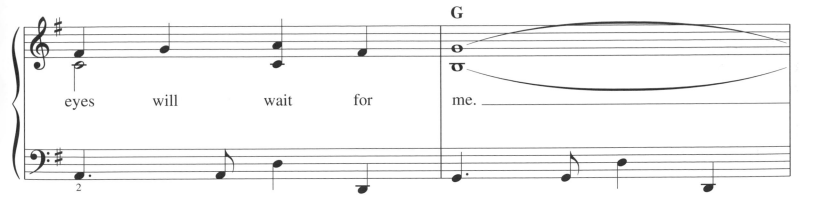

eyes   will   wait   for   me. _____

Span-ish eyes, _____

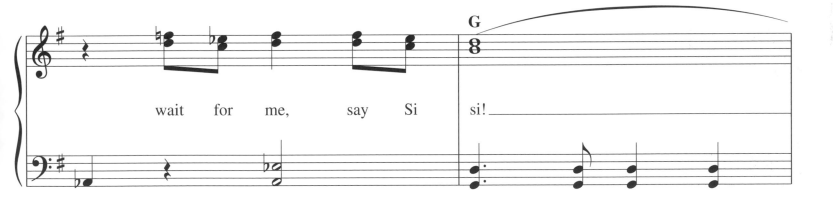

wait   for   me,   say Si   si! _____

SPEAK SOFTLY, LOVE

(Love Theme)
from the Paramount Picture THE GODFATHER

Words by LARRY KUSIK
Music by NINO ROTA

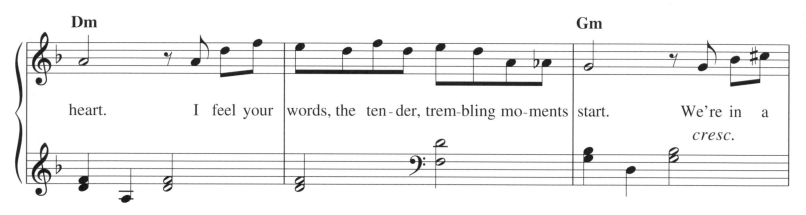

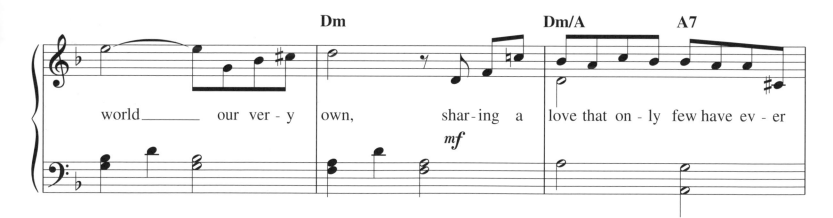

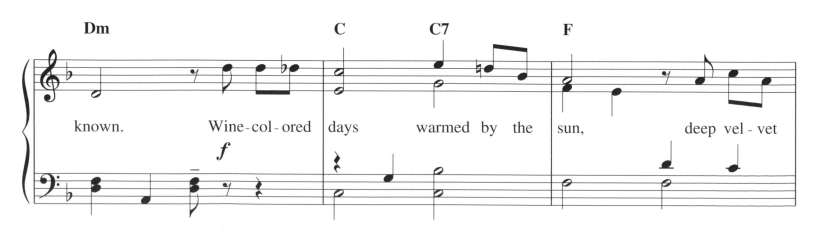

nights _____ when we are one. Speak soft-ly, love, so no one hears us but the

sky. The vows of love we make will live un-til we

die. My life is yours _____ and all be-cause you came in -

to my world with love so soft-ly, love. _____ Speak soft-ly, love. love.

STARDUST

Words by MITCHELL PARISH
Music by HOAGY CARMICHAEL

Moderately slow

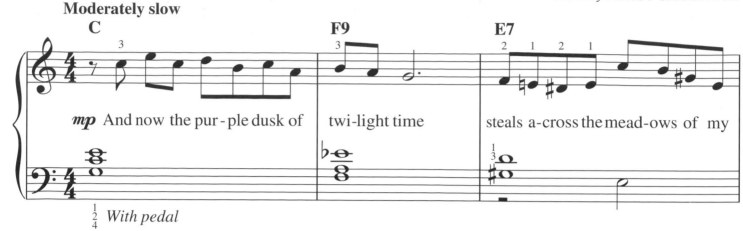

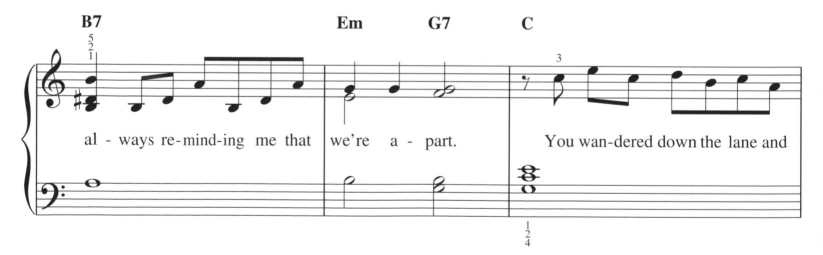

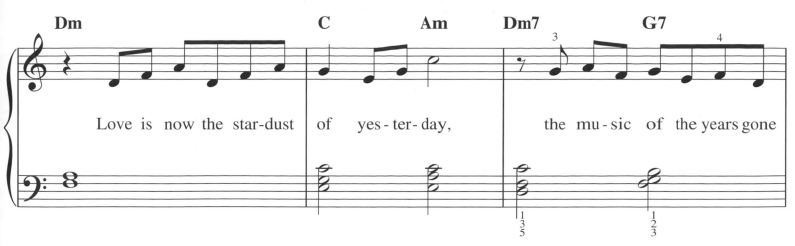

Love is now the star-dust of yes - ter- day, the mu - sic of the years gone

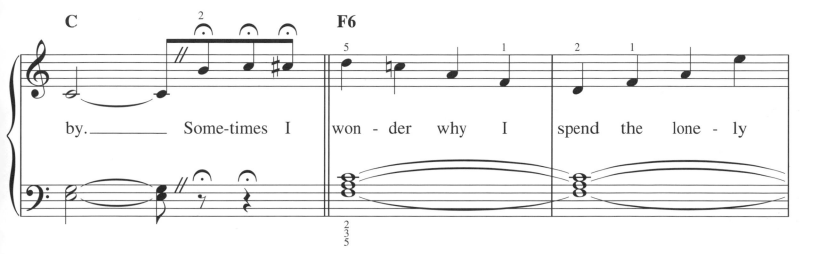

by._____ Some-times I won - der why I spend the lone - ly

night dream-ing of a song. The mel - o - dy

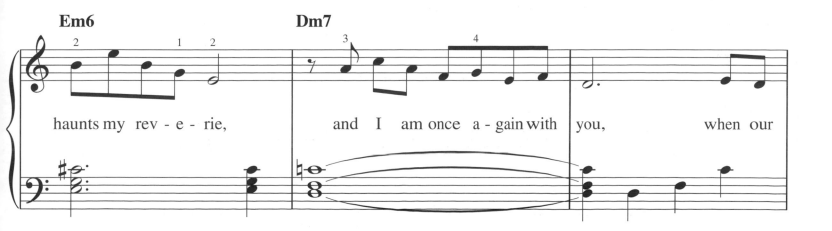

haunts my rev - e - rie, and I am once a - gain with you, when our

love was new

and each kiss an in-spi-ra- tion.____

____ But that was long a-go; now my con-sol-a-tion is

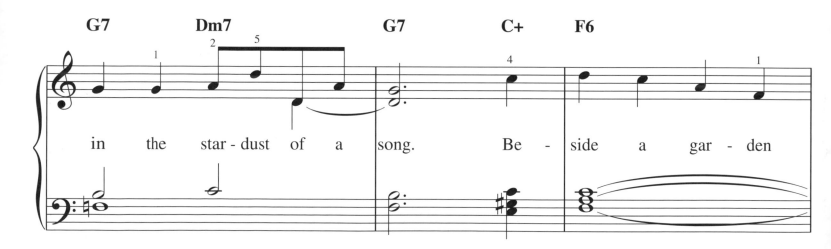

in the star-dust of a song. Be - side a gar-den

wall when stars are bright, you are in my arms. The

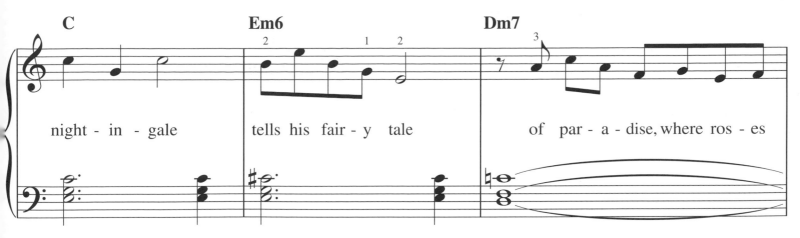

night - in - gale   tells his fair - y tale   of par - a - dise, where ros - es

grew.   Though I dream in vain,_____   in my

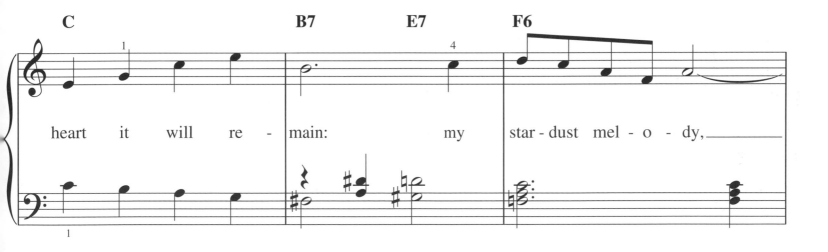

heart it will re - main: my   star - dust mel - o - dy,_____

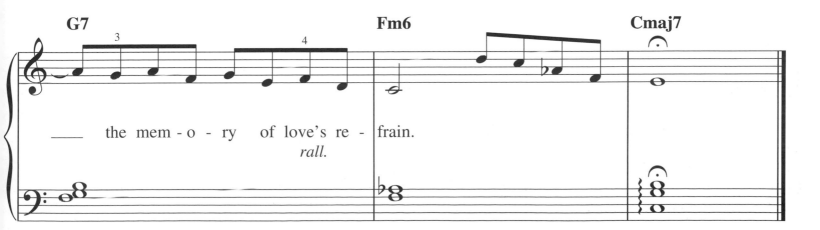

___ the mem - o - ry of love's re - frain.
rall.

STORMY WEATHER
(Keeps Rainin' All the Time)
from COTTON CLUB PARADE OF 1933
featured in the Motion Picture STORMY WEATHER

Lyric by TED KOEHLER
Music by HAROLD ARLEN

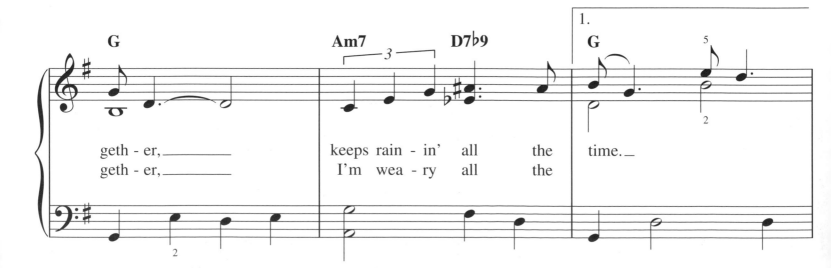

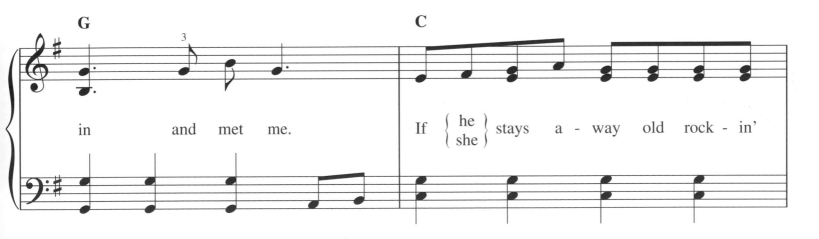

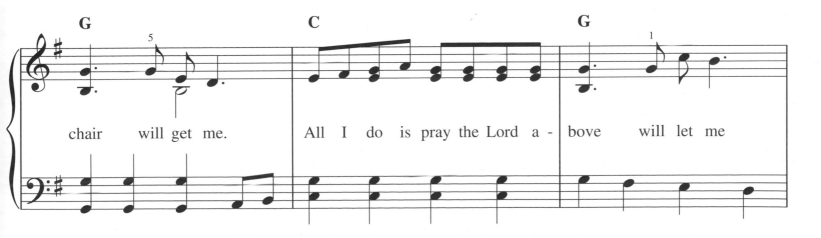

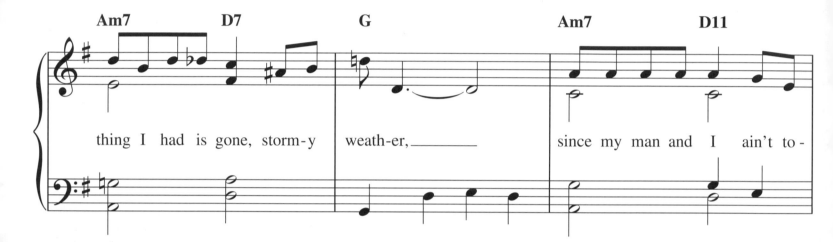

THREE COINS IN THE FOUNTAIN

from THREE COINS IN THE FOUNTAIN

Words by SAMMY CAHN
Music by JULE STYNE

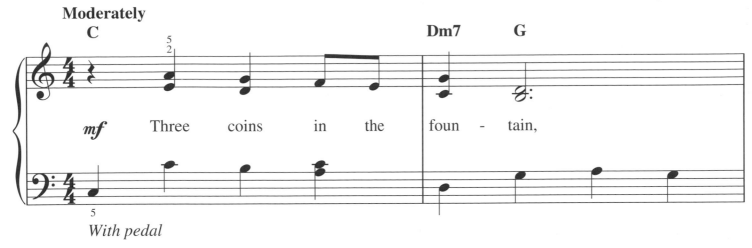

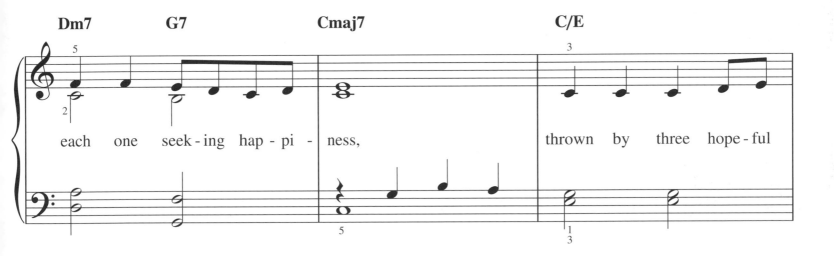

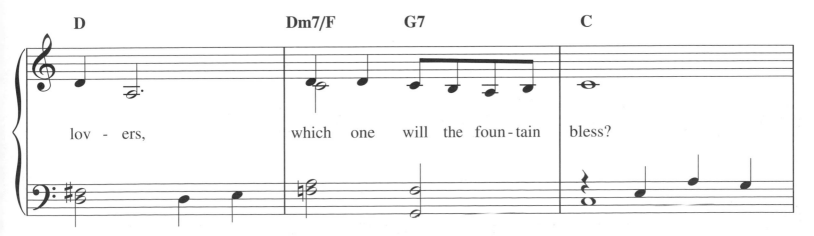

Three hearts in the foun - tain, each heart long - ing for its

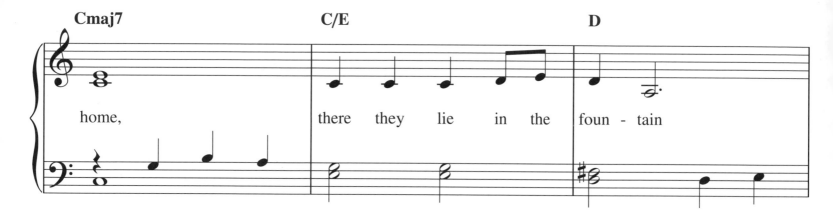

home, there they lie in the foun - tain

some - where in the heart of Rome. Which one will the foun - tain

bless? Which one will the foun - tain bless?

Three coins in the foun - tain, through the rip - ples how they

shine. Just one wish will be grant - ed,

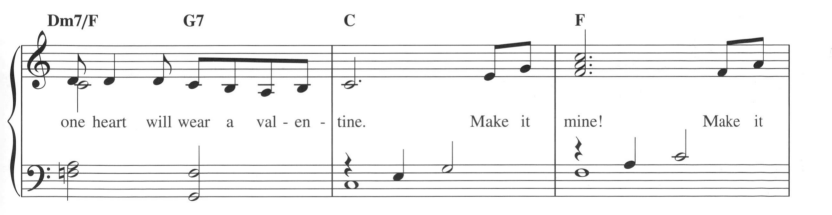

one heart will wear a val - en - tine. Make it mine! Make it

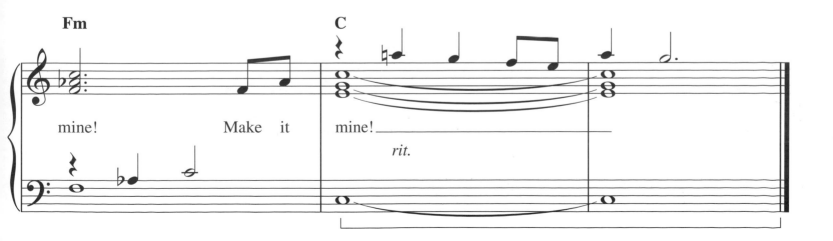

mine! Make it mine! _____

rit.

A STRING OF PEARLS
from THE GLENN MILLER STORY

Words by EDDIE DE LANGE
Music by JERRY GRAY

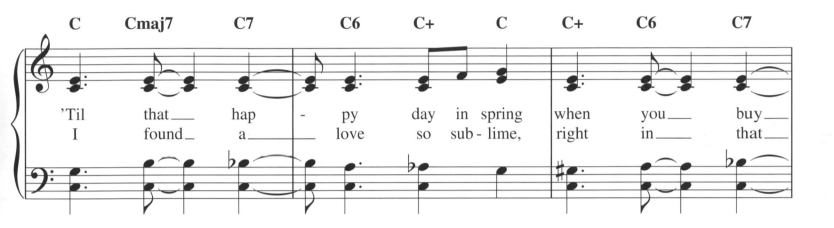

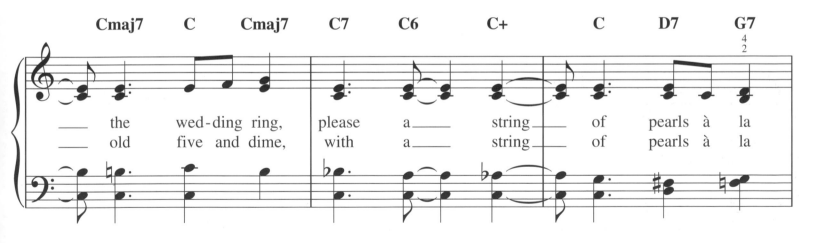

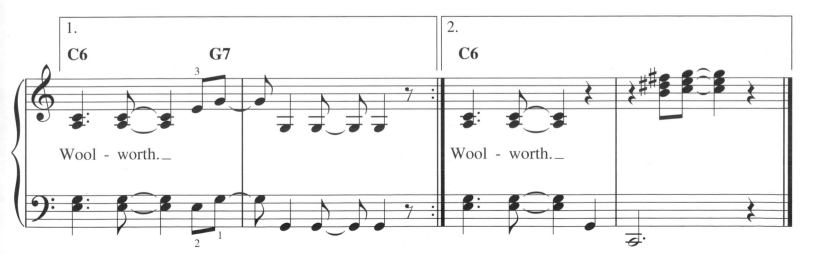

TEARS IN HEAVEN

Words and Music by ERIC CLAPTON
and WILL JENNINGS

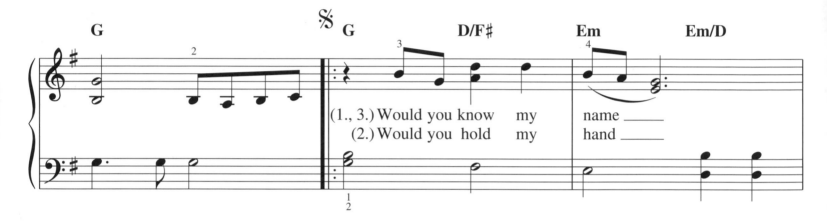

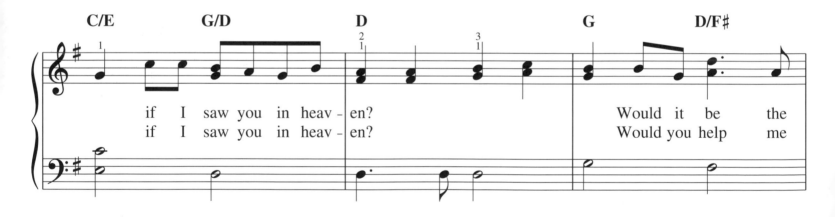

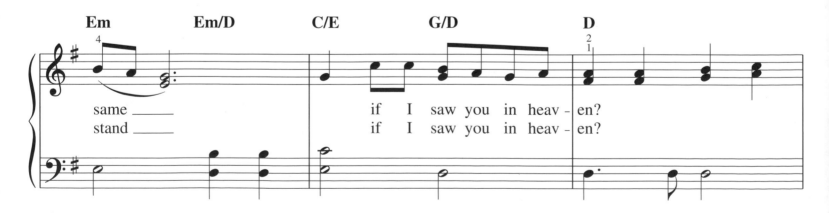

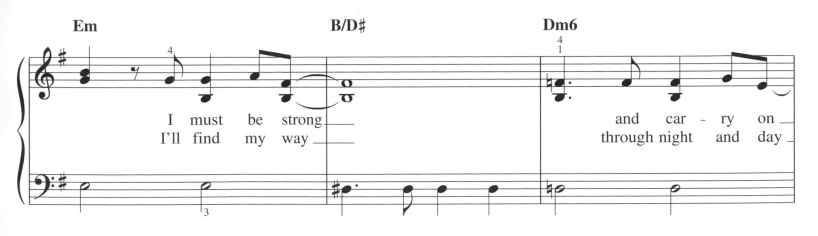

I must be strong _____ and car - ry on _____
I'll find my way _____ through night and day _____

To Coda

_____ 'cause I know _____ I don't be - long _____ here in heav -
_____ 'cause I know _____ I just can't stay _____ here in heav -

1.

en.
en.

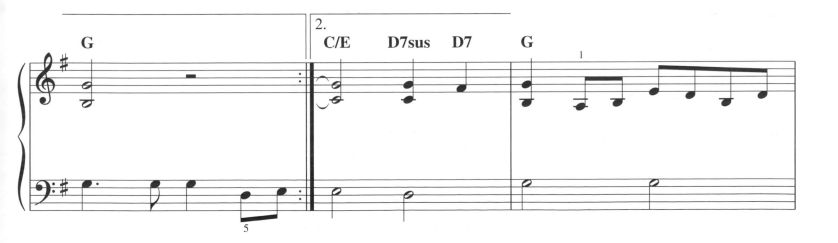

2.

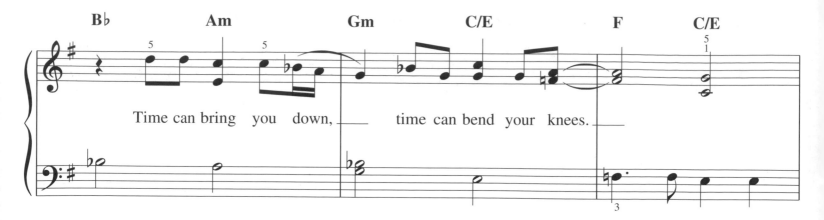

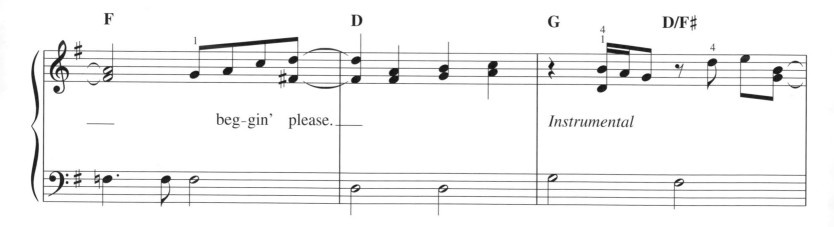

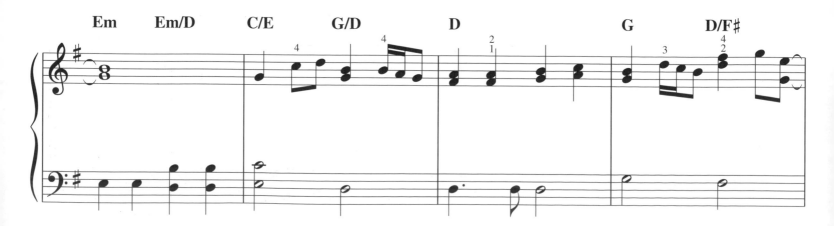

Be-yond the door

there's peace, I'm sure.___ And I know___

D.S. al Coda

there'll be no more ___ tears in heav - en.

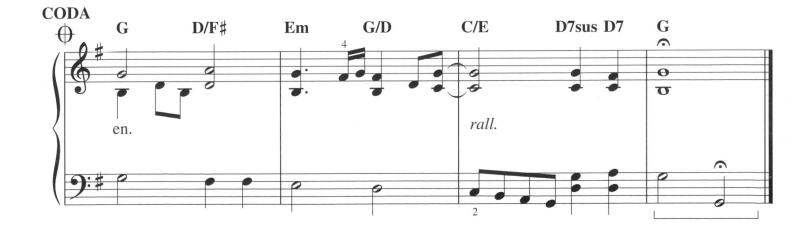

CODA

en. *rall.*

A TIME FOR US
(Love Theme)
from the Paramount Picture ROMEO AND JULIET

Words by LARRY KUSIK and EDDIE SNYDER
Music by NINO ROTA

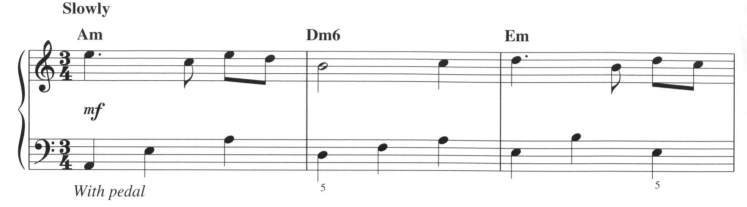

Slowly

With pedal

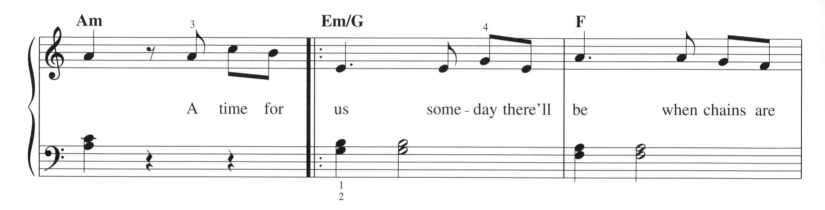

A time for us some-day there'll be when chains are

torn by cour-age born of a love that's free. A time when

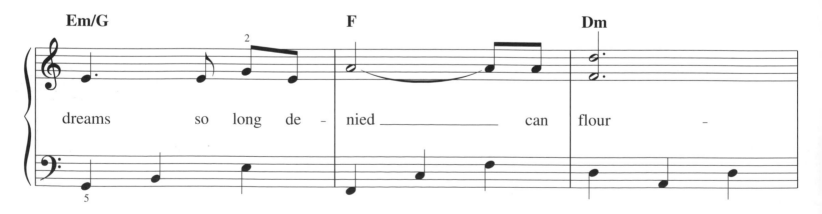

dreams so long de - nied _____ can flour -

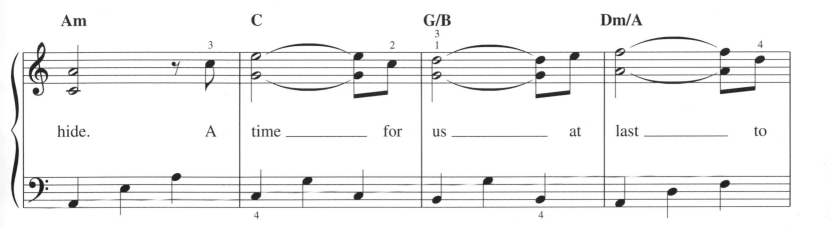

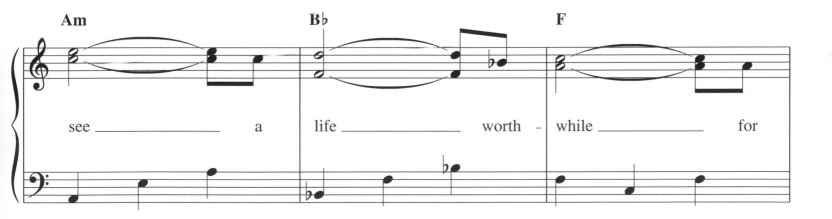

thorns   we will en - dure   as   we   pass   sure - ly through ev - 'ry

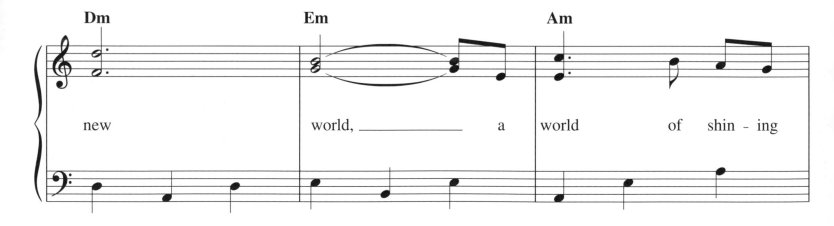

storm.   A   time   for   us   some - day there'll   be, _____   a

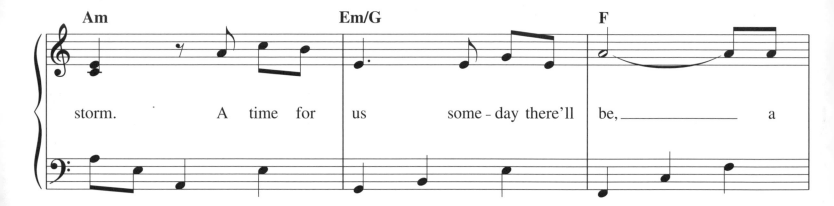

new   world, _____   a   world   of   shin - ing

hope   for   you   and   me.   A   time   for   me.

TOP OF THE WORLD

Words and Music by JOHN BETTIS
and RICHARD CARPENTER

Moderately, in 2

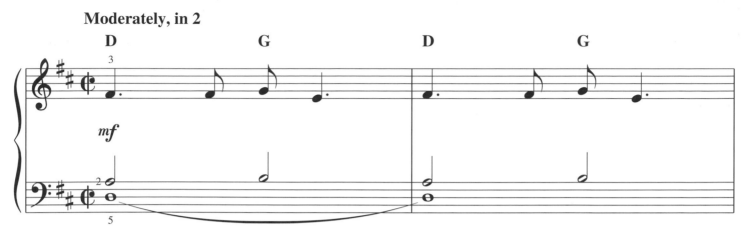

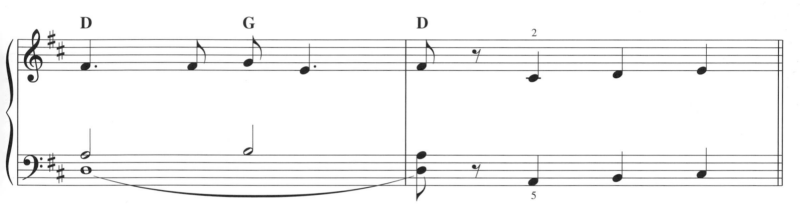

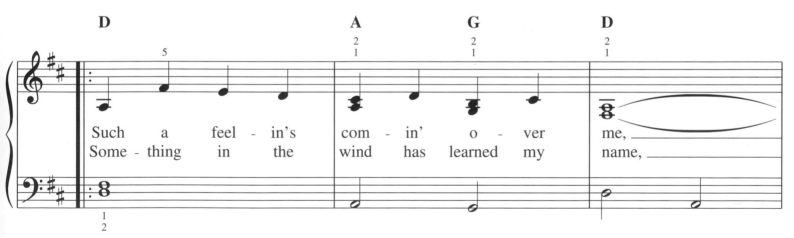

Such a feel - in's com - in' o - ver me,
Some - thing in the wind has learned my name,

____ there is won - der in ____ most ev - 'ry - thing I
____ and it's tell - in' me ____ that things are not the

D ... **G**

see, _____ not a cloud in the
same, _____ in the leaves on the

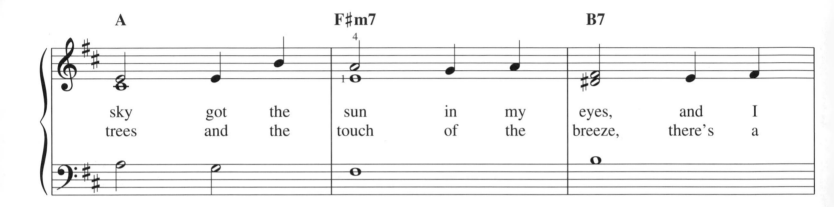

A ... **F♯m7** ... **B7**

sky got the sun in my eyes, and I
trees and the touch of the breeze, there's a

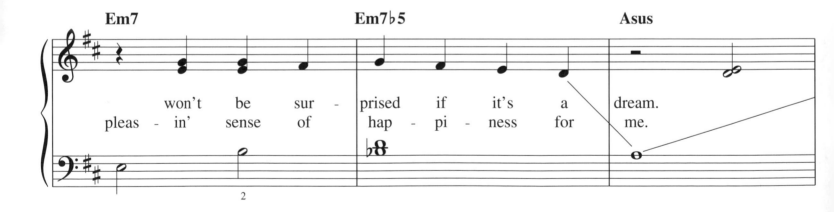

Em7 ... **Em7♭5** ... **Asus**

won't be sur - prised if it's a dream.
pleas - in' sense of hap - pi - ness for me.

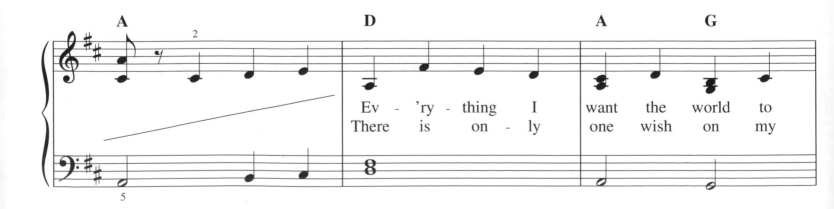

A ... **D** ... **A** ... **G**

Ev - 'ry - thing I want the world to
There is on - ly one wish on my

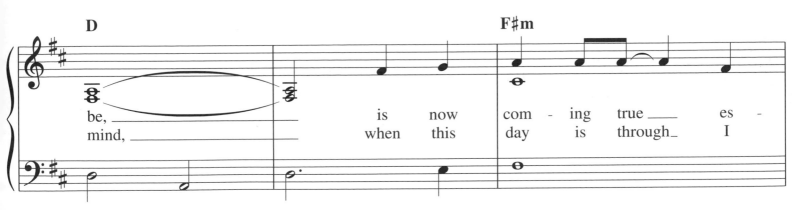

be, _____ is now com - ing true _____ es -
mind, _____ when this day is through_ I

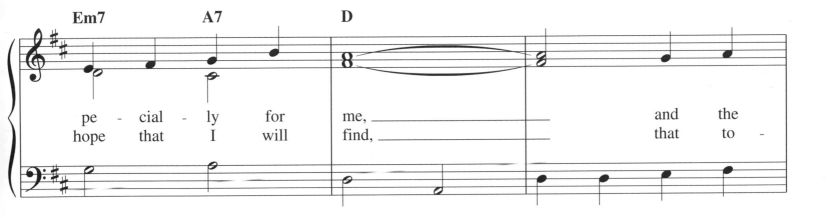

pe - cial - ly for me, _____ and the
hope that I will find, _____ that to -

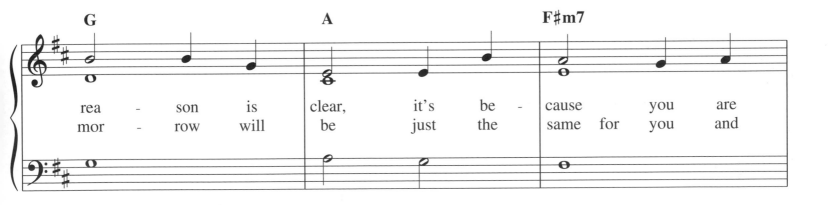

rea - son is clear, it's be - cause you are
mor - row will be just the same for you and

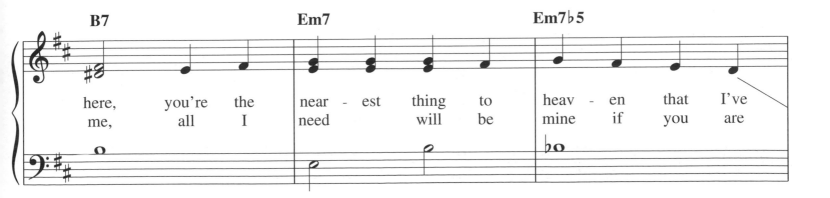

here, you're the near - est thing to heav - en that I've
me, all I need will be mine if you are

Asus   **A**   **D**

seen.}
here.}

I'm on the   top of the world

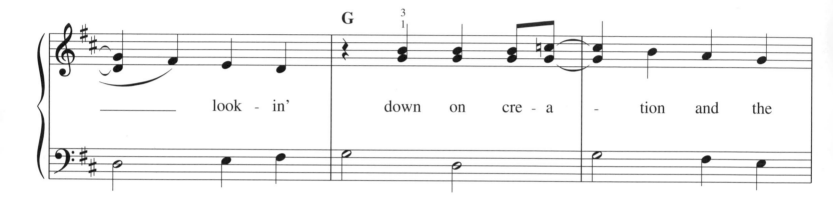

G

_____ look - in'   down on cre - a - tion and the

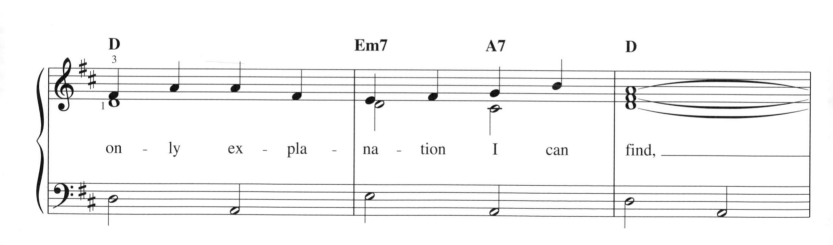

D   **Em7**   **A7**   **D**

on - ly ex - pla - na - tion I can   find, ____

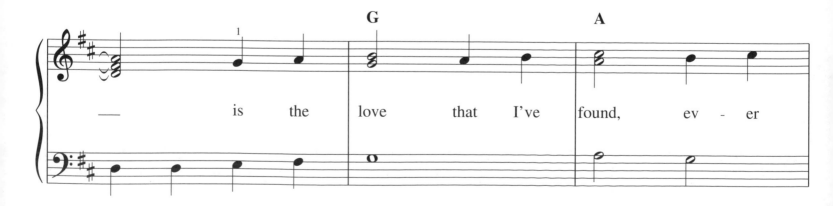

   G   **A**

—   is the   love that I've   found,   ev - er

215

since you've been a - round, your love's put me at the

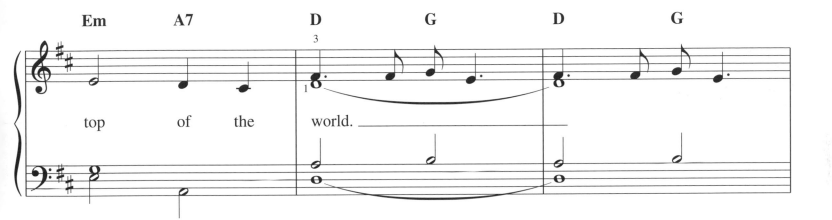

top of the world.

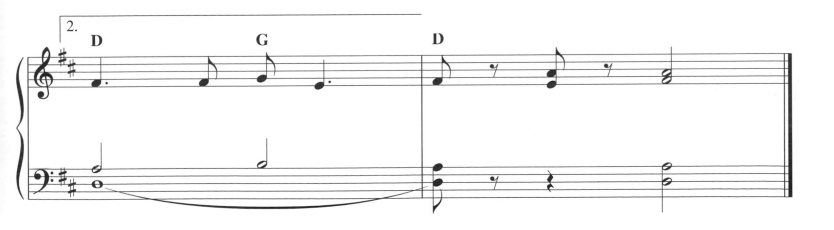

UNCHAINED MELODY
from the Motion Picture UNCHAINED

Lyric by HY ZARET
Music by ALEX NORTH

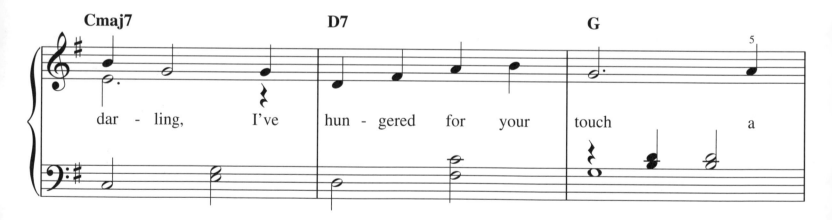

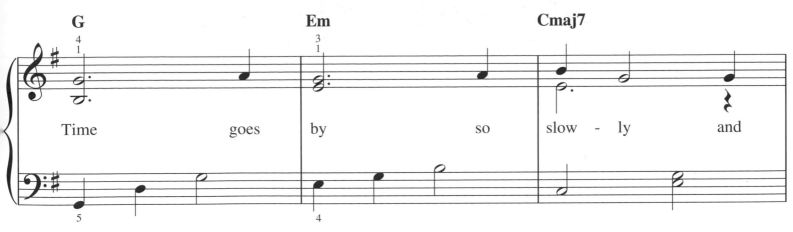

Time　　　　goes　　by　　　　so　　slow - ly　　and

time　can　do　so　much.　　　　Are　you　　　　still

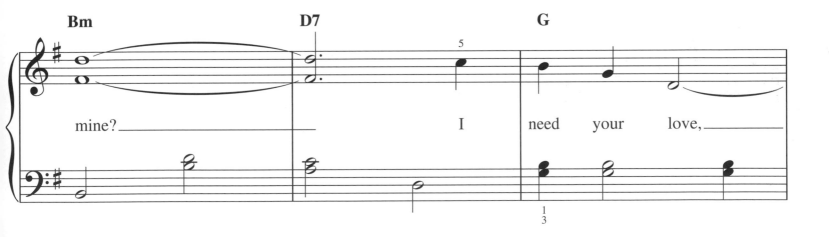

mine?＿＿＿＿＿＿＿＿　　　　I　need　your　love,＿＿＿＿

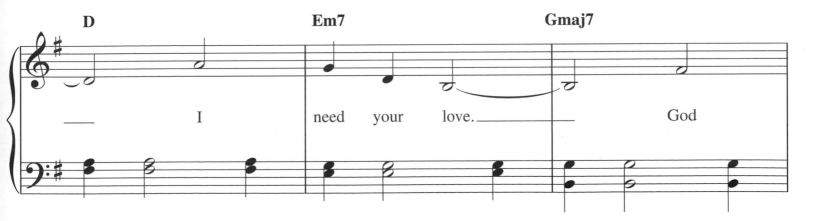

＿　　　I　need　your　love.＿＿＿＿＿　　　God

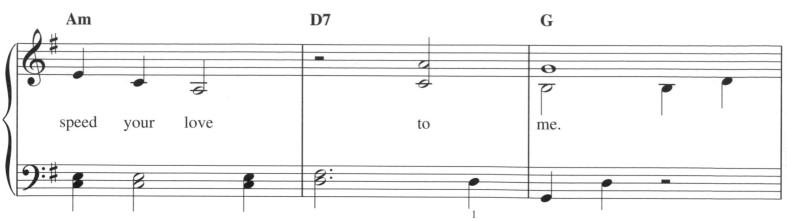

Am   **D7**   **G**

speed your love   to   me.

Slightly faster

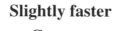

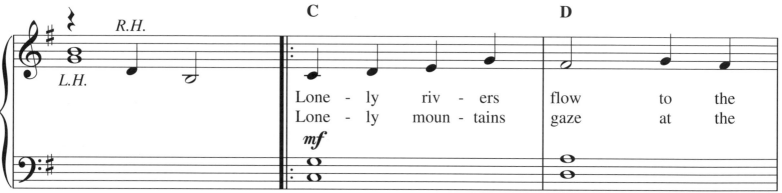

C   **D**

R.H.

L.H.

mf

Lone - ly riv - ers flow to the
Lone - ly moun - tains gaze at the

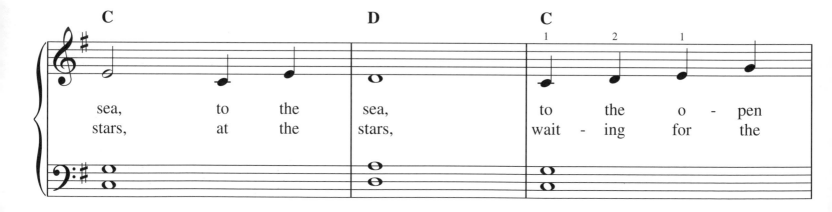

C   **D**   **C**

sea, to the sea, to the o - pen
stars, at the stars, wait - ing for the

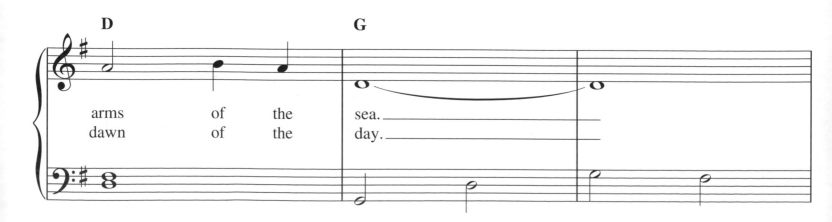

D   **G**

arms of the sea._____
dawn of the day._____

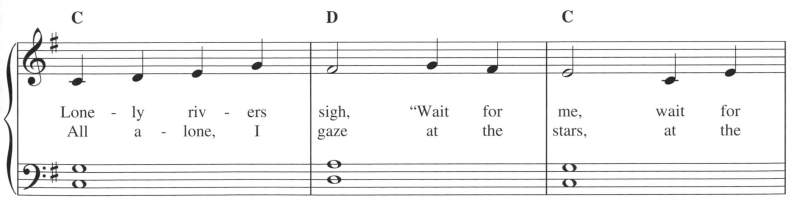

C .... **D** .... **C**

Lone - ly riv - ers sigh, "Wait for me, wait for
All a - lone, I gaze at the stars, at for the

D .... **C** .... **D**

me. I'll be com - ing home, wait for
stars, dream - ing of my love far a -
rit.

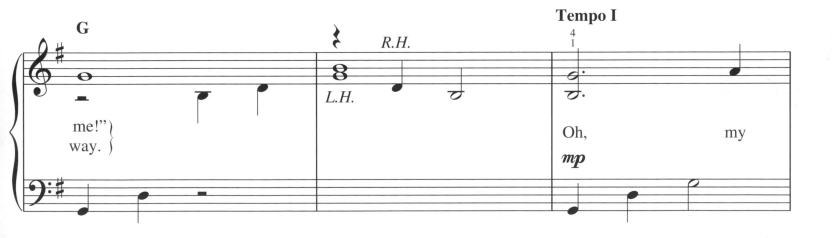

G .... *R.H.* .... **Tempo I**

me!") .... *L.H.* .... Oh, my
way. } .... *mp*

Em .... **Cmaj7** **D7**

love, my dar - ling, I've hun - gered for your

220

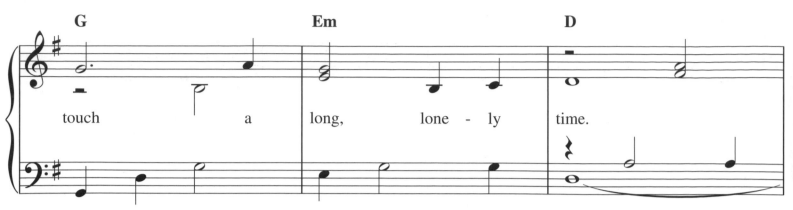

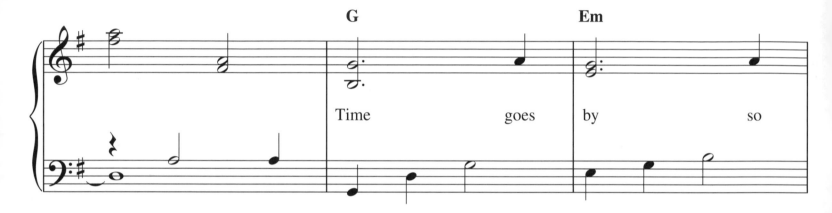

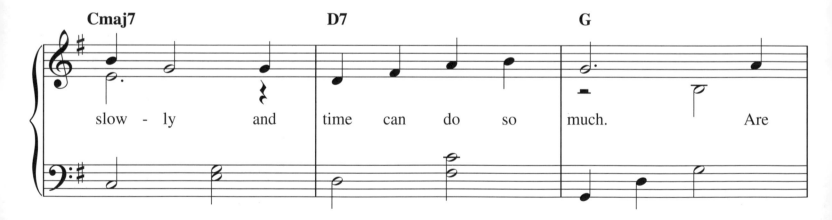

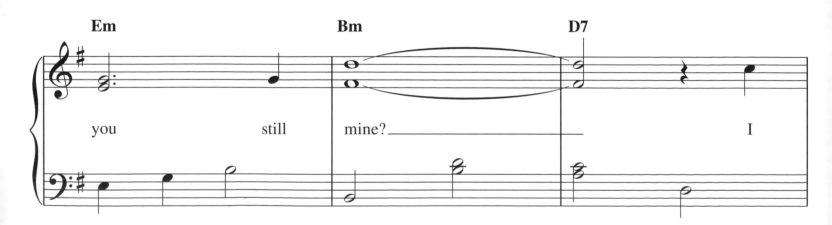

need your love,_____ I

need your love._____

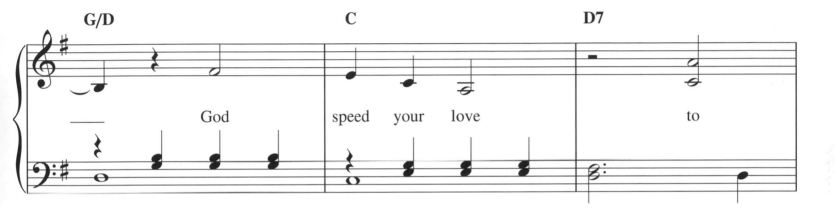

_____ God speed your love to

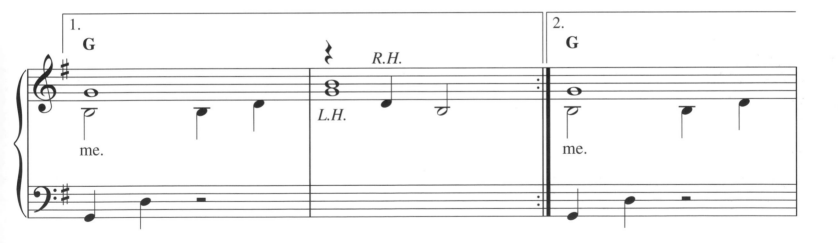

1.
me.

2.
me.

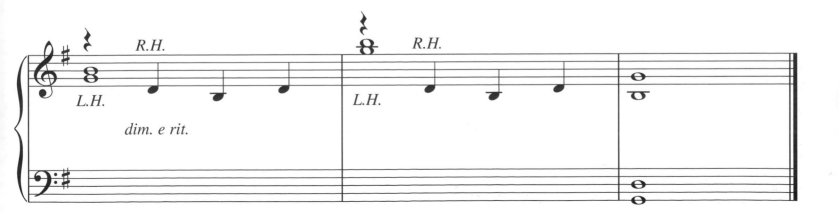

dim. e rit.

UNFORGETTABLE

Words and Music by
IRVING GORDON

Moderately

how the thought of you does things— to me. Nev - er be - fore—

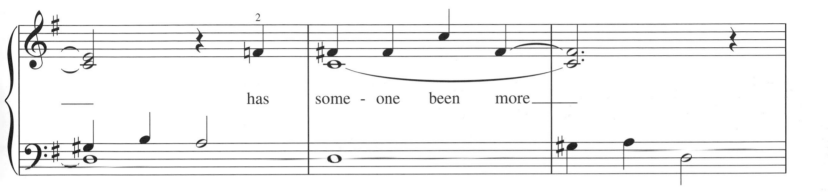

— has some - one been more—

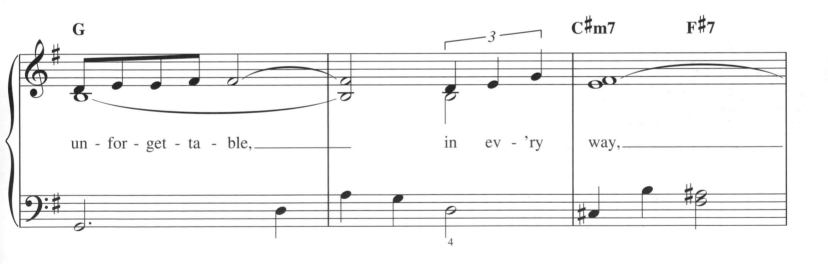

un - for - get - ta - ble,— in ev - 'ry way,—

— and for - ev - er - more,— that's how you'll

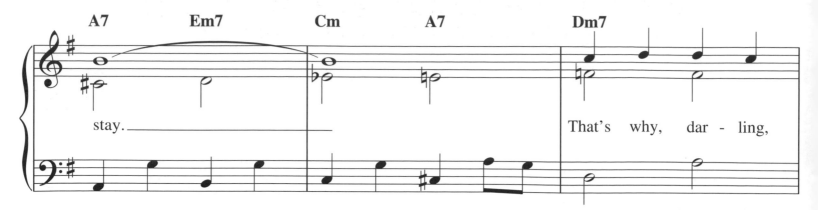

stay. _____ That's why, dar - ling,

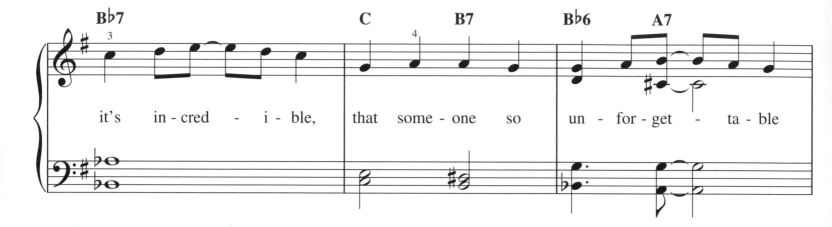

it's in - cred - i - ble, that some - one so un - for - get - ta - ble

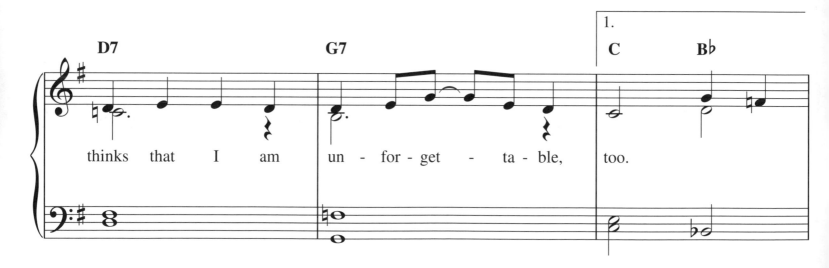

thinks that I am un - for - get - ta - ble, too.

1.

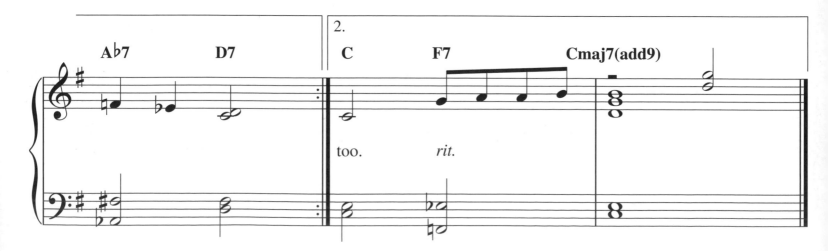

too. *rit.*

2.

WHAT KIND OF FOOL AM I?

from the Musical Production STOP THE WORLD – I WANT TO GET OFF

Words and Music by LESLIE BRICUSSE
and ANTHONY NEWLEY

Moderately slow

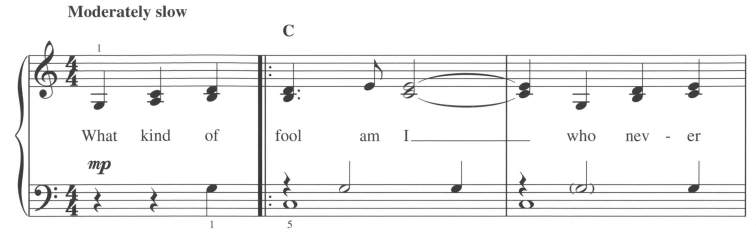

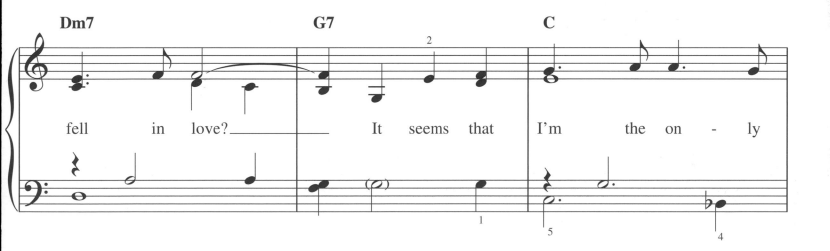

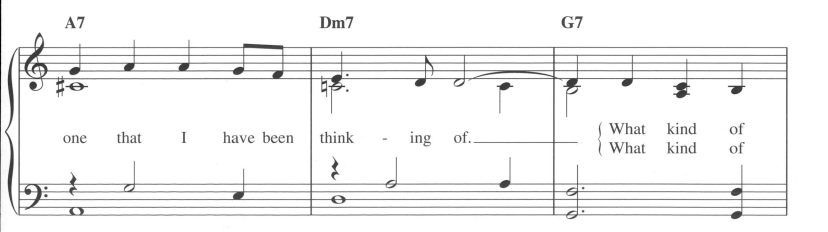

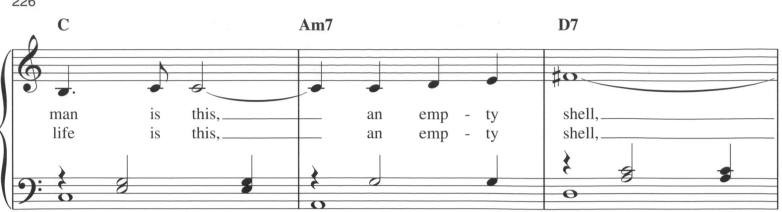

man is this,_____ an emp - ty shell,_____
life is this,_____ an emp - ty shell,_____

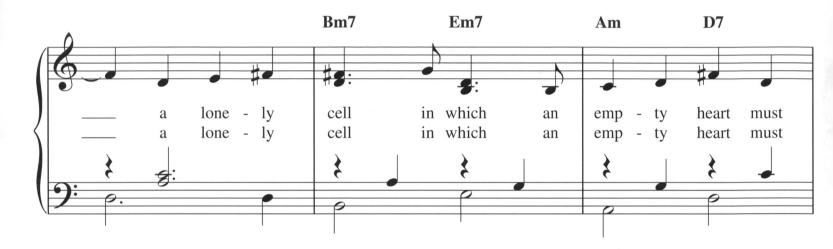

_____ a lone - ly cell in which an emp - ty heart must
_____ a lone - ly cell in which an emp - ty heart must

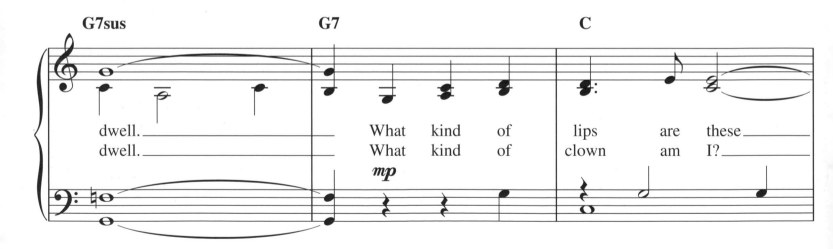

dwell._____ What kind of lips are these_____
dwell._____ What kind of clown am I?_____

_____ that lied with ev - 'ry kiss,_____ that whis - pered
_____ What do I know of life?_____ Why can't I

227

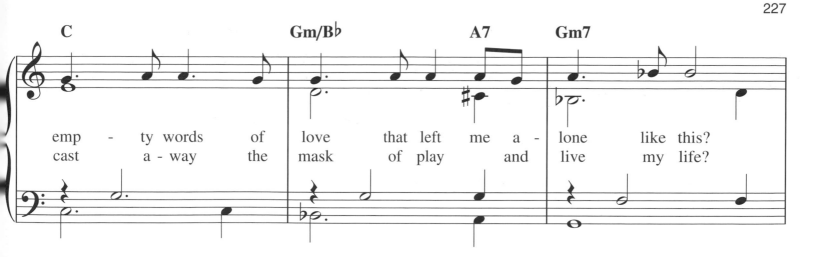

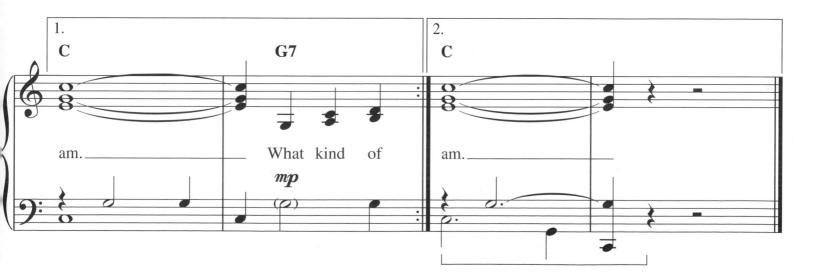

THE WAY WE WERE

from the Motion Picture THE WAY WE WERE

Words by ALAN and MARILYN BERGMAN
Music by MARVIN HAMLISCH

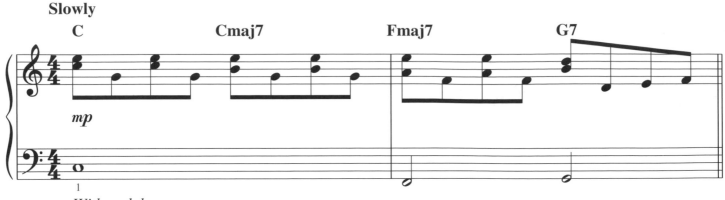

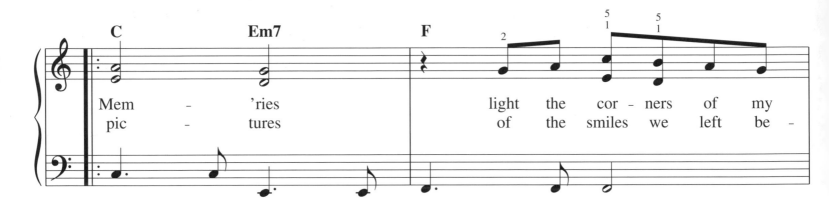

1.

Cmaj7   Am   Dm7   Gsus

were.   Scat - tered

2.

Cmaj7   Gm7   C7sus   F

were.   Can it be that it was all so

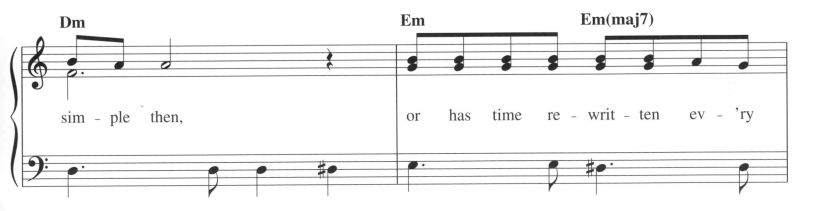

Dm   Em   Em(maj7)

sim - ple then,   or has time re - writ - ten ev - 'ry

Em7/D   A7   Dm   Dm(maj7)

line?   If we had the chance to do it

all a - gain, tell me would we? ___ Could we? ___

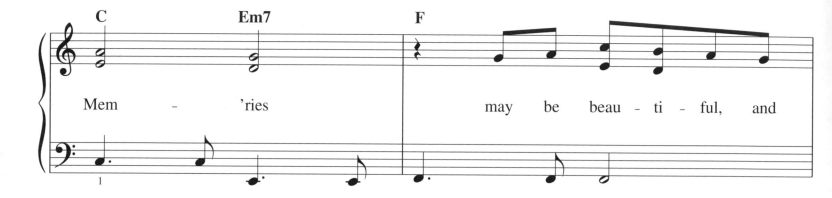

Mem - 'ries may be beau - ti - ful, and

yet, what's too pain - ful to re -

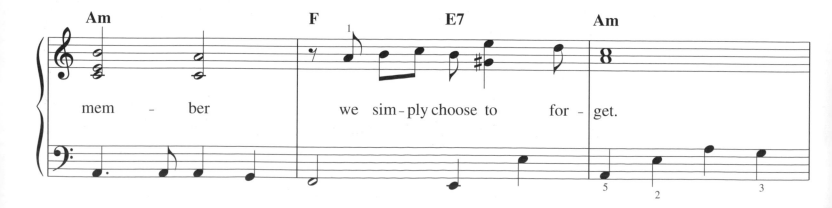

mem - ber we sim - ply choose to for - get.

So it's the laugh - ter we will re -

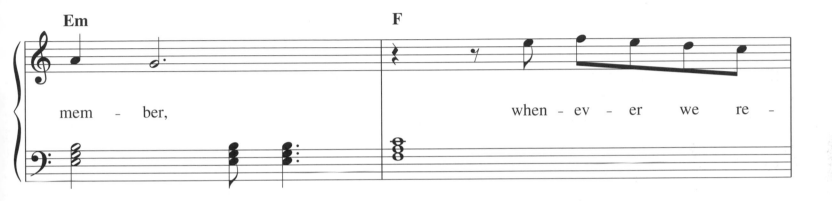

mem - ber, when - ev - er we re -

mem - ber the way we were;

the way we were. *rit.*

WE'VE ONLY JUST BEGUN

Words and Music by ROGER NICHOLS
and PAUL WILLIAMS

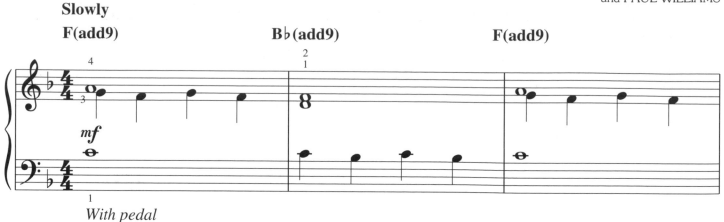

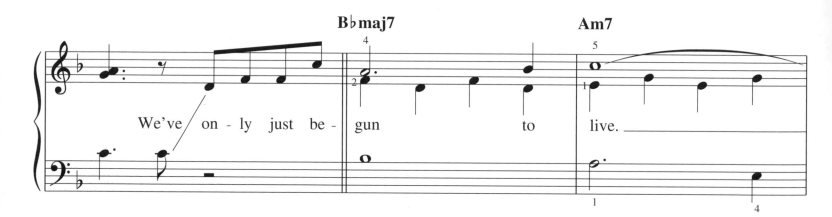

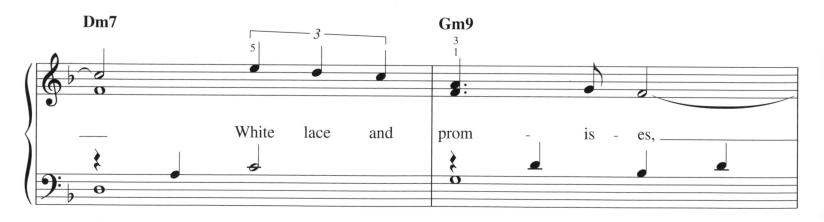

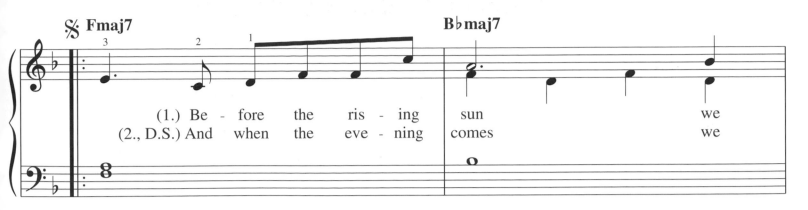

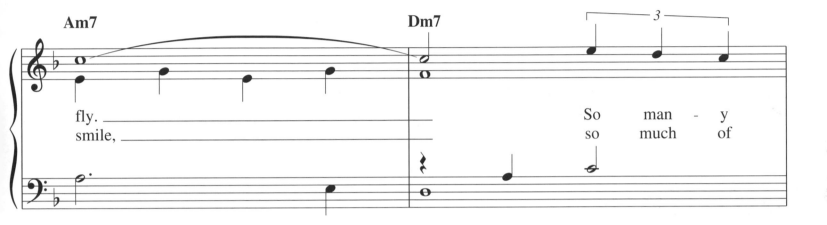

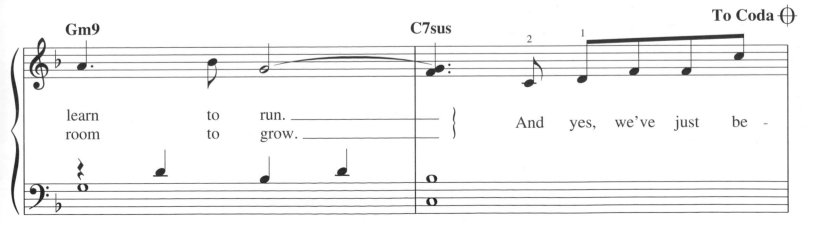

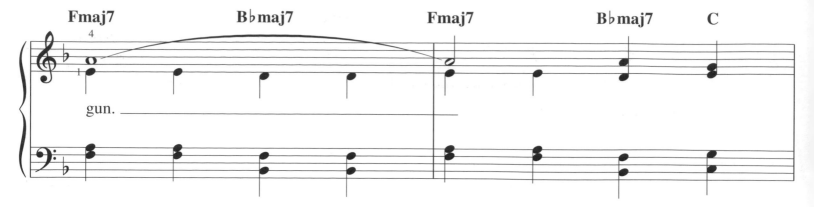

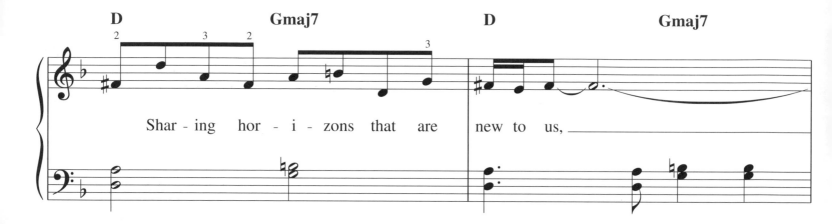

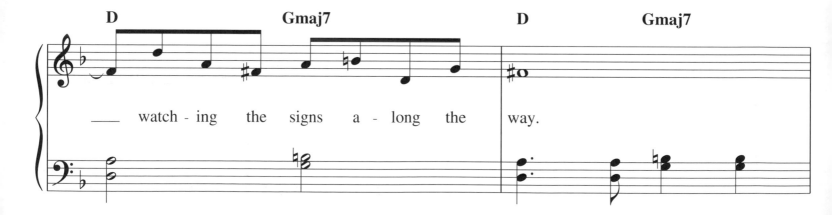

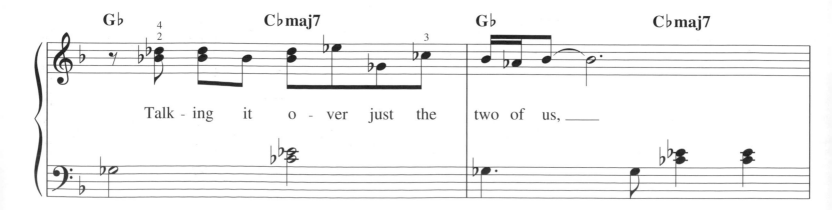

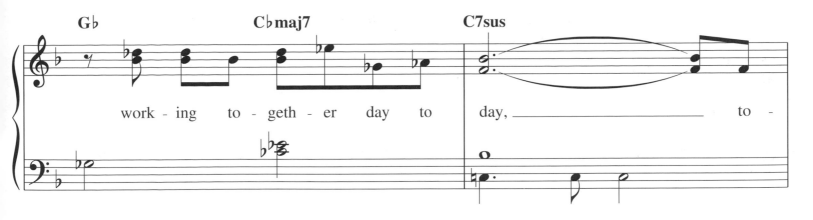

work - ing to - geth - er day to day, _____ to -

geth - er. ____ | geth - er, _____ to - geth - er. ____

CODA

gun.

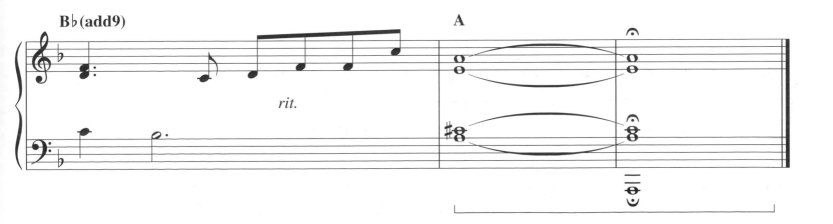

rit.

WHAT A WONDERFUL WORLD

Words and Music by GEORGE DAVID WEISS
and BOB THIELE

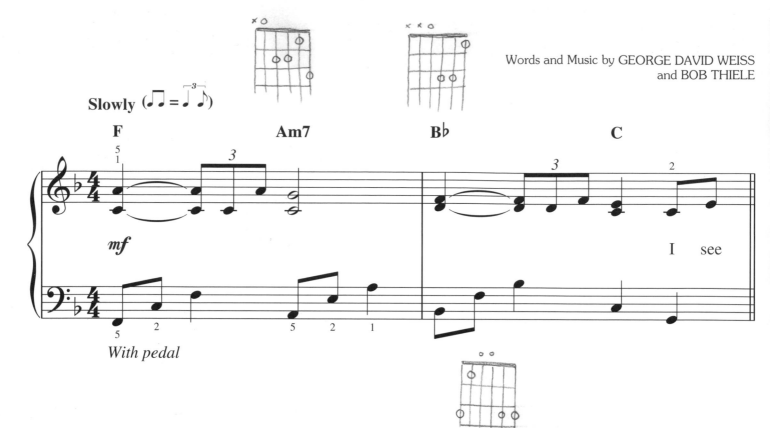

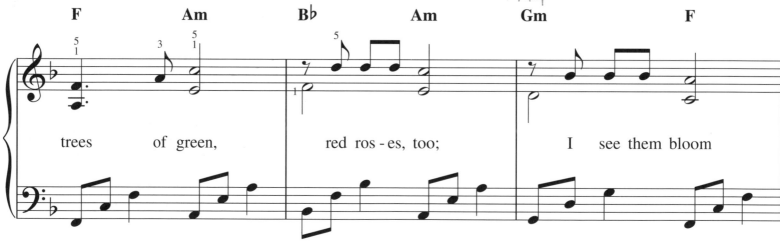

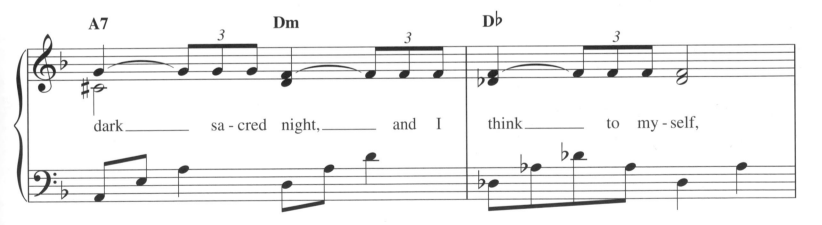

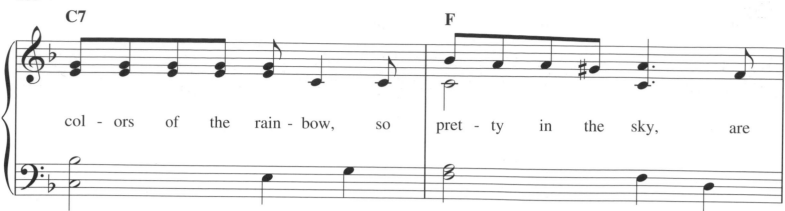

col - ors of the rain - bow, so pret - ty in the sky, are

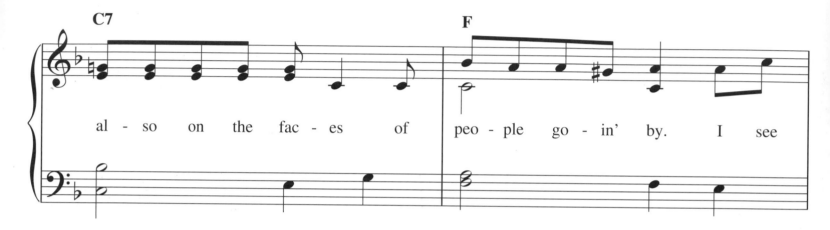

al - so on the fac - es of peo - ple go - in' by. I see

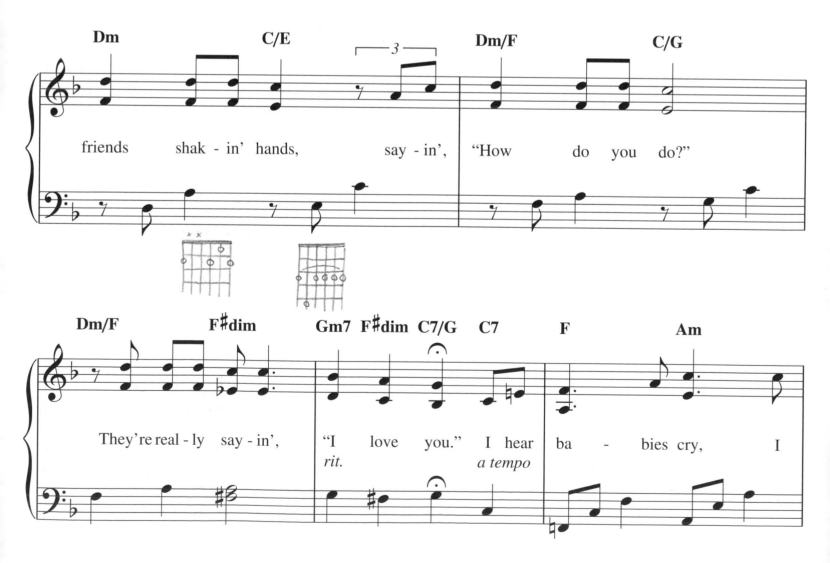

friends shak - in' hands, say - in', "How do you do?"

They're real - ly say - in', "I love you." I hear ba - bies cry, I

rit. *a tempo*

watch them grow. They'll learn much more than

I'll _____ ev - er know, _____ and I think _____ to my - self,

"What a won - der - ful world." _____ Yes, I

think to my - self, "What a won - der - ful world." _____
rit.

WHEN I FALL IN LOVE
from ONE MINUTE TO ZERO

Words by EDWARD HEYMAN
Music by VICTOR YOUNG

Moderately slow

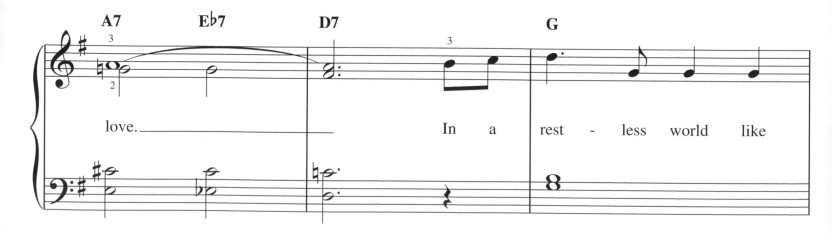

this is,   love is   end - ed be - fore it's be - gun,   and too

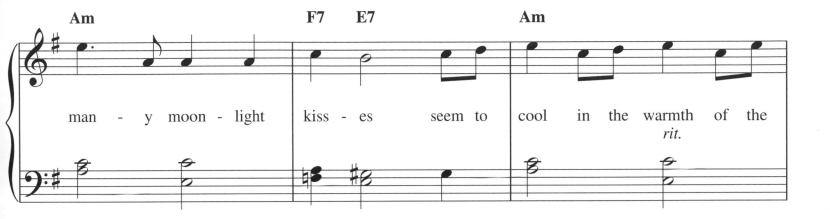

man - y moon - light   kiss - es   seem to   cool in the warmth of the

rit.

sun.   When   I   give   my   heart

a tempo

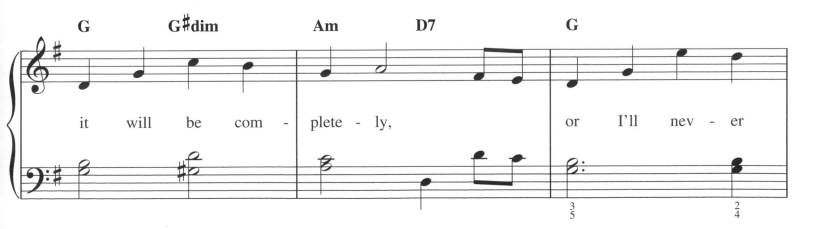

it will be com - plete - ly,   or I'll nev - er

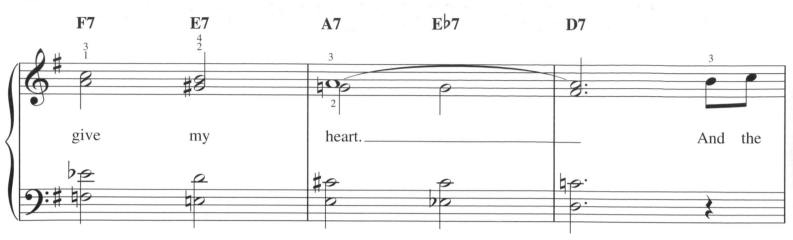

give my heart. And the

mo - ment I can feel that you feel that way

too is when I fall in love with

rit. *a tempo*

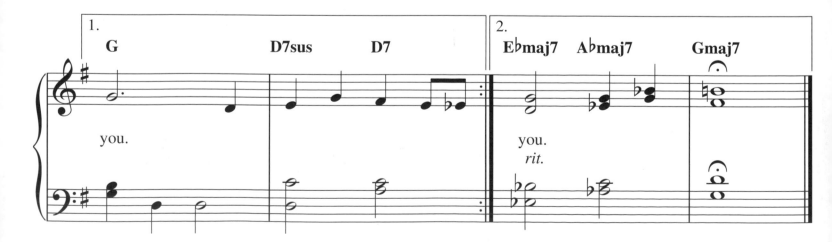

you. you.

rit.

WHEN YOU WISH UPON A STAR

Words by NED WASHINGTON
Music by LEIGH HARLINE

244

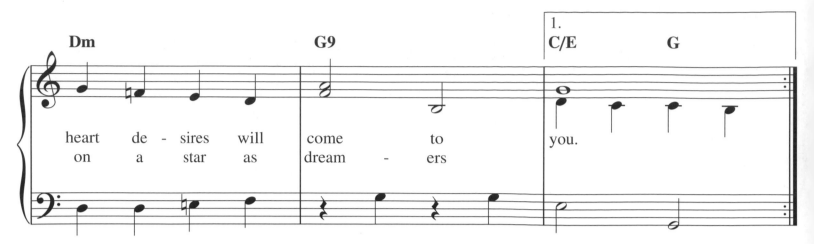

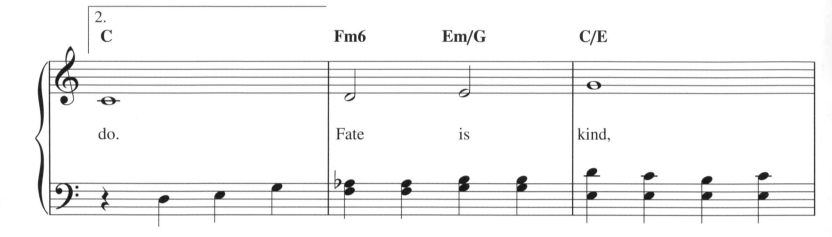

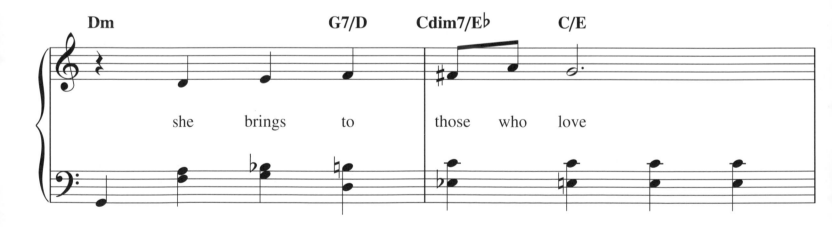

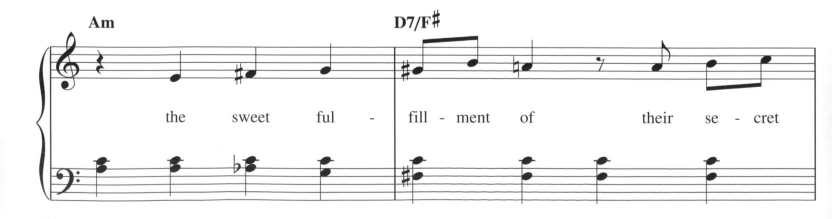

245

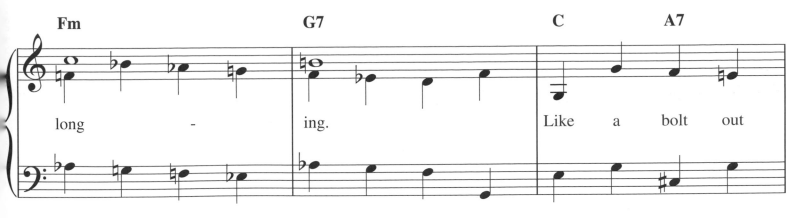

WHERE DO I BEGIN

(Love Theme)
from the Paramount Picture LOVE STORY

Words by CARL SIGMAN
Music by FRANCIS LAI

Slowly

With pedal

Where do I be-gin ___ to tell the sto-ry of how
With her first hel-lo ___ she gave a mean-ing to this

great a love can be, ___ the sweet love sto-ry that is
emp-ty world of mine; ___ there'd nev-er be an-oth-er

old-er than the sea, ___ the sim-ple truth a-bout the
love, an-oth-er time. ___ She came in-to my life and

1.
E7 · Am

love she brings to me? Where do I start?
made the liv - ing fine.

2.
E7 · Amaj7

She fills my heart.

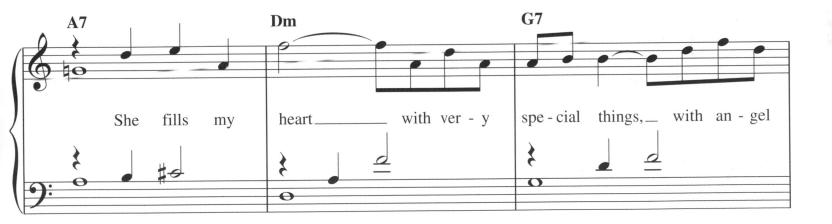

A7 · Dm · G7

She fills my heart with ver - y spe - cial things, with an - gel

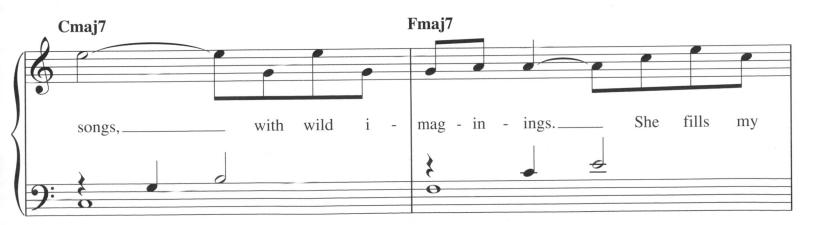

Cmaj7 · Fmaj7

songs, with wild i - mag - in - ings. She fills my

soul_____ with so much love that an - y - where I

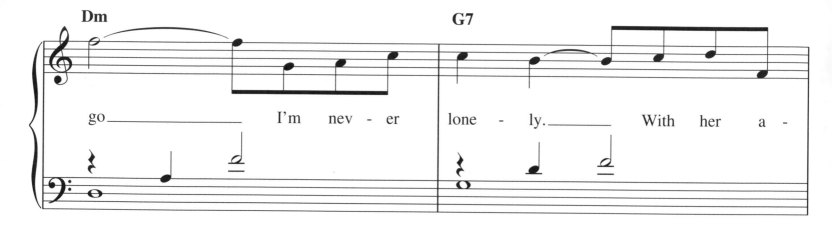

go_____ I'm nev - er lone - ly._____ With her a -

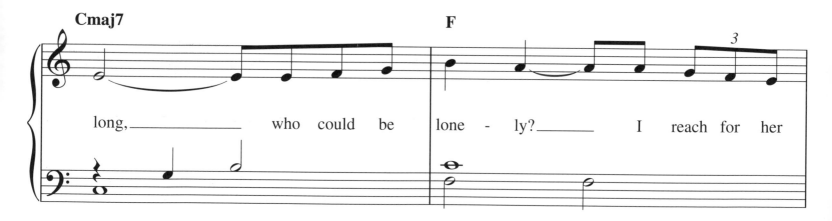

long,_____ who could be lone - ly?_____ I reach for her

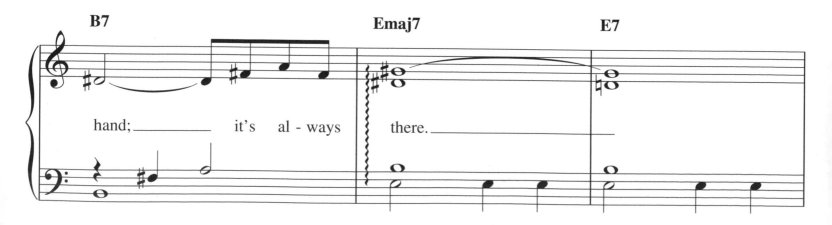

hand;_____ it's al - ways there._____

YESTERDAY

Words and Music by JOHN LENNON
and PAUL McCARTNEY

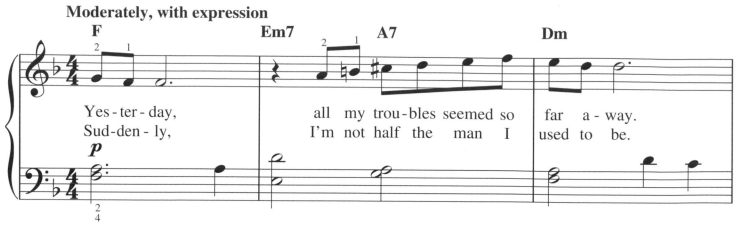

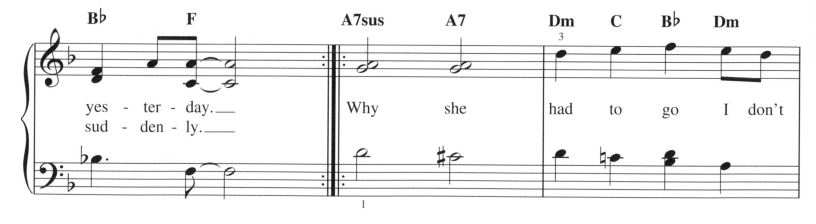

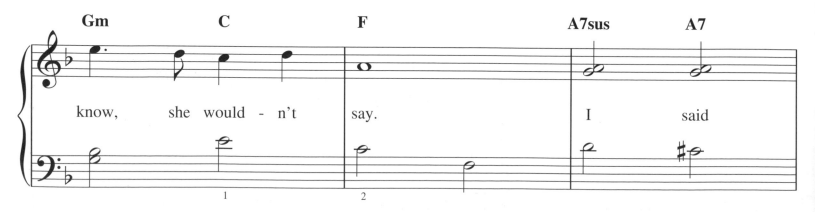

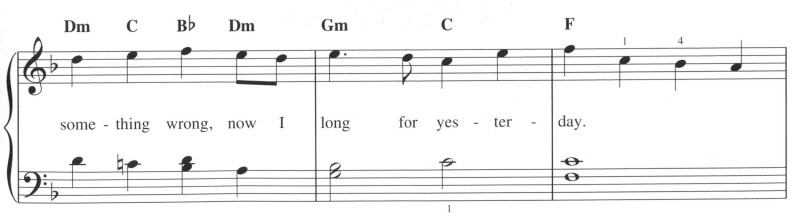

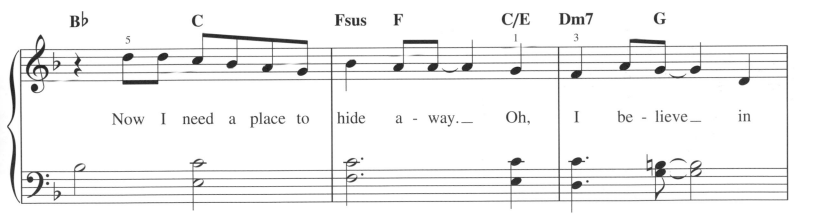

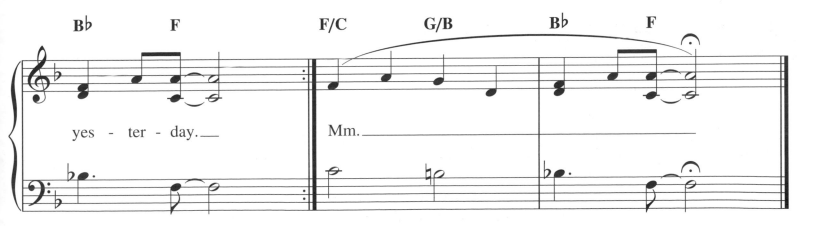

YOU ARE SO BEAUTIFUL

Words and Music by BILLY PRESTON
and BRUCE FISHER

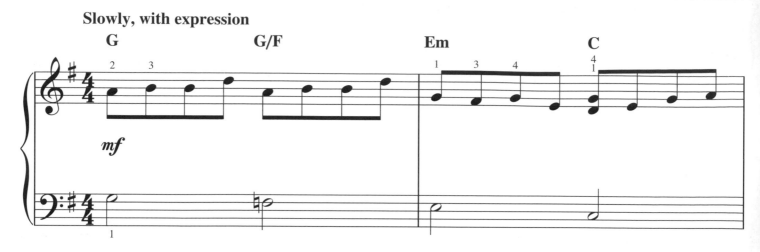

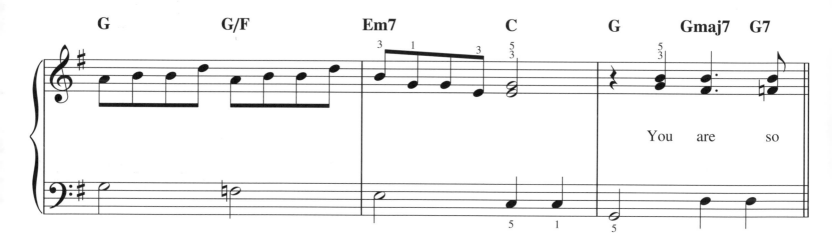

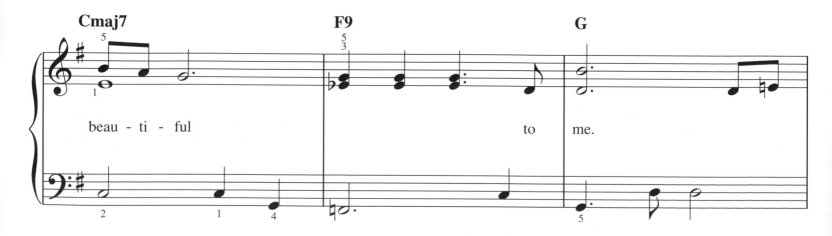

You are so beau - ti - ful to

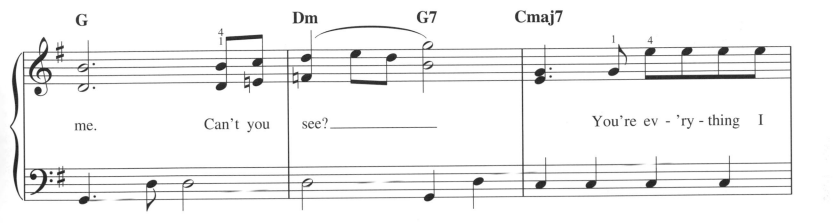

me. Can't you see? You're ev - 'ry - thing I

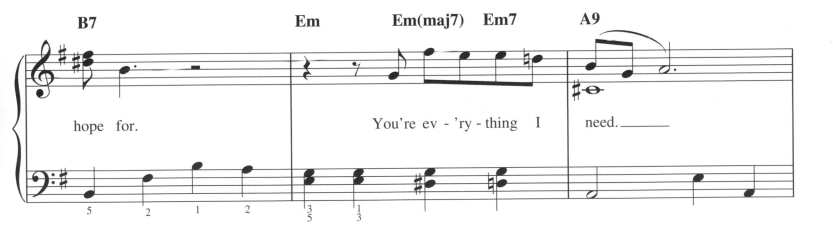

hope for. You're ev - 'ry - thing I need.

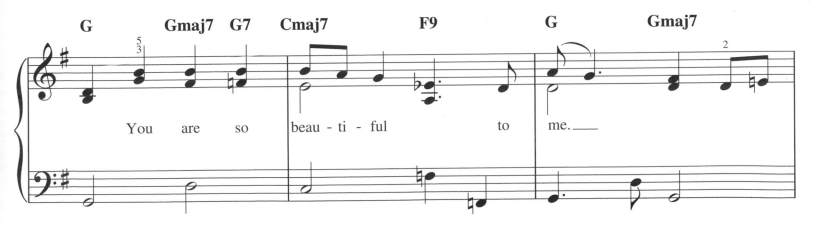

You are so beau - ti - ful to me.

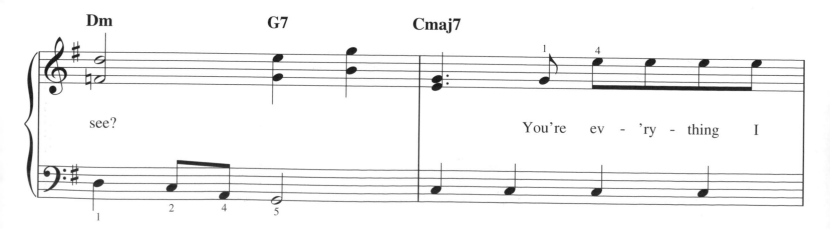

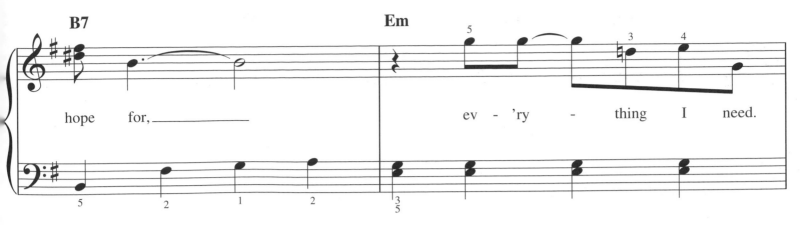

hope   for,_____

ev - 'ry - thing I need.

Freely
A13   **A tempo**

G   **Gmaj7**   **G7**

You   are   so

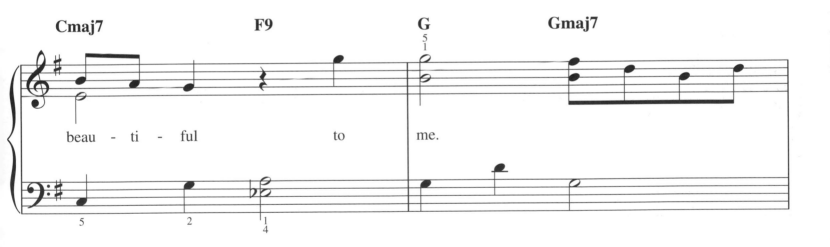

Cmaj7   **F9**   **G**   **Gmaj7**

beau - ti - ful   to   me.

Cmaj9   **F9**   **G**

YOU ARE THE SUNSHINE OF MY LIFE

Words and Music by
STEVIE WONDER

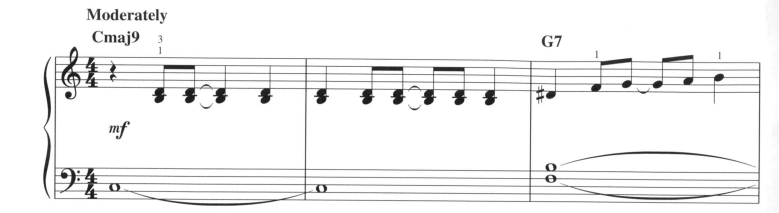

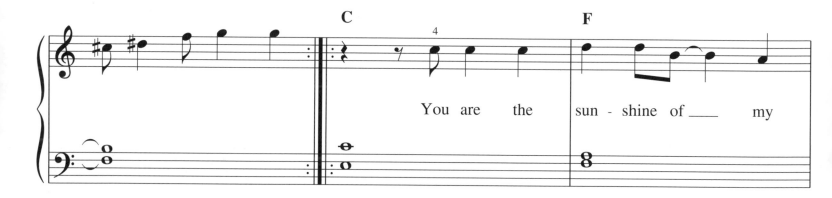

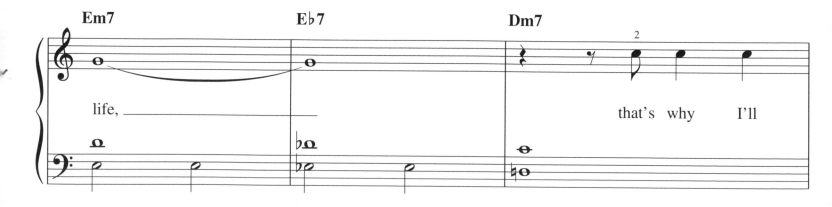

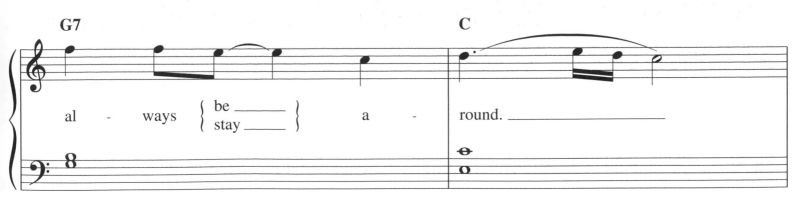

al - ways { be ____ / stay ____ } a - round. ____

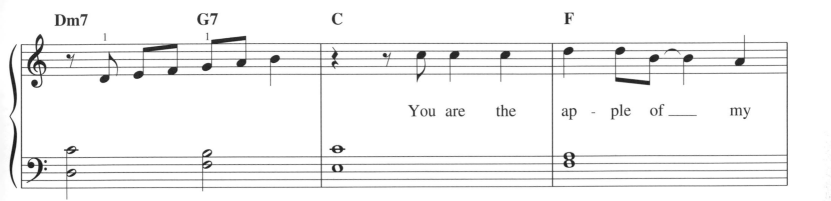

You are the ap - ple of ____ my

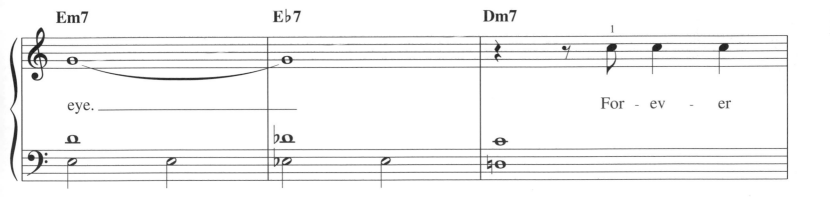

eye. ____ For - ev - er

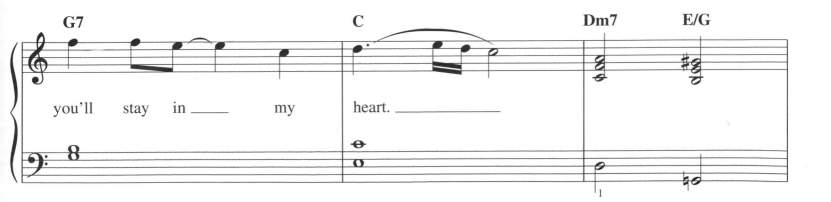

you'll stay in ____ my heart. ____

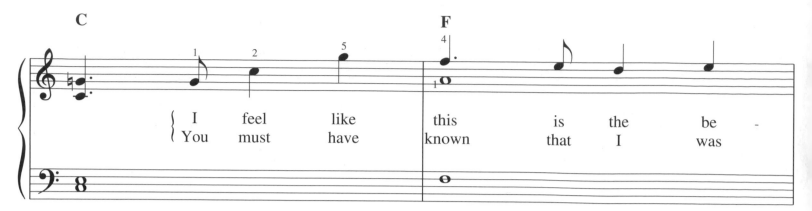

I feel like this is the be -
You must like have known is that I was

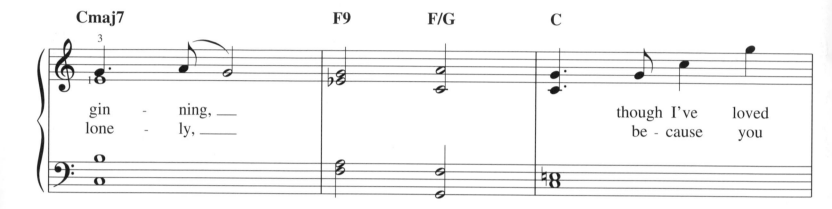

gin - ning, ___ though I've loved
lone - ly, ___ be - cause you

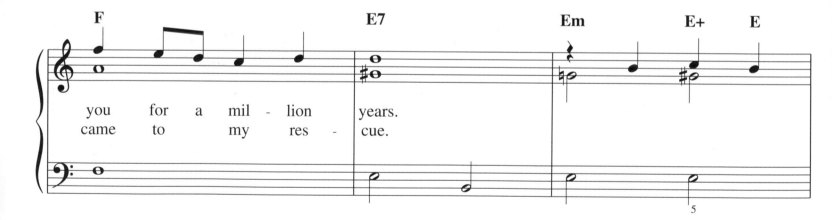

you for a mil - lion years.
came to my res - cue.

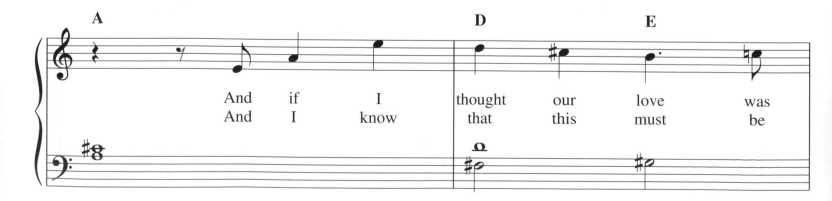

And if I thought our love was
And I know that this must be

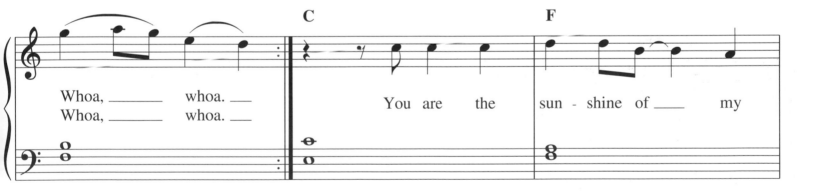

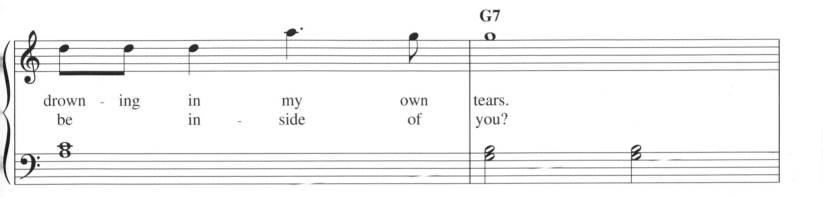

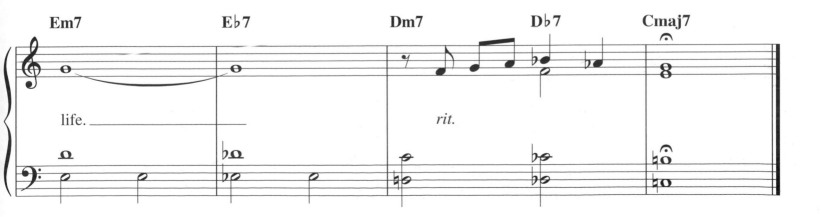

A WHOLE NEW WORLD

(Aladdin's Theme)
from Walt Disney's ALADDIN

Music by ALAN MENKEN
Lyrics by TIM RICE

Slowly and sweetly

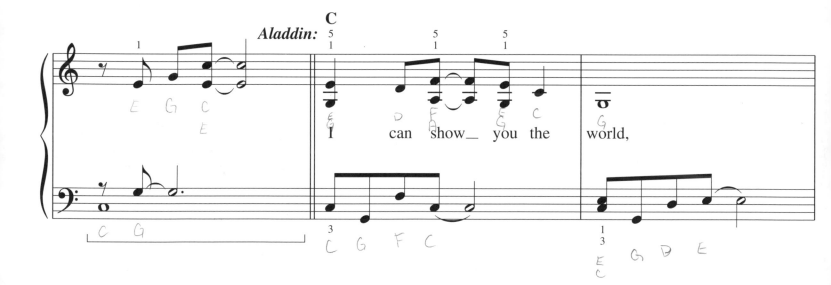

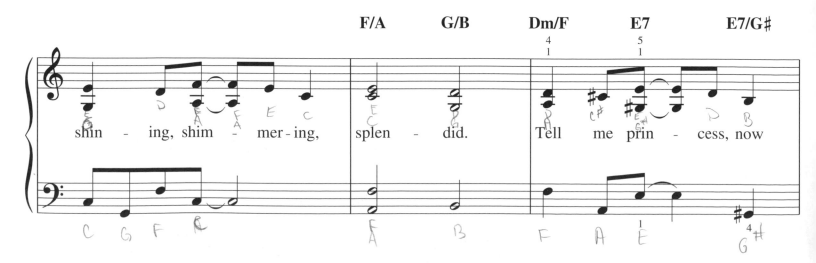

when did you last | let your heart — de - | cide?

I can o - pen your eyes | take you won - der by

won - der | o - ver, side - ways and | un - der on a

mag - ic car - pet | ride. A whole new | world

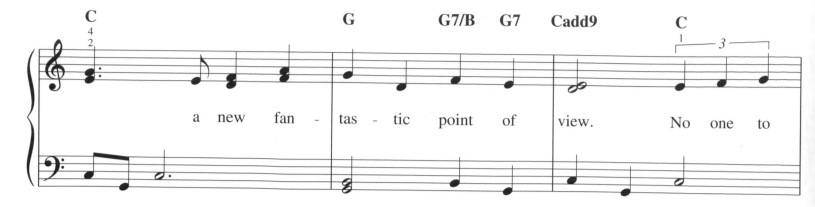

a new fan - tas - tic point of view. No one to

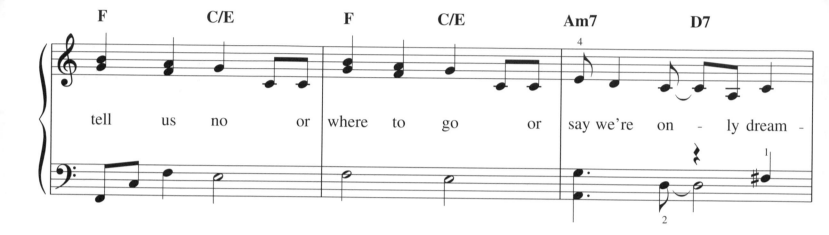

tell us no or where to go or say we're on - ly dream -

Jasmine:

ing. A whole new world a daz - zling

place I nev - er knew. But when I'm way up here it's

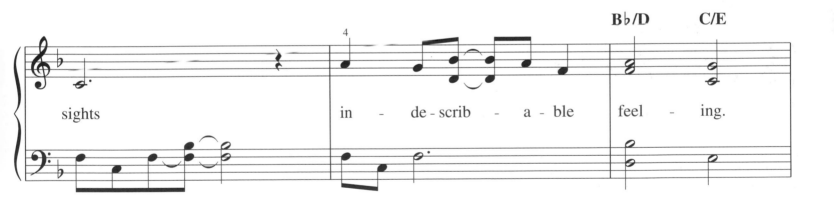

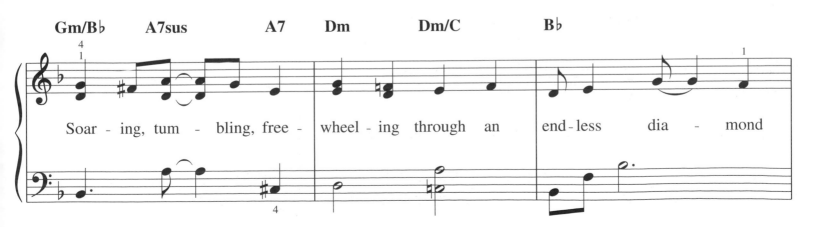

sky.   A whole new world

a hun - dred

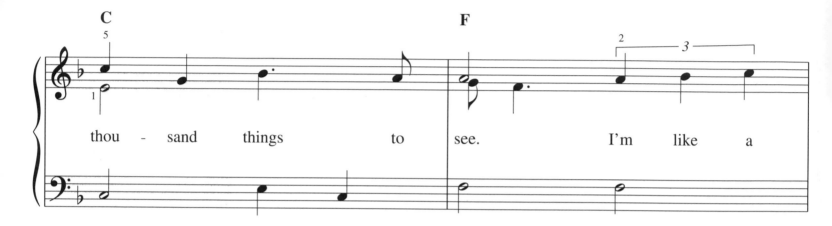

thou - sand things   to   see.   I'm   like   a

shoot - ing   star.   I've   come   so   far   I

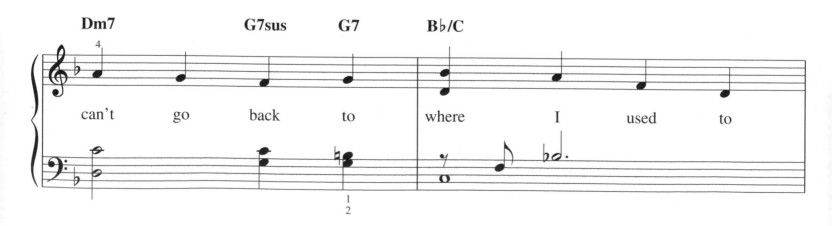

can't   go   back   to   where   I   used   to

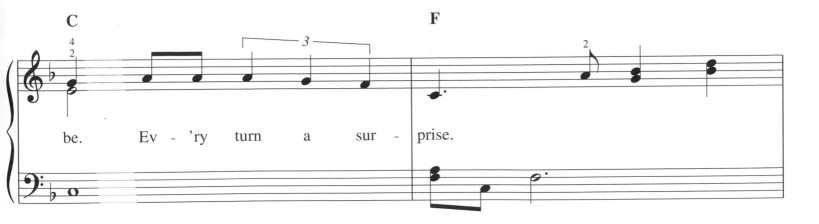

be. Ev - 'ry turn a sur - prise.

Ev - 'ry mo - ment red - let - ter. *Together:* I'll chase them

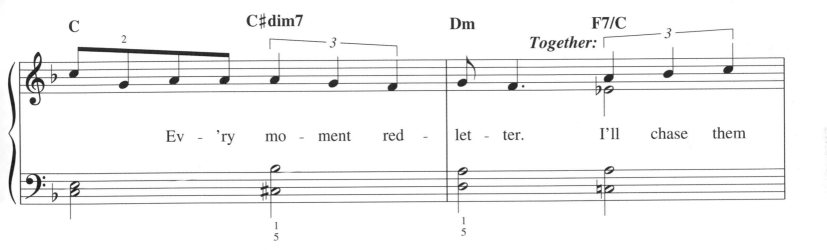

an - y - where. There's time to spare.

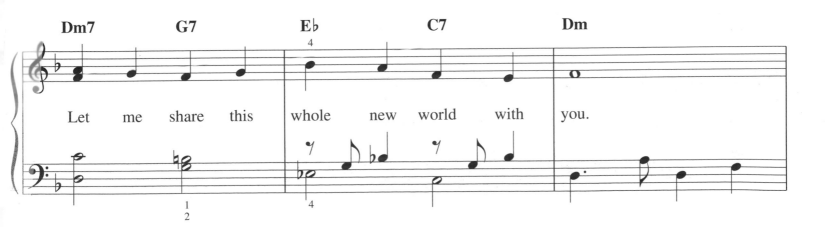

Let me share this whole new world with you.

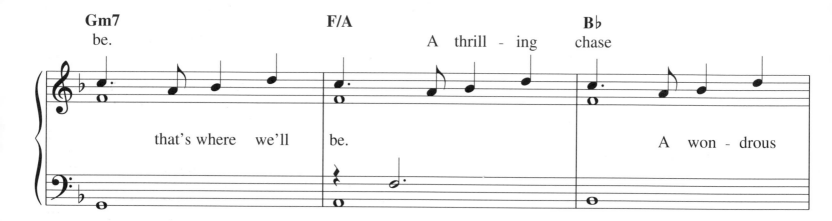

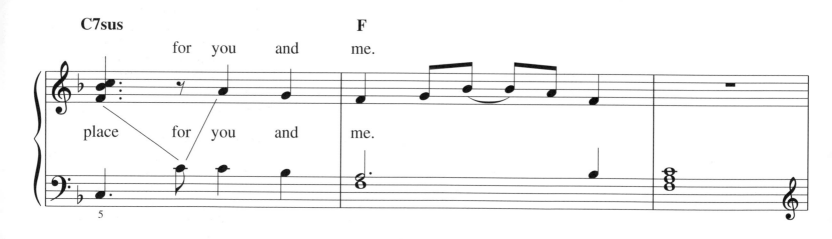

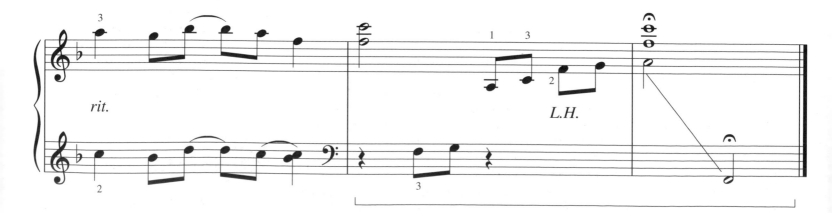

266

The Greatest Songs Ever Written

The Best Ever Collection
Arranged for Easy Piano with Lyrics.

The Best Broadway Songs Ever
67 songs: All I Ask of You • Bess, You Is My Woman • Cabaret • Comedy Tonight • Don't Cry for Me Argentina • Everything's Coming Up Roses • Getting to Know You • If I Were a Rich Man • Memory • Ol' Man River • People • Seventy-Six Trombones • Younger Than Springtime • and many more!
00300178 ....$19.95

The Best Children's Songs Ever
102 songs: Alphabet Song • The Ballad of Davy Crockett • Bingo • A Dream Is a Wish Your Heart Makes • Eensy Weensy Spider • The Farmer in the Dell • Frere Jacques • Hello Mudduh, Hello Fadduh! • I'm Popeye the Sailor Man • Jesus Loves Me • The Muffin Man • On Top of Spaghetti • Puff the Magic Dragon • A Spoonful of Sugar • Twinkle, Twinkle Little Star • Winnie the Pooh • and more.
00310360 ....$19.95

The Best Christmas Songs Ever
69 of the most-loved songs of the season: Auld Lang Syne • Blue Christmas • The Christmas Song (Chestnuts Roasting on an Open Fire) • Feliz Navidad • Grandma Got Run Over by a Reindeer • Happy Xmas (War Is Over) • I'll Be Home for Christmas • Jingle-Bell Rock • Let It Snow! Let It Snow! Let It Snow! • My Favorite Things • Old Toy Trains • Rudolph, The Red-Nosed Reindeer • Santa Claus is Comin' to Town • Toyland • You're All I Want for Christmas • and more.
00364130 ....$18.95

The Best Contemporary Christian Songs Ever
50 songs: Awesome God • The Basics of Life • Can't Live a Day • Ed Shaddai • Father's Eyes • Great Is the Lord • His Strength Is Perfect • I Can Only Imagine • Jesus Will Still Be There • Lamb of God • Oh Lord, You're Beautiful • Place in This World • Steady On • This Is Your Time • Via Dolorosa • We Can Make a Difference • and more.
00311069 ....$17.95

The Best Country Songs Ever
78 songs, featuring: Always on My Mind • Could I Have This Dance • Crazy • Daddy Sang Bass • Forever and Ever, Amen • God Bless the U.S.A. • I Fall to Pieces • Jambalaya • King of the Road • Love Without End, Amen • Mammas, Don't Let Your Babies Grow Up to Be Cowboys • Paper Roses • Rocky Top • Sixteen Tons • Through the Years • Your Cheatin' Heart • and more.
00311540 ....$17.95

The Best Easy Listening Songs Ever
75 songs: And I Love You So • Blue Velvet • Candle on the Water • Do You Know the Way to San Jose • Don't Cry Out Loud • Feelings • The Girl from Ipanema • Hey Jude • I Write the Songs • Just Once • Love Takes Time • Make the World Go Away • Nadia's Theme • One Voice • The Rainbow Connection • Sailing Through the Years • Unchained Melody • Vincent (Starry Starry Night) • We've Only Just Begun • You Are So Beautiful • and more.
00311119 ....$17.95

The Best Gospel Songs Ever
74 gospel songs, including: Amazing Grace • Blessed Assurance • Do Lord • Give Me That Old Time Religion • How Great Thou Art • I'll Fly Away • Just a Closer Walk with Thee • More Than Wonderful • The Old Rugged Cross • Precious Lord, Take My Hand (Take My Hand, Precious Lord) • Turn Your Radio On • The Uncloud Day • When the Roll Is Called up Yonder • Will the Circle Be Unbroken • and many more.
00310781 ....$19.95

The Best Hymns Ever
116 hymns: Amazing Grace • Beneath the Cross of Jesus • Christ the Lord Is Risen Today • Down by the Riverside • For the Beauty of the Earth • Holy, Holy, Holy • It Is Well with My Soul • Joyful, Joyful We Adore Thee • Let Us Break Bread Together • A Mighty Fortress Is Our God • The Old Rugged Cross • Rock of Ages • Were You There? • and more.
00311120 ....$17.95

The Best Jazz Standards Ever
71 jazzy tunes: Ain't Misbehavin' • Bye Bye Blackbird • Don't Get Around Much Anymore • Easy to Love • The Girl from Ipanema • It Don't Mean a Thing (If It Ain't Got That Swing) • The Lady Is a Tramp • My Funny Valentine • The Nearness of You • Old Devil Moon • Satin Doll • Stardust • Tangerine • and more.
00311091 ....$17.95

The Best Love Songs Ever
65 favorite love songs: Always • Beautiful in My Eyes • Can You Feel the Love Tonight • Endless Love • Feelings • Have I Told You Lately • Isn't It Romantic? • Just the Way You Are • Longer • My Funny Valentine • Saving All My Love for You • Vision of Love • When I Fall in Love • Your Song • and more.
00310128 ....$17.95

The Best Movie Songs Ever
74 songs: Alfie • Beauty and the Beast • Born Free • Circle of Life • Endless Love • Funny Girl • It Might As Well Be Spring • Theme from "Jaws" • Love Letters • Moon River • Puttin' on the Ritz • River • Somewhere Out There • Speak Softly, Love • Take My Breath Away • Unchained Melody • A Whole New World • and more.
00310141 ....$19.95

The Best Praise & Worship Songs Ever
74 songs: Agnus Dei • Better Is One Day • Come, Now Is the Time to Worship • Days of Elijah • Firm Foundation • God of Wonders • Here I Am to Worship • I Can Only Imagine • Jesus, Lover of My Soul • Lamb of God • More Precious Than Silver • Open the Eyes of My Heart • Shine, Jesus, Shine • There Is a Redeemer • We Bow Down • You Are My King (Amazing Love) • and more.
00311312 ....$17.95

The Best Rock Songs Ever
More than 60 favorites: All Shook Up • Born to Be Wild • California Dreamin' • Duke of Earl • Free Bird • Great Balls of Fire • Hey Jude • I Love Rock 'N Roll • Imagine • Let It Be • My Generation • Na Na Hey Hey Kiss Him Goodbye • Oh, Pretty Woman • Rock Around the Clock • Spinning Wheel • Takin' Care of Business • Under the Boardwalk • Wild Thing • and more.
00310444 ....$17.95

The Best Songs Ever
71 must-own classics: All I Ask of You • Blue Skies • Call Me Irresponsible • Crazy • Edelweiss • Georgia on My Mind • Imagine • Love Me Tender • Moonlight in Vermont • My Funny Valentine • Piano Man • Satin Doll • Tears in Heaven • Unforgettable • The Way We Were • When I Fall in Love • and more.
00359223 ....$19.95

More of the Best Songs Ever
72 more classic songs: Alfie • Beyond the Sea • Come Rain or Come Shine • Don't Know Why • Every Breath You Take • The Glory of Love • Heart and Soul • In the Mood • Michelle • My Cherie Amour • The Nearness of You • One • Respect • Stand By Me • Take the "A" Train • Up Where We Belong • What'll I Do? • Young at Heart • and more.
00311090 ....$19.95

EASY PIANO CD PLAY-ALONGS
Orchestrated arrangements with you as the soloist!

This series lets you play along with great accompaniments to songs you know and love! Each book comes with a CD of complete professional performances and includes matching custom arrangements in Easy Piano format. With these books you can: Listen to complete professional performances of each of the songs; Play the Easy Piano arrangements along with the performances; Sing along with the recordings; Play the Easy Piano arrangements as solos, without the CD.

GREAT JAZZ STANDARDS – VOLUME 1
Bewitched • Do Nothin' Till You Hear from Me • Don't Get Around Much Anymore • How Deep Is the Ocean • I'm Beginning to See the Light • It Might As Well Be Spring • My Funny Valentine • Satin Doll • Stardust • That Old Black Magic.
00310916 Easy Piano $14.95

FAVORITE CLASSICAL THEMES – VOLUME 2
Bach: Air on the G String • Beethoven: Symphony No. 5, Excerpt • Bizet: Habanera • Franck: Panis Angelicus • Gounod: Ave Maria • Grieg: Morning • Handel: Hallelujah Chorus • Humperdinck: Evening Prayer • Mozart: Piano Concerto No. 21, Excerpt • Offenbach: Can Can • Pachelbel: Canon • Strauss: Emperor Waltz • Tchaikovsky: Waltz of the Flowers.
00310921 Easy Piano $14.95

BROADWAY FAVORITES – VOLUME 3
All I Ask of You • Beauty and the Beast • Bring Him Home • Cabaret • Close Every Door • I've Never Been in Love Before • If I Loved You • Memory • My Favorite Things • Some Enchanted Evening.
00310915 Easy Piano $14.95

ADULT CONTEMPORARY HITS – VOLUME 4
Amazed • Angel • Breathe • I Don't Want to Wait • I Hope You Dance • I Will Remember You • I'll Be • It's Your Love • The Power of Love • You'll Be in My Heart.
00310919 Easy Piano $14.95

HIT POP/ROCK BALLADS – VOLUME 5
Don't Let the Sun Go Down on Me • From a Distance • I Can't Make You Love Me • I'll Be There • Imagine • In My Room • My Heart Will Go On • Rainy Days and Mondays • Total Eclipse of the Heart • A Whiter Shade of Pale.
00310917 Easy Piano $14.95

LOVE SONG FAVORITES – VOLUME 6
Fields of Gold • I Honestly Love You • If • Lady in Red • More Than Words • Save the Best for Last • Three Times a Lady • Up Where We Belong • We've Only Just Begun • You Are So Beautiful.
00310918 Easy Piano $14.95

O HOLY NIGHT – VOLUME 7
Angels We Have Heard on High • Deck the Hall • Ding Dong! Merrily on High! • Go, Tell It on the Mountain • God Rest Ye Merry, Gentlemen • Good Christian Men, Rejoice • It Came upon the Midnight Clear • Jingle Bells • Lo, How a Rose E'er Blooming • O Come, All Ye Faithful • O Come, O Come Immanuel • O Holy Night • Once in Royal David's City • Silent Night • What Child Is This?
00310920 Easy Piano $14.95

A CHRISTIAN WEDDING – VOLUME 8
Cherish the Treasure • Commitment Song • How Beautiful • I Will Be Here • In This Very Room • The Lord's Prayer • Love Will Be Our Home • Parent's Prayer • This Is the Day • The Wedding.
00311104 Easy Piano $14.95

COUNTRY BALLADS – VOLUME 9
Always on My Mind • Could I Have This Dance • Crazy • Crying • Forever and Ever, Amen • He Stopped Loving Her Today • I Can Love You Like That • The Keeper of the Stars • Release Me • When You Say Nothing at All.
00311105 Easy Piano $14.95

MOVIE GREATS – VOLUME 10
And All That Jazz • Chariots of Fire • Come What May • Forrest Gump • I Finally Found Someone • Iris • Mission: Impossible Theme • Tears in Heaven • There You'll Be • A Wink and a Smile.
00311106 Easy Piano $14.95

DISNEY BLOCKBUSTERS – VOLUME 11
Be Our Guest • Can You Feel the Love Tonight • Go the Distance • Look Through My Eyes • Reflection • Two Worlds • Under the Sea • A Whole New World • Written in the Stars • You've Got a Friend in Me.
00311107 Easy Piano $14.95

CHRISTMAS FAVORITES – VOLUME 12
Blue Christmas • Frosty the Snow Man • Here Comes Santa Claus • A Holly Jolly Christmas • Home for the Holidays • I'll Be Home for Christmas • Merry Christmas, Darling • Mistletoe and Holly • Silver Bells • Wonderful Christmastime.
00311257 Easy Piano $14.95

CHILDREN'S SONGS – VOLUME 13
Any Dream Will Do • Do-Re-Mi • It's a Small World • Linus and Lucy • The Rainbow Connection • Splish Splash • This Land Is Your Land • Winnie the Pooh • Yellow Submarine • Zip-A-Dee-Doo-Dah.
00311258 Easy Piano $14.95

CHILDREN'S FAVORITES – VOLUME 14
Alphabet Song • Down by the Station • Eensy Weensy Spider • Frere Jacques • Home on the Range • I've Been Working on the Railroad • Kum Ba Yah • The Muffin Man • My Bonnie Lies over the Ocean • Oh! Susanna • Old MacDonald • Row, Row, Row Your Boat • She'll Be Comin' 'Round the Mountain • This Old Man • Yankee Doodle.
00311259 Easy Piano $14.95

DISNEY'S BEST – VOLUME 15
Beauty and the Beast • Bibbidi-Bobbidi-Boo • Chim Chim Cher-ee • Colors of the Wind • Friend Like Me • Hakuna Matata • Part of Your World • Someday • When She Loved Me • You'll Be in My Heart.
00311260 Easy Piano $14.95

LENNON & McCARTNEY HITS – VOLUME 16
Eleanor Rigby • Hey Jude • The Long and Winding Road • Love Me Do • Lucy in the Sky with Diamonds • Nowhere Man • Please Please Me • Sgt. Pepper's Lonely Hearts Club Band • Strawberry Fields Forever • Yesterday.
00311262 Easy Piano $14.95

FOR MORE INFORMATION, SEE YOUR LOCAL MUSIC DEALER,
OR WRITE TO:

HAL•LEONARD®
CORPORATION
7777 W. BLUEMOUND RD. P.O. BOX 13819 MILWAUKEE, WI 53213

Disney characters and artwork © Disney Enterprises, Inc.

Prices, contents and availability subject to change without notice.

www.halleonard.com

0206

THE DEFINITIVE COLLECTIONS

These magnificent folios each feature a quintessential selection of songs. Each has outstanding piano/vocal arrangements showcased by beautiful full-color covers. Books are spiral-bound for convenience and longevity.

The Definitive Blues Collection
A massive collection of 96 blues classics. Songs include: Baby, Won't You Please Come Home • Basin Street Blues • Everyday (I Have the Blues) • Gloomy Sunday • I'm a Man • (I'm Your) Hoochie Coochie Man • Milk Cow Blues • Nobody Knows You When You're Down and Out • The Seventh Son • St. Louis Blues • The Thrill Is Gone • and more.
00311563 ....$24.95

The Definitive Broadway Collection
121 of the greatest show tunes ever compiled into one volume, including: All I Ask of You • And All That Jazz • Don't Cry for Me Argentina • Hello, Dolly! • I Could Have Danced All Night • I Dreamed a Dream • Memory • Some Enchanted Evening • The Sound of Music • The Surrey with the Fringe on Top • Tomorrow • What I Did for Love • more.
00359570 ....$24.95

The Definitive Christmas Collection
An authoritative collection of 127 Christmas classics, including: Blue Christmas • The Chipmunk Song • The Christmas Song (Chestnuts Roasting) • Feliz Navidad • Frosty the Snow Man • Happy Hanukkah, My Friend • Happy Holiday • (There's No Place Like) Home for the Holidays • O Come, All Ye Faithful • Rudolph, the Red-Nosed Reindeer • Tennessee Christmas • more!
00311602 ....$24.95

The Definitive Classical Collection
129 favorite classical piano pieces and instrumental and operatic literature transcribed for piano. Features music by Johann Sebastian Bach, Ludwig van Beethoven, Georges Bizet, Johannes Brahms, Frederic Chopin, Claude Debussy, George Frideric Handel, Felix Mendelssohn, Johann Pachelbel, Franz Schubert, Johann Strauss, Jr., Pyotr Il'yich Tchaikovsky, Richard Wagner, and many more!
00310772 ....$29.95

The Definitive Country Collection
A must-own collection of 101 country classics, including: Coward of the County • Crazy • Forever and Ever, Amen • Friends in Low Places • Grandpa (Tell Me About the Good Old Days) • Help Me Make It Through the Night • Make the World Go Away • Mammas Don't Let Your Babies Grow Up to Be Cowboys • Okie from Muskogee • Through the Years • and many more.
00311555 ....$24.95

The Definitive Dixieland Collection
73 Dixieland classics, including: Ain't Misbehavin' • Alexander's Ragtime Band • Basin Street Blues • Bill Bailey, Won't You Please Come Home? • Dinah • Do You Know What It Means to Miss New Orleans? • I Ain't Got Nobody • King Porter Stomp • Maple Leaf Rag • Original Dixieland One-Step • When the Saints Go Marching In • and more.
00311575 ....$24.95

The Definitive Hymn Collection
An amazing collection of 218 treasured hymns, including: Abide with Me • All Glory, Laud and Honor • All Things Bright and Beautiful • At the Cross • Battle Hymn of the Republic • Be Thou My Vision • Blessed Assurance • Church in the Wildwood • Higher Ground • How Firm a Foundation • In the Garden • Just As I Am • A Mighty Fortress Is Our God • Nearer, My God, to Thee • The Old Rugged Cross • Rock of Ages • Sweet By and By • Were You There? • and more.
00310773 ....$24.95

The Definitive Jazz Collection
88 of the greatest jazz songs ever, including: Ain't Misbehavin' • All the Things You Are • Birdland • Body and Soul • The Girl from Ipanema • The Lady Is a Tramp • Midnight Sun • Moonlight in Vermont • Night and Day • Skylark • Stormy Weather • Sweet Georgia Brown • and more.
00359571 ....$24.95

The Definitive Love Collection
100 sentimental favorites! Includes: All I Ask of You • Can't Help Falling in Love • Endless Love • The Glory of Love • I've Got My Love to Keep Me Warm • Isn't It Romantic? • Love Me Tender • Save the Best for Last • So in Love • Somewhere Out There • Unforgettable • When I Fall in Love • You Are So Beautiful • more.
00311681 ....$24.95

The Definitive Movie Collection
A comprehensive collection of 105 songs that set the moods for movies, including: Alfie • Beauty and the Beast • Blue Velvet • Can You Feel the Love Tonight • Easter Parade • Endless Love • Forrest Gump Suite • Theme from Jurassic Park • My Heart Will Go On • The Rainbow Connection • Someday My Prince Will Come • Under the Sea • Up Where We Belong • and more.
00311705 ....$29.95

The Definitive Rock 'n' Roll Collection
A classic collection of the best songs from the early rock 'n' roll years: 1955-1968. 95 songs, including: Barbara Ann • Chantilly Lace • Dream Lover • Duke of Earl • Earth Angel • Great Balls of Fire • Louie, Louie • Rock Around the Clock • Ruby Baby • Runaway • (Seven Little Girls) Sitting in the Back Seat • Stay • Surfin' U.S.A. • Wild Thing • Woolly Bully • and more.
00490195 ....$24.95

Prices, contents and availability subject to change without notice.

FOR MORE INFORMATION, SEE YOUR LOCAL MUSIC DEALER, OR WRITE TO:

HAL•LEONARD®
CORPORATION

7777 W. BLUEMOUND RD. P.O. BOX 13819 MILWAUKEE, WI 53213

www.halleonard.com